Military Leadership

Also of Interest

†Available in hardcover and paperback.

About the Book and Editors

Military Leadership: In Pursuit of Excellence
edited by Robert L. Taylor and William E. Rosenbach

Courage, charisma, self-reliance, self-confidence, and affection and concern for one's subordinates are the essential values for the military leader who wishes to be successful in battle, as well as in peacetime. But these values are no longer enough in a world in which complex weapons systems and support structures are wedded to traditional units and configurations. In this new environment, military virtue must be supplemented by good, basic management skills. Today's leader should possess psychological deftness in dealing with people and organizations. He or she must be able to grasp complex situations and react swiftly to challenges with judgment and balance. The true leader is capable of transforming individuals into active, responsible, and enthusiastic participants in the mission—inspiring a sense of esprit de corps.

Military leaders have always been responsible for the lives of subordinates and the fate of the nation, but never before has a text addressed the specific concerns of military leadership. The editors assembled this volume in the belief that leadership skills can be taught and, more critically, learned. The selections, culled from almost 2,000 articles, range over the vast canvas of history, tradition, management, technology, psychology, organizational theory, education, and the phenomenon of rapid technological and societal change. The articles provide examples of successful performance, but most important, they challenge the reader to think, to weigh, to compare, and to identify the full spectrum of problems and opportunities in modern leadership.

Robert L. Taylor (Lt. Col., USAF, ret.) is the Carl N. Jacobs Professor of Business and associate dean for the College of Letters and Science at the University of Wisconsin–Stevens Point. In his distinguished career as an Air Force officer, he served in a number of leadership roles, retiring in 1981 as professor and head of the Department of Management at the U.S. Air Force Academy. **Colonel William E. Rosenbach** is professor and acting head of the Department of Behavioral Science and Leadership, U.S. Air Force Academy. He has served as a staff officer and commander, including a tour at Hq USAF in the Pentagon. Awarded the Distinguished Flying Cross, he flew more than 200 combat missions in Southeast Asia. For the past ten years he has been teaching and conducting research on leadership, job attitudes, and organizational effectiveness.

Military Leadership: In Pursuit of Excellence

edited by Robert L. Taylor and William E. Rosenbach

with a foreword by Malham M. Wakin

Westview Press / Boulder and London

Copyright © 1984 by Westview Press, Inc.

Published in 1984 in the United States of America by Westview Press, Inc., 5500 Central Avenue, Boulder, Colorado 80301; Frederick A. Praeger, President and Publisher.

Library of Congress Cataloging in Publication Data
Main entry under title:
Military leadership.
    1. Leadership—Addresses, essays, lectures.
I. Taylor, Robert L., 1939–   II. Rosenbach,
William E.
UB210.M553 1984   355.3'3041   83-21769
ISBN 0-86531-729-1
ISBN 0-86531-730-5 (pbk.)

Printed and bound in the United States of America

5   4   3

307483

To Rob and Mike;
to Eric, Stefan, Laura, and Kara

Contents

Preface

We acknowledge that there are many legitimate ways to approach the study of leadership. Examinations of biography and history provide a complete study of leadership by example; yet, although we would learn a great deal about leaders, we still would not know very much about the *process* of leadership. We can also study leadership through the classics and philosophy, developing insights into human nature, but that approach by itself would not take into account the confounding effects of today's complex environment. Yet another approach is offered by management science, which allows us to quantify certain aspects of the leadership process while ignoring the equally relevant qualitative elements. These are only a few of the methods that have been employed to study military leadership. Which is most appropriate depends upon the purpose of the investigator.

We chose to select readings on leadership in general and military leadership in particular from as many different disciplines as possible, recognizing leadership as both an art and a science. Since the study of leadership is a study of human behavior in a group setting, we believe that one can become a more effective leader by studying leaders *and* leadership. We also believe that leadership skills can be taught and, more importantly, learned. Although we agree that the social sciences have contributed greatly to a better understanding of leadership as well as to the improvement of leadership, we have made a special attempt to present dissenting opinions as well.

In our experience as military followers and leaders, and as teachers and researchers, we have been frustrated with the scarcity of literature adequately developing the concept of leadership—particularly as it relates to the military. That was our motivation for putting together this interdisciplinary collection of readings. Studying the subject from various perspectives is especially important for those who want to learn about military leadership because the military draws its leaders and followers from all elements of our society. We did not try to detail specific models or theories; there are a variety of handbooks and texts that provide comprehensive reviews of the theoretical literature. Further, we avoided reports of specific research projects and explanations of the complexities of research methodologies. What we did include were readings—some old, some current—that provide an interdisciplinary overview of the critical elements in military leadership at different organizational levels and from a variety of viewpoints. There is an interesting blend of scholarly and practical perspectives.

There are four parts in our collection. Part 1 explores the nature of the leadership concept—why is it that we cannot easily specify what leadership is but seem to recognize and appreciate good leadership? Part 2 presents the oft-cited dilemma of leadership versus management and attempts to clarify the two concepts. Part 3 looks at ways requirements for successful leadership are changing and asks whether the leadership role is being sought as aggressively today as in the past. Finally, Part 4 surveys a variety of contemporary challenges and opportunities in military leadership.

We hope we can share the excitement and the feeling of growth that we experienced as a result of studying leadership from perspectives unfamiliar to us. The paradoxes are less of a concern now for they provide stimulation for studying, teaching, and living leadership.

We are especially indebted to all of those Air Force Academy cadets who confronted us with their own searching, impossible questions. We hope that they learned as much from us as we did from them. When seeking answers, we had the great fortune to have Colonel Mal Wakin as a colleague and friend; we are grateful for his advice and encouragement. Sincere thanks also go to Terrie Wacha, who assisted in the tedious research process, and Aggie Trzebiatowski, who transformed our scribbles into typewritten pages. Finally, the enthusiastic staff at Westview Press reflected the dynamic leadership of Fred Praeger, and their spirit helped us to capture the theme and purpose of this project. Many people influenced us, but we accept full responsibility for what follows.

Robert L. Taylor
William E. Rosenbach

Foreword

Recently I heard a stirring talk on leadership by a former marine lieutenant who had been wounded eight times in Vietnam. He was addressing a large group of senior cadets at the United States Air Force Academy on the evening before the new class of freshmen were to arrive; these senior cadets were charged with the responsibility of leading and training the 1,460 new "doolies." The marine lieutenant (Clebe McClary) had lost his left arm and his left eye and had undergone surgery thirty-two times, but the day he addressed these cadets he had *run* up Pikes Peak. They listened!

He draped a long piece of string across the speaker's podium and told them a story about leadership attributed to General Eisenhower. Prior to D-Day, Eisenhower is reputed to have placed a piece of string on the table around which sat his senior commanders and instructed each of them to push the string across the table. Then he reached over to grasp one end of the string and pulled it smoothly across the table. "Leadership," suggested Lt. McClary, "is most successful when you are at the head of the string and you pull your men smoothly to their tasks." The ancient Chinese Taoist, Lao Tzu, would have been very pleased with the string analogy, I thought to myself as I listened to this charismatic and courageous young marine. So too would my long-time colleague, a former engineering mechanics professor at the Air Force Academy, who frequently quoted what he referred to as Erdle's law: "You can't push on a rope."

The speaker went on to give some very practical pointers on leading troops. "If you have their hair cut short, cut yours shorter." "If you get them up at five in the morning, you get up at four-thirty." "If you want to run them five miles, you run six." Textbook authors would label this advice as encouragement to "lead by example," advice as old as leadership lore itself and yet, it seems, in need of repetition in each generation.

Leading by example is critical, of course, but we have learned from experience that example alone is not enough. The classic Greek admonition to "find a good man and imitate him" or to "do what the just person would do" in each situation points out that any old example won't do—we need to see how the expert in "goodness" judges and acts. There are "bad" examples. All of this suggests that when we follow someone's lead we would like to be going in the right direction; we would like to be confident that the leader "knows," that he or she is in control. So while the process of leadership may involve a great deal of charismatic or persuasive art, it is also clear that the leader must be competent in his or her knowledge of the situation. The fact that we want someone competent to be in control implies that leadership of human beings is a rational process. Those in control must have rational goals, must know where they are going—"*Theirs* to reason why."

Many of the authors in this volume emphasize (from different perspectives) the notions of the person of noble character who leads by example, has competent relevant knowledge, and is creative in determining goals or missions. Those like James MacGregor Burns who highlight the transformational functions of leadership seem to strike the most responsive chord for me, perhaps because of my many years of striving to become a better classroom teacher. Transformational leaders are involved in informing, educating their followers. Good leaders are good teachers. It is also the case, though often overlooked, that good teachers are good leaders, leaders in the search for truth. Socrates' likening of the teacher to a midwife who assists students in giving birth to the ideas pregnant within them is not an inappropriate analogy. The effective teacher is not merely an information giver; he or she must somehow inspire students to think and understand. This is true of all effective leaders. They are not merely ordergivers; they involve their followers in such a fashion that all accept responsibility for the mission. Ideally, then, it makes some sense to speak of the leader-follower-task situation as a transforming experience.

Bob Taylor and Bill Rosenbach, the editors of this anthology, have themselves been both college professors and military commanders. Their search for perceptive writing on leadership has been a very practical one and they have brought together here both normative and empirical views. Reading each of these chapters has provided me with insights about the leadership process that I think are worth sharing with all those who seek a better understanding of it. If we really are persuaded that we want leaders to be in control, to be leading us effectively toward proper goals, then we must prepare potential leaders in substantive fashion. This anthology is precisely the kind of tool needed for those wishing to reflect seriously on the process of leadership and for those seeking substance to impart in a course on leadership.

Malham M. Wakin, Colonel, USAF,
USAF Academy, Colorado

Part One

THE CONCEPT OF LEADERSHIP

We recognize and appreciate good leadership, yet we still search for a meaningful definition of the term. There are as many descriptions of leadership as there are people who write about it. One group of people we look to for help are those who have achieved a measure of success as leaders. Often, however, they describe leadership in ways that do not represent their own achievement. Even their biographers err in attributing success to what we *want* leaders to be rather than to the realities of the person in time and place.

Leadership is widely viewed as an influence process, dependent upon the relationship between leader and followers. Substantial agreement also exists regarding leadership situations—those events in time where the leader emerges and thrives. Leadership is a match between the person and the situation. Very often the situation is described in terms of a crisis, but we suggest that opportunities can offer equal challenges.

It is hardly surprising that military people have traditionally been concerned with the study of leadership. There is no more serious crisis than war (or the threat of war); the need for leadership is pronounced in military organizations. Providing a stable succession of capable leaders has always been a central concern for military planners.

Today, however, potential economic disasters threaten us all, and the need for capable leadership is intensifying in non-military organizations. Given the fact that economic catastrophe can be just as devastating as war, the quest for understanding leadership and identifying good leaders has become a global concern.

If we are serious about the study of leadership, we must shed the notion that meaningful concepts of leadership can only come from within; we must search everywhere for knowledge. We must also have a starting point—one that reflects the combined heritage of military leadership. Too often that base is missing or inadequate at best and folklore prevails. Part 1 provides a series of readings that, in our opinion, represent our current military ideology.

James L. Stokesbury, unlike many writers, uniquely differentiates leadership from headship in "Leadership as an Art" (Chapter 1). He focuses on the leader as a person and does not address those who merely serve (as "heads") in positions of leadership. In an attempt to define leadership, he says, we are trapped by the inadequacies of the language and often wind up with a tautological definition. Stokesbury deals with this dilemma by defining leadership as an art and suggesting that the best method for learning about leadership is to study the examples provided by history. He chose four historic leaders: the Marquis of Montrose, Alexander Suvorov, Robert E. Lee, and Henri Philippe Pétain, all of whom had little in common other than sharing attributes that Stokesbury believes constitute the art of leadership. He concludes by observing that the higher elements of leadership remain an art, whereas the lesser elements can be learned scientifically and can be treated by artifice. He ironically observes that the better times are, the less artifice works, and the more art is needed.

In Chapter 2 General Matthew B. Ridgway, former Chief of Staff of the Army, acknowledges that leadership is probably a combination of art and science, but like Stokesbury, he thinks the exercise of leadership is far more art than science. He describes the chief ingredients of leadership as character, courage, and competence, and his advice for developing leadership is to read history and biography, work hard, be humble, and be oneself. Ridgway's inability to specifically define activities or events that cause success helps demonstrate why we keep returning to the concept of leadership as an art.

The noncommissioned officer's point of view is captured in Chapter 3, "Commitment Is the Price We Pay," by Arthur L. Andrews, former Chief Master Sergeant of the Air Force. Although his focus is on the Air Force, his message has relevance for noncommissioned officers in all the military services. He believes that the basis of military professionalism is commitment, which leads to leadership by example. He challenges noncommissioned officers to take responsibility for their actions, to exhibit loyalty to their superiors, and to treat their subordinates with respect. Chief Andrews reinforces the notion that leadership is developed in the person and does not come with the position.

In "Leaders and Leadership" (Chapter 4), General S.L.A. Marshall notes that great military leaders of the past possessed a certain set of qualities—inner qualities, however, rather than outward marks of greatness. Relatively few leaders were acclaimed for leadership in their early years. Marshall's thesis is that most successful leaders are molded by the influences around them and that they have the average person's faults and vices. Leaders possess a common desire for substantial recognition and the will to earn it fairly. Too often individuals with great inner strength hold in contempt those less well endowed by nature than themselves and hence fail as leaders. Courage, humor, image, and being one's self are prescribed as the ingredients for success as a military leader.

Being one's self is a recurring theme, which suggests that leadership may well be an internalization of personal values. Malham M. Wakin argues that the consideration of ethics is imperative in the study of military leadership because of the unique function of the military. Marshall referred to military virtues, but in "Ethics of Leadership" (Chapter 5) Wakin articulates why these virtues are an absolute necessity for military leaders. He observes that the distinction between organizations that are based on the Hobbesian view of human nature, and the military, which has traditionally subscribed to the Aristotelian views of man and social organizations, is becoming less clear. According to Wakin, the leader who identifies with Aristotelian ideas is willing to subordinate his or her own interests in order to contribute to the common good of the group or society. The leader who subscribes to the Hobbesian concept, however, views his or her obligations as contractual—merely a part of the job—and hence temporary in nature. Wakin expresses concern about increasing infiltration of the Hobbesian values into the military. He also examines James McGregor Burns's concept of transactional and transformational leaders, concluding that as the distinction lessens between military specialties and civilian jobs, leadership may become less transformational and more transactional, which in turn may have a negative impact on military effectiveness.

Because we develop philosophical bases from our society and through the process of education, the essence of leadership could also be examined in terms of how we educate our leaders. Admiral James Bond Stockdale, recipient of the Congressional Medal of Honor, has absolutely no problems in dealing with how leaders should be educated. He proposes in Chapter 6 that in an age of insufficient idealism, a return to the classics of history and philosophy would help provide today's leaders with the perspective and wisdom needed to meet present dilemmas and difficulties. The Admiral makes a very good case for the study of history and philosophy, but he loses credibility when he attacks the social sciences for "having not yet outgrown an ideology of relativism, an egalitarianism of ideas, a culture-centered positivism, allegedly scientific, that most philosophers have long since called into question." The most rigorous study of leadership has come from the social sciences, in terms of theory and comprehensive empirical studies of leadership situations. However, it is true that social scientists have failed to produce finite results, so we shall let you decide if Stockdale has oversimplified his case for educating leaders "by discarding the illusions of human progress and returning to the classics where human nature is accurately portrayed."

In stark contrast to Stockdale's rather rigid approach to educating leaders, in Chapter 7 General Marshall provides the more general observation that not everyone can be taught to lead. However, if training emphasizes the importance of extra initiative, a sense of responsibility, and expert knowledge, learning leadership can be viewed as a matter of mastering techniques that will give more effective expression to the character and natural talents of every individual. Responsibility for developing leadership lies within one's self, but we should not mistake shadow for substance. Positiveness of manner and inner commitment stem only from the mastery of superior knowledge.

As we read the advice of these successful leaders, study the great leaders of history, and search for a set of ideals, we find that leadership encompasses attributes that are not easily described or defined. It is a matter of human character, which defies generalization. Hard work, courage, understanding one's strengths and shortcomings, initiative, and commitment link these chapters together with a loosely-knit theme. How and when these attributes are used depends on the individual and the situation—making leadership an art of understanding rather than a science of application.

1

Leadership as an Art

JAMES L. STOKESBURY

There is a certain sense of paradox, almost of impudence, in choosing as the opening title for a social science annual the topic, "Leadership as an Art." If one is thrown off balance by this, it is because society's perceptions have changed so radically over the past century. A hundred years ago, no one would have suspected that leadership might be anything other than an art, and impudence would have lain in asserting that there were scientific aspects to it.

Indeed, as late as fifty years ago the social sciences had still not come of age, and the most popular British historian of his time, Philip Guedalla (1923: 149), could dismiss them quite offhandedly as "light-minded young things like Psychology, with too many data and no conclusions, and Sociology, with too many conclusions and no data." In the 1960s, a distinguished American military historian used to tell his classes that the social sciences and statistical method were capable of telling us "all those things that are not worth knowing," a remark which the disgruntled humanist, pushed ever farther back behind the shrinking perimeter of his defences, teaching Latin in his office or lecturing on Napoleon to an audience that confuses the Weimar with the Roman Republic, is likely to cherish lovingly.

Now the development of computer technology has finally given the social scientist the tools he needs to amass data as never before, and to extract from it conclusions that are necessarily changing our ways of approaching problems. Social science has come of age, and the humanistic protest that "there is more to it than that" sounds increasingly plaintive. Students who used to read the classics now study executive management, and where they once learned how Caesar addressed his

James L. Stokesbury, "Leadership as an Art," pp. 23–40 in *Military Leadership*, edited by James H. Buck and Lawrence J. Korb. Copyright © 1981 by Sage Publications, Inc. Reprinted by permission.

men, or Napoleon tweaked his grenadiers' earlobes when he was pleased
with them, they now absorb graphs and mathematical formulae that are
supposed to guarantee magic results. It is a sort of acupuncture of the
mind: If you put the needle in here, the object will respond by doing
whatever it is supposed to do.

There remains, however, a place for art. The essence of science is in
mathematics and predictability. It has become more and more feasible
to forecast how more and more of any given group will respond to
certain stimuli. If the President looks forthright on television, public
confidence will strengthen; if he looks tired, or if his makeup is the
wrong shade, the stock market will drop so many points. Elections, we
are confidently told, depend on that ever-smaller number of mavericks
whose reactions simply cannot be predicted.

In a way, history is repeating itself, as it always does, with twists
and quirks. In the eighteenth century, at the height of the Enlightenment,
critics of society thought that if only they could be rid of the few
remaining irrationalities, they would then achieve the perfect society.
Old anomalous institutions like the monarchy, and especially the Church,
founded on emotion and faith rather than on the dictates of pure reason,
had to be swept away, and once they were, all would be for the best
in the best of all possible worlds, as Voltaire wrote in his jibe at Leibnitz.
Unhappily, when people destroyed the old institutions, they got the
Terror and the Napoleonic Wars, and reason turned out to be little
better a guide than tradition, or emotion, or history. One suspects a
tendency now on the part of the computer analysts to feel much as the
philosophers did in their day: If only we could reduce everything to
quantifiable factors, then we should have perfection.

Happily, we cannot, and though a great many of the things that
matter in life have been shown to be more amenable to quantitative
analysis and scientific predictability than was previously thought to be
the case, there still remains the province of art. We still respond to the
leader, in fact we hear more and more desperate cries for the emergence
of one, and the leader, to bridge that last gap between corporate
management and true leadership, still depends upon unmeasurables,
that is, on art rather than on science. The elements of his gift, or his
skill and how he develops it, are qualitative rather than quantitative,
and the problem for the humanist describing the leader is that he is
trapped by the inadequacies of the language to describe qualities that
defy precise definition. A leader, he may say, needs courage, resolution,
self-reliance, and on and on. But he can only define any one of these
terms by reference to others of them, and in the end he has produced
a tautology: The leader is a leader because he can exercise leadership.
One can hardly blame the social scientist for finding this less than

adequate, and for preferring to work with something he can pin down, i.e., can measure.

One way out of this dilemma is that history does teach by example. If it is no more than vicarious experience, it is also no less than that. It is useful to look at men whose place in history, large or small, has been guaranteed by the passage of time, and to try to extract from their careers, or episodes in them, elements that epitomize the qualities of leadership that men have most prized. In a not-quite-random sampling, consider the careers of the Marquis of Montrose, Suvorov, Robert E. Lee and Henri Philippe Pétain. These four all achieved pinnacles of leadership, but they are useful examples in that the external details of their careers had little in common. Each was from a different country, in a different century. Two were losers—most of the time, two were winners—most of the time; two fought in civil wars and two in external wars; two fought more or less unconventional wars, and two conventional. Two were in the pre-, and two in the post-industrial period. Though all are admittedly in the European tradition, that is after all our own, and it is legitimate to suggest in the aftermath of *Shogun* that some of the elements of leadership in other traditions may be so significantly different from ours as to be safely disregarded here.

The Marquis of Montrose

If the Stuart dynasty had been worthy of the devotion it inspired, there would still be a Stuart on the throne of England, and Elizabeth II would be just Mrs. Battenburg. James Graham, Marquis of Montrose, was born in 1612 and educated in Scotland and abroad. As a leading member of the Scottish nobility, he took part in the risings against the introduction of the Anglican prayerbook in Scotland in the 1630s, and was one of formost signers of the Solemn League and Covenant. When the Scottish Presbyterians became ever more insistent on their own interpretations of salvation and politics, Montrose drifted openly into the Royalist cause, and in 1644 he came out for Charles I. For the next two years, he routed army after army of Scottish troops, relying on his own brilliance as a tactician and a leader of men. His ultimate inability to hold Scotland for King Charles lay more in Charles's failure, or unwillingness, to support him fully, and Montrose's own lack of resources to overcome the tremendous power of the Campbells, the strongest of the western clans and the most determinedly anti-Stuart, than in any personal failing of his own.

Montrose's tiny army was finally routed in 1646; he himself got away to the Continent, where he remained until after the execution of Charles I. In a last chivalrous gesture, the Marquis returned to Scotland with a forlorn hope; most of his little band was shipwrecked; he himself was betrayed and sold to the Covenanters, and he was hanged in chains in Edinburgh in 1650.

It was a short but glorious career, and ever since its end the story of Montrose has seemed to epitomize all that courage and daring might achieve in the face of great odds. It is the more remarkable in that Montrose had no formal military training, though of course every gentleman of the day, and especially every great lord, was expected to know something of war. Nor did he ever have much in the way of troops. For the most part his army was made up of Irish peasants, often brought over with their families and following their own chiefs, or Scots of the Highland clans who came out for the love of fighting and the hope of booty.

Yet Montrose knew how to get the most from such men; he never asked for more than they could perform, though he asked much indeed of them. He took them into the Great Glen in the midst of winter and harried the Campbell lands when others said it could not be done, and he held his little army together in spite of reverses and the general sinking of the Royalist cause. Nothing typifies the spirit of his leadership more than his performance in his first battle, at Tippermuir. Here, with but 3,000 men, no cavalry and his musketeers down to one round per man, he met a well equipped army of 5,000 horse and foot. The Covenanters spent several hours in prayers and exhortations, but Montrose's speech to his men was short and to the point, and set precisely the right tone:

> Gentlemen! It is true you have no arms; your enemy, however, to all appearance have plenty. My advice therefore is, that as there happens to be a great abundance of stones upon this moor, every man should provide himself in the first place with as stout a one as he can well manage, rush up to the first covenanter he meets, beat out his brains, take his sword, and then I believe, he will be at no loss how to proceed! [Williams, 1975: 155]

The Irish and the Highlanders did exactly that, and when the survivors of the Covenanters fled back to Perth they had lost over 3,000 men; one of Montrose's men was killed, and a second later died of his wounds.

Such disproportionate figures as that would tend to the conclusion that Montrose's lopsided victory was no more than a fluke and that any reasonably resolute force would have defeated the Covenanters. However, Montrose did it again, at Kilsyth, in August of 1645. Once more outnumbered, by three to two this time, he attacked the over-confident Covenanters as they marched across his front. He lost three men; his enemy something more than 6,000. The clansmen and Irish slaughtered their fleeing foes for eighteen miles before they finally stopped from exhaustion.

Yet Montrose himself was not a bloody-minded man. He did his best to avoid the excesses of seventeenth-century warfare, and gave quarter where he could manage to do so. He remained a high-minded gentleman, courteous to his adversaries when he was not actively engaged in killing them, and was the very archetype of all that later Romantics saw as the virtues of the Cavalier party. He was something of a minor poet, too, and spent the night before his execution composing some appropriate lines. Probably best known, though, are the lines from *I'll Never Love Thee More* which have been attributed to him, and which sum up his career and his character as a leader:

He either fears his fate too much,
　Or his deserts are small,
That puts it not unto the touch,
　To win or lose it all. [Williams, 1975: 395–396]

Montrose had the conventional upbringing and education of the nobility of his day. His knowledge of warfare was instinctive and intuitive rather than studied, and that indeed remained the norm in the British service until well into the nineteenth century. Except for the scientific arms, engineers, and artillery, the function of British officers was to lead their men and, if necessary, to die well; the bulldog spirit was more important than technical expertise.

This was true of most armies of the eighteenth century, and most soldiers who studied war at all did so because they were interested in it, rather than because such study was a prerequisite for advancement. Knowledge could be an actual impediment in some cases; it was practically that in the career of Alexander Suvorov.

Alexander Suvorov

Born in 1729, the weak and sickly son of a former military officer who transferred into the civil service side of the Russian bureaucracy, Suvorov never wanted to be anything but a soldier. He read voraciously, and pushed his frail body to and beyond its limits. His father, much against his will, enrolled him as a cadet in the Semenovsky Regiment when he was thirteen. That was late for a Russian noble to start his military career—officers were often put on a regiment's list at birth— and Suvorov's rise was extraordinarily slow. He spent years in staff and routine work, and the ordinary chores of garrison duty. Even through the early years of the Seven Years' War he saw no action, though he was present at Kunersdorf in 1759, where Austro-Russians slaughtered half of Frederick the Great's army.

Not until 1761 did Suvorov see independent action, and from that point on he never stopped. His many years of dull service had given him a great contempt for the scheming courtier-soldiers he saw constantly promoted ahead of him, but an even greater love for the Russian soldier, conscripted for life, punished by the knout and the gauntlet, and consistently abused by his superiors. Suvorov understood such men, and empathized with them. He started making his name as a leader of Cossack irregulars, and his commander noted he was "swift in reconnaissance, daring in battle and coldblooded in danger" (Longworth, 1965: 26).

After the war, as commander of the Suzdal regiment, he rewrote the drill and tactical manuals, and spent his time working up a unit that in spirit and performance resembled Sir John Moore's light infantry more than it did other Russian formations. There was active service in Poland against the armies that tried to reverse the Polish slide toward oblivion, and Suvorov enhanced his growing fame particularly by the siege and taking of the fortress of Cracow.

Real glory came to him over the next twenty years as he was almost incessantly campaigning against the Turks in Catherine the Great's wars to expand Russia southward. His success is the more amazing in view of his constant ill health, and before one of his greatest battles, Rymnik, he was too weak to carry his own sword—but not too weak to lead his men personally on an all-night march that set up the victory.

His brilliance lay not only in intensive study allied to native military genius, but in his leadership qualities. More than any Russian before or perhaps since, he had the touch that appealed to his soldiers. On campaign he ate and slept with them, and was more than content with a pile of straw for a bed. This was a period when many Russian officers could not even address their men, having been brought up speaking French, and often those who could would not deign to do so. Suvorov, by contrast, was the common Russian writ large. In a gathering of officers, he looked like a tough weed among a bed of lilies. Regrettably, his popularity with his soldiers cost him both advancement and patronage, for just as he despised most of his fellow generals, he was hated by them. While Catherine lived he was protected, for she had learned to value his deeds more than his manners, but when she died in 1796, he was dismissed abruptly, and not recalled until Russia joined the Second Coalition against France in 1799. After a brilliant campaign in northern Italy, in which he again showed all the qualities that had made him a great soldier, he was caught up in the general Allied defeat in Switzerland, and forced to lead his starving army over the Alps and back to the Danube. Tsar Paul fired him a second time, refused to see him, and he died in disgrace in 1800.

His spirit lived on in the Russian army, however, and the great Encyclopedia Britannica edition of 1911 (Vol. 26: 173) compared the Russian Army to him in its "spirit of self-sacrifice, resolution, and indifference to losses," adding a remark which we would do well to remember in our own time: "In an age when war had become an act of diplomacy, he restored its true significance as an act of force." In 1941 and 1942, when war was universally recognized as being an act of force, Russian patriotic posters showed the ghostly figure of Suvorov, still leading Holy Mother Russia's sons into battle.

Robert E. Lee

Probably no American soldier has ever epitomized the art of leadership more fully than Robert E. Lee. Washington was often aloof, Jackson erratic for all his brilliance, MacArthur and Patton were both perhaps a little too overtly propagandistic to win the unreserved loyalties of their men, but it is safe to say of Lee that he was truly loved. On the Federal side only George H. Thomas approached Lee in this. McClellan came close for awhile, until his men found out he was so solicitous of them that he refused to risk their lives in battle, an apparently ironic fault which soldiers arc quicker to perceive as such than members of less dangerous professions.

Where Suvorov was a fierce old war-horse, and a looter and slaughterer of civilians as well, Lee was every inch a gentleman. Few soldiers have ever fought a civil war more chivalrously; Lee was in the peculiar position of having been offered the command of the army against which he was fighting, and he studiously referred to the Federals as "those people," never as "the enemy."

In spite of a brilliant record in the Mexican War and being offered the command of the Union forces, Lee did not do anything outstanding in the Confederate service until after his appointment to command the Army of Northern Virginia in June of 1862. But the new posting proved a happy mating of leader and material. Both still had much to learn, as the following campaigns showed, but they had less to learn than their opponents, and they learned it faster. The result was to produce as nearly perfect a fighting force as the world is ever likely to see again. Consider the battle of Chancellorsville, universally regarded as Lee's masterpiece. Outnumbered by better than two to one, and virtually surrounded at the outset of the battle, he ended by nearly surrounding his foes and driving them off the field in full retreat. And that against an army that was itself one of the great ones of military history!

Lee's brilliance as a commander was matched and sustained by his leadership of his men, and the love they bore him. Even in, perhaps especially in, defeat this relationship shone forth. After Pickett's immortal failure at Gettysburg, there was little sense that Lee had been wrong in sending the Confederates against the steady Union center. The famous diorama at West Point which shows the Rebels straggling back from their charge, and their officers reporting to Lee, reflects both his anguish at having sent them on such a mission, and theirs at having failed to do what he asked of them—even if flesh and blood could not do it.

Perhaps the most revealing of all episodes of Lee's career, however, is that of the fight at the Bloody Angle at Spottsylvania Court House. That was nearly a year after Gettysburg, and the shadows were gathering around the Confederacy. U.S. Grant had come out of the West to command the Union armies, and he was, as Lincoln said of him, "a man who knew his arithmetic." It was just before Spottsylvania that he wired back to Washington, "Our losses have been heavy, but so have those of the enemy. I propose to fight it out on this line if it takes all summer." Here was no McClellan, husbanding and pampering his troops to no purpose; here was a man who knew that if you killed enough men in grey and butternut brown, eventually there would be no Confederacy, and that was precisely what he intended to do. While that terrible litany of battles went on through the summer, Lee too came to recognize what fate held in store. As Grant slid south toward Richmond, Lee stopped him in the Wilderness, and entrenched next around Spottsylvania Court House, with his line forming an acute angle.

On the morning of 12 May soldiers of Hancock's II Corps swept like a blue tidal wave over the point of that angle, and the life of the Confederacy hung on a single thread. That morning Robert Lee rode among his soldiers, his sword uplifted, and proposed personally to lead the counterattack. His men would not have it, and shouting "General Lee to the rear" they went forward weeping, screaming, and cursing, to die in his place. For the rest of the day Confederates and Union soldiers fought as bitterly as men have ever done over a rotten little abatis. Lee lost one-fifth of his army, and Grant more than a tenth of his, and students who think that war is a matter of computers, or that Americans do not "know their arithmetic," would do well to study the Civil War.

Later, one day when it was all winding down to its sad finish, Lee lamented what might become of his country, and one of his aides interrupted, "General, for the last two years, these men have had no country; *you* are their country, and what they have fought for."

——— □ ———

In the twentieth century, the tasks of leadership at the highest levels of authority have become strangely complicated. On the one hand the simple growth of the population has made it increasingly difficult for a leader to touch all his potential followers; on the other, the development of modern communications methods has made it easier for a leader to project at least an image of himself to vast numbers of people. That, we may all agree, has been a mixed blessing. We have moved rapidly from the era of the newspaper image, early in the century, when the public followed with bated breath the reports of royalty and nobility visiting this fair or launching that battleship, to the era of the radio, when men as diverse as Franklin Roosevelt and Adolf Hitler discovered the uses of the ether for informing or misinforming their constituencies. And we have moved even more rapidly still to the era of the television set, the all-seeing, all-telling eye that dominates our contemporary scene. If, in the age of mass man, the leader has to reach more people than ever before, he has in the instrument of mass communication an unprecedented means of doing so.

Such problems were in their infancy, and but imperfectly perceived, at the time of the First World War. Until 1914 men were convinced that modern masses could meet and overcome any challenge by the application of modern technology. There was then what now looks like a charmingly naive confidence that anything might be achieved. Had not man recently learned to fly? A few years earlier, when the machine gun was developed, writers had praised the new tool as a means by which the savages and natives of backward territories might be civilized and Christianized the more rapidly. That was the era of Samuel Smiles and self-help, and if you believed you could do better, then by golly you *could* do better.

That complacent confidence had evaporated by 1917. It had been slaughtered on the "corpsefield of Loos," blown apart on the slopes of Vimy Ridge, and ground into the mud on the Somme and Verdun. In April, when General Robert Nivelle led the French armies once more to defeat in the Second Battle of the Aisne, they finally broke and mutinied. It was for France the greatest crisis of the war, and the government resolved it by the appointment of the one man who typified the army's ideal of leadership, General Philippe Pétain.

Philippe Pétain

Pétain had already made his mark several times over the years, and until fairly recently that mark had always been a black one. As a junior officer he had thoroughly identified with his men in the Chasseurs alpins, much as Suvorov had done in an earlier time. Like his famous predecessor, he was as unpopular with his superiors as he was popular with his men, and one of his fitness reports contained the always-quoted remark, "If this officer rises above the rank of major it will be a disaster for France." His chief problem was not his personality, though, it was his studying of modern tactics which led him to fly in the face of accepted French military dogma. In the late nineteenth century the French, falling behind Germany in all the statistics of great power status, convinced themselves that such statistics meant nothing, and that French spirit was irresistible. They adopted the idea of the all-conquering offensive as an article of religious faith, and Ferdinand Foch became its high priest. Pétain was the heretic in the congregation. He believed in the superior power of the defensive, and to all paeans on the attack at all costs he replied with a laconic "Fire kills." By 1914 he was a disgruntled colonel, on the verge of retirement.

The outbreak of the war changed all that, and Pétain, twelve years a captain, went from colonel to lieutenant-general in three months. He did well at the Marne, got command of the second Army in mid-1915, and a year later his name was a household word, for when the Germans launched the great Verdun offensive, Pétain was sent to stop it.

He did so, at enormous cost in men and material. He instituted a rotation system, and it is estimated that 60 percent of the French army passed through the fighting at Verdun at one phase or another of the battle. He organized the supply system, sending an endless chain of men and materials up the *voie sacrée*. When the battle finally ended, the French had lost more than a quarter of a million men, but they had held Verdun, and Pétain's name, whatever it might become in another war, was irrevocably linked with this greatest of the Third Republic's victories.

So it was that when the army at last refused duty after Nivelle's vainglorious Aisne offensive—a sort of Fredericksburg writ [at] large— Pétain was appointed to the supreme command, and set about to restore order and morale. He did so by the simplest of measures: He showed the soldiers that someone in authority was interested in them. That does not seem like much, but it was far more than most French soldiers had received so far in the war.

British writers charge that after Pétain the French army was relatively inactive, and took little offensive part in the war. That is certainly true, but the fact derived more from the enormous wastage of the army before Pétain took it over; in terms of generalship he did little but recognize reality. That, indeed, had always been his specialty, and accounted for his prewar unpopularity. As a leader, however, as a restorer of morale, a man who empathized with his troops and won their loyalty and respect, he had few equals in the twentieth century. That accounts in large part for the way in which he was greeted as a savior when he assumed power in 1940. His ultimate tragedy was that he lived too long, and the sad later years of his career should not obscure the enormous impact of his leadership on the soldiers of France in 1916, 1917, and 1918.

A Common Thread

All four of these men, in their own time and since, have been acknowledged as masters of the art of leadership. Do these cursory examinations of their careers reveal any general characteristics, from which it is possible to extract some of the essence of leadership? The answer is both yes and no. No, because there tends to be relatively little in common between them except that they were all soldiers, and, of course, great leaders. But the conditions of war under which Pétain labored were not very similar to those of Montrose's day, and the personality of a Robert Lee was not very much like that of Suvorov. There are, however, some elements that can be isolated.

Each of these leaders believed in his men, in their power to rise to the heights of endeavor to which he called them. It is often preached that loyalty is a two-way street; unhappily it is less often practiced. The potential leader cannot demand the unswerving loyalty of his followers unless he is willing to return it. If he sees his men only as instruments to further his own career, he is not going to be very successful. Napoleon once remarked to Metternich that he could use up a million men a month, "for what does a man like me care for such as these," but that was after the legend was established, indeed, that was when Napoleon was already on the way down, and events were to prove he could *not* use up a million men a month. The leader who says, "You must be loyal to me, but I need think only of my next fitness report" will not go far.

These men also believed in a cause which transcended themselves and their own desires or ambitions. Those causes may in our own day be difficult to discern, but that is more our problem than theirs. Montrose believed both in the right of the Stuarts to rule Britain, and in his own concept of freedom of religion. Suvorov served the dynastic state in the person of Catherine the Great. Robert E. Lee believed in the Confederacy, in fact epitomized what was best in it, and Pétain was similarly the embodiment of France, the real France of small villages and infinitely tenacious peasantry—in spite of a reputation for frivolity, the French are among the most dour nations on earth—and he inspired the same attitudes in his men.

It is probable that their followers believed less in these causes than they did in the men who led them. Montrose's Irish and Highlanders followed their own lords to war, and were no doubt but dimly aware of the constitutional principles involved in the English Civil War. Suvorov's peasant soldiers were not asked if they cared to aggrandize Russia when they were dragged off to the army for life. It was the humane treatment, the fact that he was actually interested in them, that made them follow Suvorov, and that made him subsequently a Russian legend, for surely there has not been much of that sort of leadership in Russian history since then. For the most part, leadership as practiced in Russia has been of the remote and awe-inspiring—or indeed fear-inspiring—variety.

Charles de Gaulle (1960: 65), who had some considerable professional interest in the problem, commented on this facet of leadership. He wrote between the wars,

> It is, indeed, an observable fact that all leaders of men, whether as political figures, prophets, or soldiers, all those who can get the best out of others, have always identified themselves with high ideals. Followed in their lifetime because they stand for greatness of mind rather than self-interest, they are later remembered less for the usefulness of what they have achieved than for the sweep of their endeavors.

It is safe to say that de Gaulle and Bernard Montgomery agreed on little, but they both agreed on that. Montgomery (1961: 17) thought that one of the prime requisites for leadership was "selflessness, by which I mean absolute devotion to the cause he serves with no thought of personal reward or aggrandisement."

The student is apt to retort that neither de Gaulle nor Montgomery, both of whom were acknowledged as great leaders, particularly lived up to this requirement. Both of them would insist, in rebuttal, that indeed they had. Both saw themselves, however historians have seen them, as essentially selfless men. Here is de Gaulle (1960: 64) again: "Every man of action has a strong dose of egotism, pride, hardness, and cunning. But all those things will be forgiven him, indeed they will be regarded as high qualities, if he can make of them the means to achieve great ends." He would therefore argue that selflessness does not mean self-abnegation; one may be ruthlessly thrusting and ambitious, provided that ambition is directed in the service of something that is perceived as a greater good, and equally provided that the leader has the ability to convey to his followers the importance of that greater good, and not just his own ambition.

Military history is littered with the names of great and good men who were not quite hard enough, and whose disinclination to get their men killed caused only more suffering in the long run; consider again McClellan's solicitousness for his men, which may well have prolonged the Civil War by years, or Ian Hamilton's reluctance to interfere with his subordinate commanders at Gallipoli, which threw away a campaign that might well have been won on the first day. Some writers maintain that one of the few deficiencies of Sir Harold Alexander as a field commander was his preference for the soft word, and it may have cost him the capture of most of the German army south of Rome in May of 1944. Napoleon summed it up when he sent Brune down to clean up the Vendée in 1800; he told his general it was better to kill ten thousand now, than to be too soft and have to kill a hundred thousand later on.

The leader therefore not only has to believe in his men, and have that belief reciprocated; he has to be able to inspire them to risk their lives for some greater end which they may only very dimly perceive, and he has to have himself the courage to demand that they do so. It is of course in this particular that military leadership differs from other kinds.

As we are now nearly a decade away from an active war, there is a tendency, unfortunate but perhaps inevitable in such periods, to regard military leadership as little different from directing, for example, a large company or a political entity. If a man can run a railroad, he ought to be able to run the United States Army, so we say. This, as it happens, is not the case, though the example of Montrose, moving smoothly from civilian to military leadership in his society, might seem to suggest that it was. In such times as these, we try to repress the knowledge that the military obligation, the "profession of arms," in Sir John Hackett's phrase, demands a greater commitment: It demands, in the last analysis, that men agree to die if necessary in fulfilling their tasks. That is rather a different affair from the possibility of losing one's job if one does not do well. The man who raises his right hand and dons a uniform is saying, in so many words, "I shall perform a certain task, and if necessary I shall put my life on the line to succeed in it." Not many trade unions, and not many managerial staff, would be willing to make that sort of statement (though if they were required to do so, Chrysler might have started making small cars several years ago). If the military leader has the advantage of trained and disciplined followers, he also has the disadvantages of the much higher risks of their profession.

This is not, it appears, an unnecessary laboring of the obvious. In recent years, in spite of having the television bring war into our front rooms, there has been a very real sense of suppression of this basic fact. People are not "killed," they are "wasted," or "terminated" in common parlance, and statisticians succumb to the same impulse that makes undertakers describe people as having "passed away"; bodies at the funeral home are "resting" rather than "dead." It may well be that this is a most unfortunate attitude, and that if there were clearer recognition that someone who is "killed" is "dead," there would be fewer temptations to resort to war as "an extension of politics," a mistaken definition which Clausewitz only too belatedly recognized.

The Problem of War

The problem of war, and of leadership, is that if your soldiers are brought to acknowledge the necessity of achieving their objective or dying in the effort, so are the enemy's. It is that which calls forth the leader's ability to deal with the unforeseen, "the contingent element inseparable from the waging of war [which] gives to that activity both its difficulty and its grandeur" (de Gaulle, 1960: 16). "Whimsy, the irrational or unpredictable event or circumstance, *Fortuna*" (Record, 1980: 19), these are the things that are not susceptible to computer analysis, these are what makes war an art, and therefore leadership an art as well.

There are of course those parts of the trade, or art, that can be studied, and therefore learned. There have been few great leaders who were not knowledgeable about the mechanics of the business; you cannot be an inspiring leader if you neglect the logistics that feed your men. They will not give you their confidence if you forget to bring up the reserve ammunition, or if you leave them with no way out of an ambush, or even if you consistently schedule two columns to use the same crossroads at the same time. All of that level of operation is subject to scientific principles, and can be taught. Any reasonably intelligent person can learn the routine of siting a battery, or even of administering a battalion. One can go very far on basic managerial skills, and one cannot do much without them. One of the difficulties, in fact, of dealing with the question of leadership is the tendency not to distinguish between the aspects of it that relate to making sound military decisions, and the aspects that relate to leading men in battle. The last people to insist that science was nothing, art and spirit were all, were the French military advocates of *l'attaque à l'outrance,* the *furia francese,* before World War I, and all they managed to do was kill off the better part of their army in the first couple of weeks of the war, as Pétain had all too accurately foreseen. It has been pointed out that if Waterloo was won on the playing fields of Eton, Gallipoli and Singapore were also lost there. It would therefore again be a mistake to insist on too wide a cleavage between science and art, and to say that either one was all, the other nothing. Every aspect of life has elements of both in it. To repeat the example above, there is an art to siting a battery, but it must be done on scientific principles, as the British discovered when they tried to unlimber within range of the Boer rifle pits at Colenso; they lost 1100 men, and ten out of twelve of their guns, for a Boer loss of less than fifty. The higher elements of leadership remain an art, though the lesser ones can be learned scientifically, can be treated, as it were, by artifice.

Ironically, the better times are, the less artifice works, and the more art is needed. We live in what is undeniably the most prosperous society that has ever existed, with better conditions for more people than has so far been possible in human history. Artifice does not work, because our servicemen are for the most part sufficiently intelligent and so- phisticated to see through it. Our society has become so free that preoccupation with freedom as an end in itself has led us to neglect the responsibilities and the obligations that have always been thought to accompany it. No state in history has been able to say to its citizens that they need not, if they do not choose, take any part in defending the unit against the outside world. Most states resorted to conscription of a sort; even Britain, if for two centuries it had no obligatory service, had the press gang when necessary, which was a type of lottery con- scription: If you happened to be in the wrong place at the wrong time, you got caught. The United States, however, has only rarely in its history had to resort to a form of conscription that was always far more selective than it was universal. In recent years we have based our security forces on the thesis that enough money will answer our needs, and that if we pay our servicemen sufficiently, they will continue to be servicemen in spite of the siren song of civilian life, a thesis which does not seem, by and large, to be proving correct. The nature of the obligation, once again, and the constraints of military life, are such that even our society does not produce sufficient to pay enough men enough money to fulfill our needs.

To this fact that prosperity breeds a disinclination for the military life must be added the further one that our recent experience has not been such as to enhance the prestige and morale of the military forces. Our position in this respect is summed up, oddly enough, by de Gaulle (1960: 71–72) writing about France after World War I:

The aversion felt for war in general has crystallized around the army. This is an anthropomorphic phenomenon of the same kind as that which makes us dread the dentist even more than the toothache. . . . But the *mystique* of our times must not be allowed to discourage or to humiliate those who wield the sword of France. What better guarantee can be offered to a people gorged with good things, looked at from abroad with embittered resentment, and whose frontiers are so drawn that a single lost battle may put its very capital in jeopardy, than the efficiency of its armed forces.

It is perfectly normal that after a period of unhappy foreign adventuring Americans should prefer to remain at home, that after a long wasting war which was actively opposed by a substantial portion of the population the military services, the most visible target for both fiscal retrenchment and public resentment, should be unpopular. But such attitudes, now hopefully diminishing in the face of returning awareness that there still is a world out there, and that it is not a very friendly one, make the task of leadership, and the exercise of it, all the more difficult.

────── □ ──────

The more difficult such leadership becomes, the more it requires skill approaching art. One is still left with the problem of precisely what that is, or how to inculcate it into one's potential leaders. But this is by no means a new problem. Ever since society departed, somewhere in the last century, from a stratified system in which certain persons were thought by right of birth to be capable of exercising leadership, men have attempted to grapple with it. Lord Palmerston, when pressed to support the idea of examinations for the civil and military service, wrote to a friend, "Success at an examination is certainly not a decisive proof of Fitness for official employment, because after all, examination is chiefly a test of memory acting upon previous Study, and there are other qualities besides Memory and Studious Habits required to make a Good official Man" (Ridley, 1972: 683).

How to produce the Good official Man, or how to recognize him, has remained one of the besetting problems of our time. If we believe, as our whole history attests we do, in the career open to talent, then talent must be recognizable and rewarded as such. But how to recognize it, and how to cut through the "media hype" that tries to convince us today that a man can walk on water, and the day after he is elected or put in command that he cannot walk at all?

De Gaulle (1960: 127), again, groped for a solution. "Enlightened views and supreme wisdom," he said,

. . . are all a matter of intuition and character which no decree can compel, no instruction can impart. Only flair, intelligence and above all, the latent eagerness to play a part which alone enables a man to develop ability and strength of character, can be of service. It all comes to this, that nothing great will ever be achieved without great men, and men are great only if they are determined to be so.

"Intuition," "character," "flair," "greatness through determination to be great," all these are unsatisfactory to the social scientist as explanations of why men do the things they do. They are, in other words, in the province of art. Leadership remains the most baffling of the arts, and in spite of all the tricks that supposedly make it manageable, it will remain that way. As long as we do not know exactly what makes men get up out of a hole in the ground and go forward in the face of death at a word from another man, then leadership will remain one of the highest and most elusive of qualities. It will remain an art.

References

DeGaulle, C., *The Edge of the Sword* (G. Hopkins, trans.), New York: Criterion, 1960.

Encyclopedia Britannica, "Suvárov" (vol. 26), Cambridge: Cambridge University Press, 1911, pp. 172–173.

Guedalla, P., *Men of War,* London: Hodder and Stoughton, 1923.

Longworth, P., *The Art of Victory,* New York: Holt, Rinehart & Winston, 1965.

Montgomery, B., *The Path to Leadership,* London: Collins, 1961.

Record J., "The Fortunes of War," *Harper's* (April 1980), pp. 19–23.

Ridley, J., *Lord Palmerston,* London: Panther, 1972.

Williams, R., *Montrose, Cavalier in Mourning,* London: Barrie and Jenkins, 1975.

2

Leadership

General MATTHEW B. RIDGWAY

In discussing the subject of leadership, I am struck by two diametrically opposite concepts. One conceives leadership as an exact science capable of being understood and practiced by anyone. This view is ably developed by Colonel Sherman L. Kiser, US Army, Retired, in his book, *The American Concept of Leadership*. An opposite concept holds that "no amount of learning will make a man a leader unless he has the natural qualities of one." This latter view was that of General Sir Archibald P. Wavell, and is expounded in his published lectures in *Generals and Generalship*. One concept treats leadership as a science; the other as an art.

I incline strongly to the Wavell concept. While recognizing that there are many principles, or truths, pertaining to the exercise of leadership, and while firmly believing that powers of leadership can be greatly increased in any individual through knowledge of these principles and practice in their application, I still think the variables of human nature combined with those of combat, and to a lesser degree with those in peacetime training, make the exercise of leadership far more of an art than a science.

There is, of course, a great deal of bad leadership as well as of good. It, too, deserves study so that its pitfalls may be avoided. But in general, I believe bad leadership is the result either of violation of basic principles, or the lack or failure to develop one or more of the qualities of good leadership. In any event, I want to speak now of the good type of military leadership with some specific reference later to combat leadership of large units—the division, corps, and army.

The chief ingredients of leadership, as I have known it to be exercised by those whose careers I have studied, or under whose command I was

Reprinted by permission from *Military Review*, LVI:10 (October 1966), pp. 40–49.

privileged to serve, are three. I call them the three C's—character, courage, and competence.

Character is the bedrock on which the whole edifice of leadership rests. It is the prime element for which every profession, every corporation, every industry searches in evaluating a member of its organization. With it, the full worth of an individual can be developed. Without it—particularly in the military profession—failure in peace, disaster in war, or, at best, mediocrity in both will result.

Types of Character

We often use this word "character" carelessly. There are those of notoriously evil character, as well as those of an exemplary one. Yet in its usual acceptation it stands for those magnificent traits which placed George Washington first among his countrymen and, in fact, made him the Father of his Country—the unanimous choice for our first Presidency. It stands for the time-honored code of the officer corps. It stands for self-discipline, loyalty, readiness to accept responsibility, and willingness to admit mistakes. It stands for selflessness, modesty, humility, willingness to sacrifice when necessary, and, in my opinion, for faith in God. Let me illustrate.

During a critical phase of the Battle of the Bulge, when I commanded the 18th Airborne Corps, another corps commander just entering the fight next to me remarked: "I'm glad to have you on my flank. It's character that counts." I had long known him, and I knew what he meant. I replied: "That goes for me, too." There was no amplification. None was necessary. Each knew the other would stick however great the pressure; would extend help before it was asked, if he could; and would tell the truth, seek no self-glory, and everlastingly keep his word. Such feeling breeds confidence and success.

Self-Discipline

Only those who have disciplined themselves can exact disciplined performance from others. When the chips are down, when privation mounts and the casualty rate rises, when the crisis is at hand, which commander, I ask, receives the better response? Is it the one who has failed to share the rough going with his troops, who is rarely seen in the zone of aimed fire, and who expects much and gives little? Or is it the one whose every thought is for the welfare of his men, consistent with the accomplishment of his mission; who does not ask them to do what he has not already done and stands ready to do again when necessary; who with his men has shared short rations, the physical discomforts and rigors of campaign, and will be found at the crises of action where the issues are to be decided?

I know your answer: self-disciplined, self-controlled, and so in control of others, no matter how tough the going—Washington at the Battle of Long Island and at Valley Forge; Grant at Shiloh; Mackenzie of the 4th Cavalry in his epic raid; the junior officer pursuing hostile Indians in sub-zero weather on our western plains, closing up at dark for a dawn attack, with no fires permitted and only cold rations, if any, before H-hour—much the same many times in Korea, I might add, and I am sure under equally arduous conditions in Vietnam today; the young ship commander named Kennedy, his patrol torpedo boat sunk in action, his crew safely on the beach, then swimming out in shark-infested waters to try to intercept a friendly destroyer and rescue his men.

The world's annals and our own are studded with the names of such men, of all services and all grades. Always ready to assume responsibilities, they could always assign them to others and know they would be willingly accepted. True to themselves and to their conscience, their men sense they will be true to them, giving them full credit, and frankly admitting mistakes and accepting responsibility when they themselves are to blame.

General Washington wrote to Congress from Valley Forge:

. . . without arrogance or the smallest deviation from truth, it may be said that no history now extant, can furnish an instance of an Army's suffering such uncommon hardships as ours have done, and bearing them with the same patience and fortitude. To see men without clothes to clothe their nakedness, without blankets to lie on, without shoes, by which their marches might be traced by the blood from their feet, and almost as often without provisions as with; marching through frost and snow, and at Christmas taking up their winter quarters within a day's march of the enemy, without a house or hut to cover them till they could be built, and submitting to it without a murmur, is a mark of patience and obedience which in my opinion can scarce be paralleled.

And what Washington did not say—a mark of his own unexcelled leadership.

An eyewitness report of Lee after Pickett's failure stated:

His face did not show the slightest disappointment, care or annoyance, and he addressed to every soldier he met a few words of encouragement; "All will come right in the end, we'll talk it over afterwards," And to a Brigade Commander speaking angrily of the heavy losses of his men: "Never mind, General, all this has been my fault. It is I who have lost this fight, and you must help me out of it the best way you can."

For leadership through willingness to admit mistakes and instantly to accept responsibility, I think, history can offer few examples to surpass this.

Willingness to Sacrifice

Archibald Rutledge once wrote that there can be no real love without a willingness to sacrifice. Tuck this away in your inner minds. It may pay off in some crisis coming to you in the years now hidden beyond the horizon. Do you love your country and its flag? Do you love the branch in which you are serving, the men with whom you will be privileged to share service and to command? If you do, then you will be prepared to sacrifice for them, if your responsibilities or the situation so demands. The commander of Torpedo Squadron 8 at Midway; the four army chaplains on the torpedoed *SS Dorchester* off Iceland in predawn darkness in February 1942; the many aircraft commanders who have ordered "abandon ship," then stuck overlong to the controls to insure that their last man was out.

Courage, the second "C," could well be treated as a trait of character, as, indeed, it is. Yet it deserves, I believe, a separate category, for I know of not one recipient of history's accolade for battle leadership of enduring fame who was not known for great gallantry.

Physical and Moral Courage

There are two kinds of courage, physical and moral, and he who would be a true leader must have both. Both are products of the character-forming process, of the development of self-control, self-discipline, physical endurance, of knowledge of one's job and, therefore, of confidence. These qualities minimize fear and maximize sound judgment under pressure and—with some of that indispensable stuff called luck—often bring success from seemingly hopeless situations.

Putting aside impulsive acts of reckless bravery, both kinds of courage bespeak an untroubled conscience, a mind at peace with God. An example is Colonel John H. Glenn who was asked after his first rocket flight if he had been worried, and who replied: "I am trying to live the best I can. My peace had been made with my Maker for a number of years, so I had no particular worries."

Examples of physical courage are neither confined to combat nor limited to a stouthearted few, but are common throughout the world among men and women of every color, creed, race, and age, in peace as well as in war. However, examples of moral courage are less well known. They can be considered as proof of true greatness of soul. Where the individual has not measured up, he has generally failed fortune's bid to fame.

To me such incidents most frequently found in war are those where the career of the leader is at stake, and where his actions or decisions will determine the saving or slaughter of many of his men. History is full of these cases. The lure of glory, the fear of being thought afraid, of losing personal power and prestige, the mistaken idea that blind obedience to orders has no alternative—all have been followed by tragic losses of lives with little or no gain.

History often glosses over the countless thousands of lives which have been fruitlessly sacrificed to the pull of power, prestige, and publicity. Haig's Flanders Campaign in 1917 is a conspicuous example. Here, 100,000 men were sacrificed for the gain of 1,000 yards of almost bottomless morass.

It is easy to gamble with other peoples' money, and sometimes easier still with other men's lives, particularly when your own is in no great danger. You remember the commanders' conference prior to one of the big offensives of World War I, when a corps commander—whose command post was miles behind the front—spoke out during a lull in the meeting, saying: "I'd give 10,000 men to take that hill." And a liaison officer from a frontline infantry unit remarked to a brother officer standing beside him in the back of the room: "Generous, isn't he?"

Opposition to Orders

The military services deal harshly, as they should, with failure to carry out orders in battle. The commander present on the scene is entitled to full, instant, and enthusiastic execution of orders by subordinates. Yet when faced with different situations from those anticipated, as well as in the transition from plans to orders, there sometimes comes the challenge to one's conscience, the compelling urge to oppose foolhardy operations before it is too late, before the orders are issued and lives are needlessly thrown away.

Or the leader may be faced with the decision: Shall I take the responsibility of discarding the original mission? Shall I take the initiative and strive for success along different lines? He will have to put those questions to his conscience. "Blind obedience," said Napoleon Bonaparte, "is due only to a superior present on the spot at the moment of action." I concur.

I still support a statement of mine of some years ago:

It has long seemed to me that the hard decisions are not the ones you make in the heat of battle. Far harder to make are those involved in speaking your mind about some harebrained scheme which proposes to commit troops to action under conditions where failure seems almost certain, and the only results will be the needless sacrifice of priceless lives. When all is said and done, the most precious asset any nation has is its youth, and for a battle commander ever to condone the unnecessary sacrifice of his men is inexcusable. In any action you must balance the inevitable cost in lives against the objectives you seek to attain. Unless the results to be expected can reasonably justify the estimated loss of life the action involves, then for my part I want none of it.

General George C. Marshall, one of the noblest men who has worn an American uniform since Washington, once said of decisions of this kind: "It is hard to get men to do this, for this is when you lay your career, perhaps your commission, on the line."

Twice in my personal experience as a division commander I felt compelled to protest against tactical decisions that were about to be assigned to my 82d Airborne Division.

The first occasion was the planned drop on Rome in September 1943. I have recounted the incident in some detail in my book, *Soldier.* Recently, however, published memoirs of German generals then present in the Rome area have confirmed my views. One passage from the account of that incident illustrates the point I wish to make: "When the time comes that I must meet my Maker, the source of most humble pride to me will not be accomplishments in battle, but the fact that I was guided to make the decision to oppose this plan, at the risk of my career, right up to the Theater Commander."

The drop was not ordered.

The second experience was a proposed attack by the 82d across the Volturno River where the Germans had brought the Allied advance to a halt. The sector chosen involved getting across an unfordable river and, then, after an advance of roughly 1,000 yards across open flat terrain, the attack and seizure of a line of hills, curving away from the river on one flank, then like a bow curving back almost to the stream again on the other flank of the zone of attack, so that the assaulting troops would be under concentrated fire from the front and both flanks.

While the proposal to use the 82d was a high compliment—since it was the weakest numerically, and much the most lightly armed of any of the divisions in the 5th Army—I could only view the proposed operation as a suicide mission that would result in the loss of most of the assaulting troops and, then, with small chance of success. I could not accept such a mission without protest. But first I decided to discuss the plan with General Lucien K. Truscott, Commanding General, US

3d Infantry Division, a field commander conspicuous for competence and gallantry, and an old friend. He said he wouldn't touch it with a 40-foot pole, even with his heavier division. So I spoke my mind, first to the corps commander, under whom the operation was to be mounted—and I recall I used the word "fantastic"—and, finally, to the army commander. The plan was canceled.

In action and out, there is often a thin dividing line between recklessness, boldness, and caution. Even later study of battle records may fail to erase that line, for it is next to impossible to reconstruct the exact picture as it was thrown on the screen of the commander's brain at any particular crisis of combat. Yet experience, your own and that of others which you have absorbed, together with commonsense, will be your best guides, and with good luck will see you through.

Physical Fitness

Physical fitness comes under competence, the third of my three basic ingredients of leadership. It plays a great part. My own earlier training at Fort Leavenworth, Fort Benning, Fort Sam Houston with the 2d Division, with the 33d Infantry in the Panama area, and with the airborne paid off in battle—first as a division, then as a corps, and, finally, as an army commander. Because of strenuous and unremitting physical training, I was able to keep up with the best of my troops in the hottest sectors and the toughest terrain and climate.

Let me mention briefly what I think the standards should be for commanders of large units. The division commander should have the physical endurance, stamina, and reserves of his best infantry battalion commanders, because that is where he belongs—with them—a good part of the time; the corps commander, those of his infantry regimental commanders; and the army commander just about the same.

And remember this, since no one can predict today when you may be thrown into combat, perhaps within hours of deplaning in an overseas theater—as happened to thousands in Korea, and as I have no doubt to many in Vietnam—you will have no time to get in shape. You must be in shape all the time.

There is another element in battlefield leadership which I want to mention and illustrate. It is a cardinal responsibility of a commander to foresee insofar as possible where and when crises affecting his command are likely to occur. It starts with his initial estimate of the situation—a continuing mental process from the moment of entering the combat zone until his unit is pulled out of the line. Ask yourself these questions. What are the enemy capabilities? What shall I do, or what could I do, if he should exercise that one of his capabilities which would be most dangerous to me, or most likely to interfere with the accomplishment of my mission?

Personal Presence

As commander of a division or smaller unit, there will rarely be more than one crisis, one really critical situation facing you at any one time. The commander belongs right at that spot, not at some rear command post. He should be there before the crisis erupts, if possible. If it is not possible, then he should get there as soon as he can after it develops. Once there, then by personal observation of terrain, enemy fires, reactions, and attitudes of his own commanders on the spot—by his eyes, ears, brain, nose, and his sixth sense—he gets the best possible picture of what is happening and can best exercise his troop leadership and the full authority of his command. He can start help of every kind to his hard-pressed subordinates. He can urge higher commanders to provide additional fire support, artillery, air, other infantry weapons, and, in the future, perhaps, nuclear strikes.

No other means will provide the commander with what his personal perceptions can provide, if he is present at the critical time and place. He can personally intervene, if he thinks that necessary, but only to the extent that such intervention will be helpful and not interfere with his subordinates. He is in a position to make instant decisions, to defend, withdraw, attack, exploit, or pursue.

If, at this time, he is at some rear command post, he will have to rely on reports from others, and time will be lost, perhaps just those precious moments which spell the difference between success and failure. Notwithstanding the console capabilities of future television in combat, I still believe what I have said is true. In any event, keep this time factor ever in mind. It is the one irretrievable, inextensible, priceless element in war.

Relief of Commanders

The occasion for the relief of commanders may regrettably arise. If it does, there are three points to consider: Is your decision based on personal knowledge and observation, or on secondhand information? What will the effect be on the command concerned? Are you relieving a commander whose men think highly of him—even with affection— regardless of professional competence? And, finally, have you a better man available?

Every man is entitled to go into battle with the best chance of survival your forethought as a leader can provide. What best helps you discharge this responsibility? Sharing things with your men; to be always in the toughest spots; always where the crisis is, or seems most likely to develop; always thinking of what help you can give your commanders who are executing your orders; doing your utmost to see that the best in rations, shelter, first aid, and evacuation facilities are available; being generous with praise, swift and fair with punishment when you have the facts, intolerant of demonstrated failure in leadership on which lives depend, yet making full allowances for human weaknesses and the stresses and strains of battle on individuals.

Know Your Men

Know your men, and be constantly on the alert for potential leaders—you never know how soon you may need them. During my two years in command of the 82d Airborne Division in World War II, I was in close and daily touch with every regimental and most battalion commanders. Before acceding to command of the division, and while I was General Omar N. Bradley's assistant division commander, I had learned to call by name every infantry officer in the division.

Later, by frequent exchange of views with the infantry regimental commanders and the divisional artillery commander, I knew in advance whom they had earmarked for battalion command. I do not recall any instance where I thought the regimental commander had not picked the right man. The payoff came in Normandy. I went in with 12 infantry battalion commanders—four regiments—and I had 14 new ones when we came out, for some battalions lost as many as three commanders during the 33 days we were in that fight.

The qualities of a leader are not limited to commanders. The requirements for leadership are just as essential in the staff officer, and in some respects more exacting, since he does not have that ultimate authority which can be used when necessary and must rely even more than his commander on his own strength of character, his tact and persuasion in carrying out his duties.

Between the commander and his chief of staff in a division or larger unit there should be thorough mutual respect, understanding, and confidence with no official secrets between them. Together they form a single dual personality, and the instructions issuing from the chief of staff must have the same weight and authority as those of the commander himself.

But this does not mean that a commander who delegates such authority to his chief of staff can allow his chief to isolate him from the rest of his staff. If that happens, the commander will soon find himself out of touch, and the chief of staff will be running the unit.

There is a fine balance here. The chiefs of staff sections should know that they always have access to their commander. He should see them and visit their sections with sufficient frequency to understand their problems, to let them know he appreciates their efforts, and that he stands ready to help where he can.

Inform Subordinates

Closely akin to the relationship with staff officers is keeping in close personal touch with your principal subordinate commanders—in the division, with your brigade and separate battalion commanders; in the corps, with your division commanders, their chiefs of staff, and as many of the commanders of attached corps units as you can; and in the army, with corps and division commanders and their chiefs of staff. There is always time for these visits; administrative work can be done at night. By day you belong with your troops.

Keep them informed of your thinking and plans. When you have the concept of an operation first in mind, consult your principal commanders without delay and get their reactions. No matter how sound a tactical plan may be, the chances of successful execution will be greatly increased if you have first secured the willing acceptance by commanders responsible for execution of the missions you plan to assign them. Insure that they receive notice of your decision and the principal details of your plan as approved in ample time to permit them and their subordinates to make their necessary reconnaissances and issue their orders.

These are some of the reasons why I hold that leadership is not a science, but an art. It conceives an ideal, states it as an objective, and then seeks actively and earnestly to attain it, everlastingly persevering, because the records of war are full of successes coming to those leaders who stuck it out just a little longer than their opponents.

Some suggestions for leadership are:

- Read widely and wisely all the history and biography possible. Soak up all the personal experiences you can of battle-tested brother officers. This broadens your understanding of an art of which you can never hope to know all.
- Study thoughtfully the records of past successful leaders and adapt their methods to yours.
- Work hard to keep fit. That little extra stamina may some day pull you out of some deep holes.
- Work hard, in your own way, at being tops at your job.

- Keep the three C's—character, courage, and competence—always before your mind, and with faith in God, be yourself.
- Remember there are many others on your team, and be inwardly humble. Every man's life is equally precious, although all are at the disposal of our country, and the contribution each makes in battle is of equal potential value.

3

Commitment Is the Price We Pay

Chief Master Sergeant of the Air Force
ARTHUR L. ANDREWS

During my first year as Chief Master Sergeant of the Air Force, I was on the road for twenty-three days a month, and visited more than 100 installations or sites worldwide. During those travels I saw the best and the worst. However, one overall impression is clear: The enlisted force is striving to make the Air Force bigger, better, and stronger. They work hard to better the United States Air Force and better themselves.

During my travels I kept in touch with the Air Force's senior leaders. They know what I see and hear because, like me, they have an open-door policy. Because enlisted people tell me their feelings, I can relay their thoughts to the senior leadership. However, this communication process is not a one-way street: I, in turn, tell the enlisted force what our senior leaders are doing to better the Air Force and what they expect of the enlisted force and why. We must always have such honest and direct two-way communication.

Our senior leaders are currently working on many important issues: the new GI Bill; dental Champus; per-diem equity; and this year's pay bill, to name just a few. Your thoughts on these issues are known, but as you and I voice our concerns, do we uphold our end of the bargain to earn these benefits? Are we going that extra step?

We need to. We are responsible for tasks that must be done, and done right to the best of our abilities. We can never stop striving to do our absolute best. We must never say, "There, that's good enough," and sit back and take it easy. There is no room for mediocrity in the

Reprinted with permission from *Air Force Magazine,* 65:9 (September 1982), pp. 105–106. Copyright © 1982, Air Force Association.

34   *Arthur L. Andrews*

Air Force. The Air Force *does not* exist to provide a "job" and a comfortable way of life. We don't have jobs in the United States Air Force; we are part of a calling.

Tradition and Commitment

Let us reflect for just a moment on a word we hear a lot about in the Air Force. And that word is *tradition.* Our tradition, as military professionals. The day we accept the premise that the Air Force is nothing more than another occupation, or even primarily an occupation, this country is in grave danger. All of us are dues-paying members of one of the more demanding and honorable professions in the world: the United States Air Force. And you and I are paying those dues in the only coin that is acceptable in our profession: *commitment.* Commitment is the price we pay to be noncommissioned officrs in the Air Force. By definition, commitment is the act of pledging or entrusting, or setting something apart or putting it to purpose. An Air Force career—our lifestyle—is all of those things.

Again, our military career is not just another job. It calls for self-sacrifice, not self-interest. It calls for self-discipline, not self-indulgence. In more concrete terms, it calls for alerts, deployments, worldwide airlift missions, PCS moves, etc., etc. National defense is not a business that opens its doors at 8:00 A.M. and closes at 5:00 P.M., Monday through Friday. National defense is not an enterprise whose only branch offices are located in the sunbelt states. National defense calls for a special kind of dedication and a motivation to serve and excel.

Some of us in fact do complain about the assignment system. We too often want to select where we want to go and what we want to do. But nobody has explained to me how I would go about telling the Chief of Staff and the Secretary of the Air Force that we are going to close down the northern-tier bases and pull out of our remote locations because no one wants to serve there this year.

A few of us, and I'm happy to say only a few of us, tend to forget that our commitment began when we enlisted. We used phrases such as "I do solemnly swear... support and defend the Constitution... bear true faith and allegiance ... obey the orders of the officers appointed over me ... so help me God." We made a pledge, a solemn promise. When we made the pledge, we were, by implication, entrusting our well-being to the Air Force. The Air Force became responsible to a very large degree for seeing that we are properly fed, housed, kept healthy, and trained. So the commitment is, in that sense, a two-way street.

As we grow in grade and responsibility and become part of the leadership of the Air Force, we must become more deeply involved on both sides of that street. We have to be held accountable for living up to that pledge, but we also, as leaders, have to assume a share of the Air Force commitment. We must ensure that our people are properly cared for, and also make sure they hold up their end of the bargain. As leaders and noncommissioned officers, we are responsible to accomplish the mission and to look after the well-being of our people. When these objectives conflict, the mission prevails—that is the price of that commitment.

Leadership by Example

Our sense of tradition and commitment is linked to *leadership*. I stress leadership, "leadership by example," because I believe in it and I think we need to improve on it. Noncommissioned officers are responsible for leadership today and tomorrow. We are charged with taking young men and women today and leading them to positions of greater responsibility. The optimistic leader sees and readily accepts that very challenge. The true leaders know their units are the best and do everything in a positive manner.

The leader treats the letters PME, Professional Military Education, as a stepping-stone to success, not just another school, not just another TDY. The leader is not afraid to delegate the authority to go along with the responsibility. The true leader has faith in his or her subordinates and, most of all, complete confidence and trust.

A leader never degrades his or her superiors; leadership by example is always first and foremost. We, and I mean all of us, have got to get rid of that "I'm afraid I will turn them off" attitude by correcting and demanding compliance to long-established rules and regulations. Ask yourself, when was the last time I corrected a peer or a subordinate? When did you last tell someone to get into shape or, for that matter, how many times have we sidestepped a sloppy individual, simply because we didn't want to get involved in a hassle? We *must* set the example. Silence of that sort is not golden; rather, it is very dangerous.

The true leaders belong to the *we* society, not the *me* group. They understand that good leadership instills pride and discipline in every phase of our subordinates' careers, and that professionalism is something we must never lose sight of. Our noncommissioned officers of the 1980s must accept the extra responsibility that comes with a leadership career in this very challenging decade.

If we do not accept that extra responsibility, our units, work groups, associates, and yes, even our country will certainly be the ultimate losers. We have so very much to gain as individuals and, of course, as a nation by having solid followers and solid leaders. We can be anything we set our hearts and minds to be.

4

Leaders and Leadership

General S.L.A. MARSHALL

In that gallery of great Americans whose names are conspicuously identified with the prospering of the national arms in peace and war, there are almost as many types as there are men.

There were a certain few qualities they had to possess in common or their names would never have become known beyond the county line.

But these were inner qualities, often deeply buried, rather than outward marks of greatness that men recognized immediately upon beholding them.

Some almost missed the roll call, either because in early life their weaknesses were more apparent than their strengths, or because of an outward seeming of insignificance, which at first fooled their contemporaries.

In the minority are the few who seemed marked for greatness almost from the cradle, and were acclaimed for leadership while still of tender years.

Winfield Scott, a brigadier in the war of 1812 when brigadiers were few, and Chief of Staff when the Civil War began, is a unique figure in the national history.

George Washington, Adjutant of the State of Virginia at 21, is one other military infant prodigy who never later belied his early fame.

The majority in the gallery are not like these. No two of them are strikingly alike in mien and manner. Their personalities are as different, for the most part, as their names. Their characters also ran the length of the spectrum, or nearly, if we are talking of moral habit rather than of conscientious performance of military duty. Some drank their whiskey

---

Reprinted from *The Armed Forces Officer* (Washington, D.C.: Government Printing Office, 1975), pp. 47–57.

neat and frequently; others loathed it and took a harsh line with any subordinate who used it.

One of the greatest generals in American history, celebrated for his fighting scarcely more than for his tippling, would walk from the room if any man tried to tell an off-color story in his presence. One of the most celebrated and successful of our World War II admirals endeared himself to millions of men in all ranks by his trick of gathering his chief subordinates together just before battle, issuing his orders sternly and surely, and then relaxing long enough to tell them his latest parlor story, knowing that finally it would trickle down through the whole command.

In Korea, one infantry division commander was a skilled banjo player. Up at the front, he formed a small orchestra of enlisted men and fitted into it. Between fire fights, they played for troops. The men loved him for it. Later, he became one of the Army's ranking generals and was named to one of its top posts. His name: Arthur G. Trudeau.

Among the warriors in this gallery are men who would bet a month's pay on a horse race. There are duellists and brawlers, athletes and aesthetes, men who lived almost saintly lives and scholars who lived more for learning than for fame.

Some tended to be so over-reclusive that they almost missed recognition; others were hail-fellow-well-met in any company.

Their methods of work reflected these extreme variations in personal type, as did the means they used to draw other men to them, thereby setting a foundation for real success.

Part of their number commanded mainly through the sheer force of ideas; others owed their leadership more to the magnetism of dynamic personality.

In the very few there was the spark of genius. All things seemed to come right with them at all times. Fate was kind, the openings occurred, and they were prepared to take advantage of them.

But the greater number moved up the hill one slow step at a time, not always sure of their footing, buffeted by mischance, owning no exalted opinion of their own merits, reacting to discouragement much as other men do, but finally accumulating power as they learned how to organize the work of other men.

While a young lieutenant, Admiral Sims became so incensed when the United States would not take his word on a voucher that he offered to resign.

General Grant signally failed to organize his life as an individual before a turn of the wheel gave him his chance to organize the military power of the United States in war.

General Sherman, who commanded the Army for almost 15 years, was considered by many of his close friends to be a fit subject for confinement as a mental case just before the Civil War.

General Meade, one of the calmest and most devoted of men in his family relationships, lacked confidence in his own merits and was very abusive of his associates during battle.

Admiral Farragut, whose tenderness as an individual was demonstrated during the 16 years in which he personally nursed an invalid wife, was so independent in his professional thought and action that both in and out of the Navy he was discredited as a "climber." He got into wretched quarrels with his superiors mainly because he felt his assignments afforded him no distinction. The Civil War gave him his opportunity.

General Winfield Scott, as firm a commander as any in our history, plagued the Army with his petty bickering over rank, seniority, and precedent.

Being human, they had their points of personal weakness. A newly appointed ensign or second lieutenant also has chinks in his armor, and sometimes views them in such false proportion that he doubts his own potential for high responsibility.

There is not one perfect life in the gallery of the great. All were molded by the mortal influences surrounding them. They reacted in their own feelings, and toward other men, according to the rise and fall of their personal fortunes. They sought help where it could be found. When disappointed, they chilled like anyone else. But along with their professional talents, they possessed in common a desire for substantial recognition, accompanied by the will to earn it fairly, or else the Nation would never have heard their names.

All in all it is a much mixed gallery. If we were to pass it in review and then inspect it carefully, it would still be impossible to say: "This is the composite of character. This is the prototype of military success. Model upon it and you have the pinnacle within reach."

The same thing would no doubt hold true of a majority of the better men who commanded ships, squadrons, regiments, and companies under these commanders, and at their own level were as superior in leadership as the relatively few who rose to national prominence because of the achievements of the general body.

The same rule will apply tomorrow. Those who come forward to fill these places, and to command them with equal or greater authority and competence, will not be plaster saints, laden with all human virtue, spotless in character, and fit to be anointed with a superman legend by some future Parson Weems. They will be men with ambition and a strong belief in the United States and the goodness of a free society. They will have some of the average man's faults and maybe a few of his vices. But certainly they will possess the qualities of courage, creative intelligence, and physical robustness in more than average measure.

What we know of our great leaders in the current age should discourage the idea that only a genius may scale the heights. Trained observers have noted in their personalities and careers many of the plain characteristics each man feels in himself and mistakenly regards as a bar to preferment.

Drew Middleton, the American correspondent, wrote of General Carl "Tooey" Spaatz: "This man, who may be a heroic figure to our grandchildren, is essentially an unheroic figure to his contemporaries. He is, in fact, such a friendly, human person that observers tend to minimize his stature as a war leader. He is not temperamental. He makes no rousing speeches, writes no inspirational orders. Spaatz, in issuing orders for a major operation involving 1,500 airplanes, is about as inspiring as a groceryman ordering another five cases of canned peas."

An interviewer who called on General Ira C. Eaker when he was leading the 8th Air Force against Germany found "a strikingly soft-spoken, sober, compact man who has the mild manner of a conservative minister and the judicial outlook of a member of the Supreme Court. But he is always about two steps ahead of everybody on the score, and there is a quiet, inexorable logic about everything he does." Of his own choice, Eaker would have separated from military service after World War I. He wanted to be a lawyer, and he also toyed with the idea of running a country newspaper. In his off hours, he wrote books on aviation for junior readers. On the side, he studied civil law and found it "valuable mental training."

On the eve of the Guadalcanal landing, General A. A. Vandegrift's final order to his command ended with the stirring and now celebrated phrase: "God favors the bold and strong of heart." Yet in the afterglow of later years, the Nation read a character sketch of him that included this: "He is so polite and so soft-spoken that he is continually disappointing the people whom he meets. They find him lacking in the fire-eating traits they like to expect of all marines, and they find it difficult to believe that such a mild-mannered man could really have led and won the bloody fight." When another officer spoke warmly of Vandegrift's coolness under fire, his "grace under pressure," to quote Hemingway's phrase, he replied: "I shouldn't be given any credit. I'm built that way."

The point is beautifully taken. Too often the man with great inner strength holds in contempt those less well endowed by nature than himself.

Brilliance of intellect and high achievement in scholarship are an advantage, though in the end they have little or no payoff if character and courage are lacking. Thousands of officers who served in Vietnam, some dubious about the wisdom of the national policy, questioning whether the tight rein on operations made military sense, still believed that "My country right or wrong" is the only course possible for one who has taken the oath.

No, brain trusting and whizz kidding are not what it takes. Of 105 major generals who served in World War I, 56 had failed to score above the middle of their class in mathematics. Of 275 in World War II, 158, or 58 percent, were in the middle group or among the dubs in the same subject. General William C. Westmoreland, who commanded in Vietnam and was later Army Chief of Staff, had punched practically none of the buttons. As for military schooling, for over 30 years after graduating from West Point, he attended only Cooks and Bakers School and the Airborne School. One of his outstanding subordinates, a two-star general, respected and loved by all who served under him, had joined the service at the age of 15 out of reform school to straighten himself out. By sweat and study, he won his sergeant's stripes at 18 and his commission at 21. He made his resolve and stayed with it, which was the main thing. The solution of every problem, every achievement is, as Justice Holmes said, a bird on the wing; and he added, one must have one's whole will on one's eye on that bird. One cannot be thinking of one's image, or one's place in history—only of that bird.

While there are no perfect men, there are those who become relatively perfect leaders of men because something in their makeup brings out in strength the highest virtues of all who follow them. That is the way of human nature. Minor shortcomings do not impair the loyalty or growth of the follower who has found someone whose strengths he deems worth emulating. On the other hand, to recognize merit, you must yourself have it. The act of recognizing the worthwhile traits in another person is both the test and the making of character. The man who scorns all others and thinks no one else worth following parades his own inferiority before the world. He puts his own character into bankruptcy just as surely as does that other sad sack of whom Thomas Carlyle wrote: "To recognize false merit, and crown it as true, because a long trail runs after it, is the saddest operation under the sun."

Sherman, Logan, Rawlins, and the many others hitched their wagons to Grant's star because they saw in him a man who had a way with other men, and who commanded them not less by personal courage than by patient work in their interest. Had Grant spent time brooding over his own civilian failures, he would have been struck with a disorderly camp and would never have gotten out of Illinois. He was not dismayed by his own shortcomings. Later he said: "I doubt that any of my officers ever discovered that I hadn't bothered to study tactics."

The nobility of the private life and influence of General Robert E. Lee and the grandeur of his military character are known to every American school boy. His peerless gifts as a battle leader have won the tribute of celebrated soldiers and historians throughout the world. Likewise, the deep religiosity of his great lieutenant, Stonewall Jackson, the fiery zeal and almost evangelical power with which he lifted the hearts of all men who followed him, are hallmarks of character that are vividly present in whatever context his name happens to be mentioned.

If we turn for a somewhat closer look at Grant, it is because he, more than any other American soldier, left us a full, clear narrative of his own growth, and of the inner thoughts and doubts pertaining to himself which attended his life experience. There was a great deal of the average man in Grant. He was beset by human failings. He could not look impressive. He had no sense of destiny. In his great hours, it was sweat, rather than inspiration, dogged perseverance, rather than the aura of power, that made the hour great.

Average though he was in many things, there was nothing average about the strong way in which he took hold, applying massive common sense to the complex problems of the field. That is why he is worth close regard. His virtues as a military leader were of the simpler sort that plain men may understand and hope to emulate. He was direct in manner. He never intrigued. His speech was homely. He was approachable. His mind never deviated from the object. Though a stubborn man, he was always willing to listen to his subordinates. He never adhered to a plan obstinately, but nothing could induce him to forsake the idea behind the plan.

History has left us a clear view of how he attained to greatness in leadership by holding steadfastly to a few main principles.

At Belmont, his first small action, he showed nothing to indicate that he was competent as a tactician and strategist. But the closing scene reveals him as the last man to leave the field of action, risking his life to see that none of his men had been left behind.

At Fort Donelson, where he had initiated an amphibious campaign of highly original daring, he was not on the battlefield when his army was suddenly attacked. He arrived to find his right wing crushed and his whole force on the verge of defeat. He blamed no one. Without more than a fleeting hesitation, he said quietly to his chief subordinates: "Gentlemen, the position on the right must be retaken." Then he mounted his horse and galloped along the line shouting to his men: "Fill your cartridge cases quick; the enemy is trying to escape and he must not be permitted to do so." Control and order were immediately reestablished by his presence.

At Shiloh the same thing happened, only this time it was worse; the whole Union Army was on the verge of rout. Grant, hobbling on crutches from a recent leg injury, met the mob of panic-stricken stragglers as he left the boat at Pittsburgh Landing. Calling on them to turn back, he mounted and rode toward the battle, shouting encouragement and giving orders to all he met. Confidence flowed from him back into an already beaten Army, and in this way a field nearly lost was soon regained, with decisive help provided by Buell's Army.

The last and best picture of Grant is on the evening after he had taken his first beating from General Lee in the campaign against Richmond. He was new with the Army of the Potomac. His predecessors, after being whipped by Lee, had invariably retreated to a safe distance. But this time, as the defeated army took the road of retreat out of the Wilderness, its columns got only as far as the Chancellorsville House crossroad. There the soldiers saw a squat, bearded man sitting horseback, and drawing on a cigar. As the head of each regiment came abreast of him, he silently motioned it to take the right-hand fork—back toward Lee's flank and deeper than ever into the Wilderness. That night, for the first time, the Army sensed an electric change in the air over Virginia. It had a man.

"I intend to fight it out on this line" is more revealing of the one supreme quality that put the seal on all of U.S. Grant's great gifts for military leading than everything else that the historians have written of him. He was the essence of the spirit that moderns call "seeing the show through." He was sensitive to a fault in his early years, and carried to his tomb a dislike for military uniform, caused by his being made the butt of ridicule the first time he ever donned a soldier suit. As a junior officer in the Mexican War, he sensed no particular aptitude in himself. But he had participated in every engagement possible for a member of his regiment, and had executed every small duty well, with particular attention to conserving the lives of his men. This was the school and the course that later enabled him to march to Richmond, when men's lives had to be spent for the good of the Nation.

In more recent times, one of the great statesmen and soldiers of the United States, Henry L. Stimson, has added his witness to the value of this force in all enterprise: "I know the withering effect of limited commitments and I know the regenerative effect of full action." Though he was speaking particularly of the larger affairs of war and national policy, his words apply with full weight to the personal life. The truth seen only halfway is missed wholly; the thing done only halfway had best not be attempted at all. Men can't be fooled on this score. They will know every time when the arrow falls short for lack of a worthwhile effort. And when that happens, confidence in the leader is corroded, even among those who themselves were unwilling to try.

There have been great and distinguished leaders in our military Services at all levels who had no particular gifts for administration and little for organizing the detail of decisive action either within battle or without. They excelled because of a superior ability to make use of the brains and command the loyalty of well-chosen subordinates. Their particular function was to judge the goal according to their resources and audacity, and then to hold the team steady until the goal was gained. So doing, they complemented the power of the faithful lieutenants who might have put them in the shade in any IQ test. Wrote Grant: "I never knew what to do with a paper except to put it in a side pocket or pass it to a clerk who understood it better than I did." There was nothing unfair or irregular about this, it was as it should be. All military achievement develops out of unity of action. The laurel goes to the man whose powers can most surely be directed toward the end purposes of organization. The winning of battles is the product of the winning of men. That aptitude is not an endowment of formal education, though the man who has led a football team, a class, a fraternity or a debating society is the stronger for the experience he has gained. It is not unusual for those who have excelled in scholarship to despise those who have excelled merely in sympathetic understanding of the human race. But in the military Services, though there are niches for the pedant, character is at all times at least as vital as intellect, and the main rewards go to him who can make other men feel toughened as well as elevated.

- Quiet resolution.
- The hardihood to take risks.
- The will to take full responsibility for decision.
- The readiness to share its rewards with subordinates.
- An equal readiness to take the blame when things go adversely.
- The nerve to survive storm and disappointment and to face toward each new day with the scoresheet wiped clean, neither dwelling on one's successes nor accepting discouragement from one's failures.

In these things lie a great part of the essence of leadership, for they are the constituents of that kind of moral courage that has enabled one man to draw many others to him in any age.

It is good, also, to look the part, not only because of its effect on others, but because, from out of the effort made to look it, one may in time come to be it. One of the kindliest and most penetrating philosophers of our age, Abbé Ernest Dimnet, has assured us that this is true. He says that by trying to look and act like a socially distinguished person, one may in fact attain to the inner disposition of a gentleman. That, almost needless to say, is the real mark of the officer who takes great pains about the manner of his dress and address, for as Walt Whitman said: "All changes of appearances without a change in that which underlies appearances are without avail." All depends upon the spirit in which one makes the effort. By his own account, U.S. Grant, as a West Point cadet, was more stirred by the commanding appearance of General Winfield Scott than by any man he had ever seen, including the President. He wrote that at that moment there flashed across his mind the thought that some day he would stand in Scott's place. Grant was unkempt of dress. His physical endowments were such that he could never achieve the commanding air of Scott. But he left us his witness that Scott's military bearing helped kindle his own desire for command, even though he knew that he could not be like Scott.

Much is said in favor of modesty as an asset in leadership. It is remarked that the man who wishes to hold the respect of others will mention himself not more frequently than a born aristocrat mentions his ancestor. However, the point can be labored too hard. Some of the ablest of the Nation's military commanders have been anything but shrinking violets; we have had now and then a hero who could boast with such gusto that this very characteristic somehow endeared him to his men. But that would be a dangerous tack for all save the most exceptional individual. Instead of speaking of modesty as a charm that will win all hearts, thereby risking that through excessive modesty a man will become tiresome to others and rated as too timid for high responsibility, it would be better to dwell upon the importance of being natural, which means neither concealing nor making a vulgar display of one's ideals and motives, but acting directly according to his dictates.

This leads to another point. In several of the most celebrated commentaries written by higher commanders on the nature of generalship, the statement is made rather carelessly that to be capable of great military leadership a man must be something of an actor. If that were unqualifiedly true, then it would be a desirable technique likewise for any junior officer; he, too, should learn how to wear a false face and play a part that cloaks his real self. The hollowness of the idea is proved by the lives of such men as Robert E. Lee, W. T. Sherman, George C. Marshall, Omar N. Bradley, Carl A. Spaatz, William H. Simpson, Chester A. Nimitz, Harold K. Johnson, Matthew B. Ridgway, Lew Walt, Creighton W. Abrams and John S. McCain, Jr., to mention only a few. As commanders, they were all as natural as children, though some had great natural reserve, and others were warm and much more outgoing. They expressed themselves straightforwardly rather than by artful striving for effect. There was no studied attempt to appear only in a certain light. To use the common word for it, their people did not regard them as "characters." This naturalness had much to do with their hold on other men.

Such a result will always come. He who concentrates on the object at hand has little need to worry about the impression he is making on others. Even though they detect the chinks in the armor, they will know that the armor will hold.

On the other hand, a sense of the dramatic values, coupled with the intelligence to play upon them skillfully, is an invaluable quality in any military leader. Though there was nothing of the "actor" in Grant, he understood the value of pointing things up. To put a bold or inspiring emphasis where it belongs is not stagecraft but an integral part of the military fine art of communicating. System that is only system is injurious to the mind and spirit of any normal person. One can play a superior part well and maintain prestige and dignity, without being under the compulsion to think, speak, and act in a monotone. In fact, when any military commander becomes over-inhibited along these lines because of the illusion that this is the way to build a reputation for strength, he but doubles the necessity for his subordinates to act at all times like human beings rather than robots.

Coupled with self-control, consideration and thoughtfulness will carry a man far. Men will warm toward a leader when they come to believe that all the energy he stores up by living somewhat within himself is at their service. But when they feel that this is not the case, and that his reserve is simply the outward sign of a spiritual miserliness and concentration on purely personal goals, no amount of restraint will ever win their favor. This is as true of him who commands a whole Service as of the leader of a squad.

To speak of the importance of a sense of humor would be futile, if it were not that what cramps so many men isn't that they are by nature humorless as that they are hesitant to exercise what humor they possess. Within the military profession, this is as unwise as to let the muscles go soft or to spare the mind the strain of original thinking. Great humor has always been in the military tradition. The need of it is nowhere more delicately expressed than in Kipling's lines:

My son was killed while laughing at some jest,
    I would I knew
What it was, and it might serve me in a time
    When jests are few.

Marcus Aurelius, Rome's soldier philosopher, spoke of his love for the man who "could be humorous in an agreeable way." No reader of

Grant's *Memoirs* (one of the few truly great autobiographies ever written by a soldier) could fail to be impressed by his light touch. A delicate sense of the incongruous seems to have pervaded him; he is at his whimsical best when he sees himself in a ridiculous light. Lord Kitchener, one of the grimmest warriors ever to serve the British Empire, warmed to the man who made him the butt of a practical joke. There is the unforgettable picture of Admiral Beatty at Jutland. The *Indefatigable* had disappeared beneath the waves. The *Queen Mary* had exploded. The *Lion* was in flames. Then word came that the *Princess Royal* was blown up. Said Beatty to his Flag Captain, "Chatfield, there seems to be something wrong with our—ships today. Turn two points nearer the enemy." Admiral Nimitz, surveying the terrible landscape of the Kwajalein battlefield for the first time, said gravely to his staff: "It's the worst devastation I've ever seen except for that last Texas picnic in Honolulu." There is a characteristic anecdote of General Patton. He had just been worsted by higher headquarters in an argument over strategy. So he sat talking to his own staff about it, his dog curled up beside him. Suddenly he said to the animal: "The trouble with you, too, Willy, is that you don't understand the big picture." General Eisenhower, probably more than any other modern American commander, had the art of winning with his humor. He would have qualified under the English essayist Sydney Smith's definition: "The meaning of an extraordinary man is that he is eight men in one man; that he has as much wit as if he had no sense, and as much sense as if he had no wit; that his conduct is as judicious as if he were the dullest of human beings, and his imagination as brilliant as if he were irretrievably ruined."

In Korea, just before the first battle of Pork Chop Hill began, Lt. Thomas V. Harrold heard a loud wailing from the Communist trench and asked his company its meaning.

"They're prayer singing," said an interpreter. "They're getting ready to die."

Said Harrold: "Then I guess we ought to be singing too."

And not a bad idea. The 1st Marine Division, fighting its way back from the Chosin Reservoir in December 1950, was embattled amid the snows from the moment the column struck its camp at Hagaru. By midnight, after heavy loss through the day, it had bivouacked at Kotori, still surrounded, still far from the sea. Maj. Gen. Oliver P. Smith was alone in his tent. It was his bad moment. The task ahead seemed hopeless. Suddenly he heard music. Outside some truckers were singing the Marine Hymn. "All doubt left me," said Smith. "I knew then we had it made."

Concerning leadership within the terms here set forth, the final thought is that there is a radical difference between training and combat conditions.

In training the commander may be arbitrary, demanding, and a hard disciplinarian. But so long as his sense of fair play in handling his men becomes evident to them, and provided they become aware that what he is doing is making them more efficient than their competition, they will approve him, if grudgingly, stay loyal to him, and even possibly come to believe in his lucky star.

They are more likely to do it, however, if he takes a fatherly interest in their personal welfare. But that feeling doesn't have to come naturally to a man for him to win the respect of troops. If he knows his business, they're on his team.

When it comes to combat, something new is added. Even if they have previously looked on him as a father and believed absolutely that being with him is their best assurance of successful survival, should he then show himself to be timid and too cautious about his own safety, he will lose hold of them no less absolutely. His lieutenant, who up till then under training conditions has been regarded as a mean creature or a sniveler, but on the field suddenly reveals himself as a man of high courage, can take moral leadership of the company away from him, and do it in one day.

On the field there is no substitute for courage, no other binding influence toward unity of action. Troops will excuse almost any stupidity; excessive timidity is simply unforgiveable. This was the epitome of Captain Queeg's failure in *The Caine Mutiny*. Screwball that he was, and an oppressor of men, his other vices would have been tolerable had he, under fire, proved himself somewhat better than a coward.

5

Ethics of Leadership

Colonel MALHAM M. WAKIN

A leader is best
When people barely know that he exists,
Not so good when people obey and acclaim him,
Worst when they despise him.
"Fail to honor people,
They fail to honor you;"
But of a good leader, who talks little,
When his work is done, his aim fulfilled,
They will all say, "We did this ourselves."
— Lao Tzu, Sixth Century B.C.;
Verse 17 of the *Tao Teh Ching*

It is possible to infer much more from this verse in the *Tao Teh Ching* concerning ethics and leadership than its author could have intended so many centuries ago. Lao Tzu saw human leadership at its best when it imitated the most harmonious ways of nature, flowing smoothly like a natural stream, without harshness or aggressive struggle, and marked always by a gentleness that naturally pulled subordinates to their tasks. This is a view totally inimical to that of the leader as an egoistic order-giver who forces compliance from subordinates by threats, and claims sole credit for any positive results of their efforts. With some trepidation, I would like to reflect on these two extreme characterizations of superior-subordinate relationships, pursuing a fundamental notion first suggested to me in a paper delivered by William May,[1] and developing the ethical implications of adopting one mode of leadership rather than another. Following these reflections, I hope to be able to establish the critical

Malham M. Wakin, "Ethics of Leadership," pp. 95–111 in *Military Leadership*, edited by James H. Buck and Lawrence J. Korb. Copyright © 1981 by Sage Publications, Inc. Reprinted by permission.

importance of ethical considerations to military leadership in the light of the unique function of the military profession.

Social Contract or Polity?[2]

In the many criticisms of military leadership which have been published in recent years, much attention has been given to the image of a ruthless, ambitious careerist, intent upon furthering his own interests in his climb up the hierarchical ladder in spite of or even because of the high personal cost he may extract from contemporaries, subordinates, or the actual military mission itself. This is one of the anecdotal statements made by an Army major who was interviewed during the Army War College's research for their *Study on Military Professionalism* (1970: B-1-2): "My superior was a competent, professional, knowledgeable military officer who led by fear, would doublecross anyone to obtain a star, drank too much and lived openly by no moral code. He is now a Brigadier General!" But the "careerists" are not a peculiar military phenomena; they are to be found in many of our professions. And it is not as though ethical considerations are irrelevant for these professional climbers— they have an ethic, but as Max Lerner puts it, "It is the wrong one." Lerner (1975: 11) refers to this ethic in contemporary business parlance as the "bottom line" ethic.

> For a politician, the ethic is to get power and hold on to it; for a lawyer, it is to win his case and get his fee . . . for a corporate executive, the ethic is to win out in the lethally competitive struggle for profits, markets, stock values. The bottom line is what counts, whatever the means used. It is the cancer of the professions.

How does one find oneself caught up in this bottom line ethic, not only without sensitivity for the means employed but often with the seeming conviction that promotion (the symbol of success) is evidence of virtue? The means employed "worked"; can there still be ethical questions to ask? Promotion itself provides vindication for the means employed. One possible explanation of this "ethic" is that it is an understandable extended outcome of a certain position on the nature of man, advocated in its most primitive form by Thomas Hobbes.

Hobbes is used as one of the classic representatives of egoism in most textbooks of moral philosophy. His view of man in the *Leviathan* begins with the assumption that all men are equal in the state of nature; that is, as they appear in the world considered apart from any formal social or political structure. In this primal condition, every man has an equal right to everything and moral terms have no meaning. There can be no right or wrong if every person has a right to everything; the fundamental rule of behavior involves personal survival by the use of one's own devices. This natural condition of man is chaotic, savage, and marked by violence. Indeed Hobbes tells us that "during the time men live without a common power to keep them all in awe, they are in that condition which is called war; and such a war, as is of every man, against every man." Life for man in such condition is "solitary, poor, nasty, brutish, and short" (*Leviathan:* Ch. 13). But man is also endowed with reason which ultimately leads him to conclude that if he is to survive, he must seek peace with other men. He must give up his right to harm other men if he can persuade them to do likewise and enter into an agreement, a social contract with them. However, the mere fact of the existence of an agreement does not change human nature. It is still the case that "of the voluntary acts of every man, the object is some *good to himself*" (*Leviathan:* Ch. 14). So to guarantee that men will abide by their agreements, tremendous powers must be granted to government (the real leviathan) so that men will live up to their social contract out of fear of punishment. For the first time, moral terms have meaning once the agreement is made: Living up to the contract is "justice"; breaking it is injustice. All laws passed by the agreed-upon government become moral obligations; morality itself rests on the agreement—it is man-made and not found either in nature or in accordance with nature. Moral rules are legislated (see Melden, 1955).

This brief elaboration of Hobbes's account of the nature of man and the origins of government through a social contract is relevant to any analysis of military leadership. The Hobbesian view of man is held by several commentators on the military profession to be essential to the military ethic (see Huntington, 1957: Ch. 3). This view might also be at the root of the moral comfortableness of the careerist mentioned previously. If self-interest is the primary focus of human action, or if, more to the point, it *ought* to be, then one may feel morally justified if hierarchical ambitions are realized even at high cost to others. Here, we may reflect on William May's suggestion that social contract theories "tracing the origin of the state to a supreme evil" (namely man's predatory nature) give rise to adversary relationships on every side. May made specific reference to John Locke's version of the social contract theory rather than to that of Hobbes, perhaps because Locke is viewed as having more direct influence on the framers of the American Constitution. Locke, of course, did not share Hobbes's extreme egoistic view of man although he placed great stress on innate human rights, especially the right to private property. For both Hobbes and Locke, however, it seems accurate to conclude that governments are essentially founded in negative fashion to provide security to the individual from the threat posed by other men.

If one stops for a moment to place the Hobbesian contractual view into the context of the military profession, it is easy to develop the least attractive picture of military leadership. Orders can be seen as justified *because* the military leader gives them (he is authorized by contract to do so), not because they make sense or are appropriate to the task addressed. A legitimate answer to the query "Why?" on this analysis would always be, "Because the general said so." Further if Hobbes's version of psychological egoism were correct, one could hardly expect to find any examples of self-sacrifice or subordination of the good of the self to the good of the unit, service, or nation. And yet, if we analyze the critical and essential functions that are uniquely military (more on this later), we see immediately that self-sacrifice rather than self-interest is an essential ingredient both of military leadership and of military service in general. Self-interest theories of ethics and the view of human nature in which they are grounded are simply not appropriate for the military profession (nor indeed for any of the professions focused on service to the greater society).

In one sense at least the military profession is more akin to the classical Greek notion of polity than to the communities of the social contract theorists. The fundamental mission of the military under a constitutional government must be associated with the common good, the good of the community it serves. When the military or any branch of the military places its own interests ahead of the nation's overall interest, we soon see elements of the militarism that Alfred Vagts (1959), General Hackett (1962), and others have adequately described. Militarism is, as it were, careerism writ large, and both are grounded in the ethics of self-interest. In reflecting on Aristotle's position that man's natural habitat is the society of other men and that human development seems intended by nature to take place in the social context, Hackett (1962: 45) suggests that a properly functioning military may be an ideal societal form.

> Living in a group demands some subordination of the self to the interests of the group. The military contract demands the total and almost unconditional subordination of the interests of the individual if the interests of the group should require it. This can lead to the surrender of life itself. It not infrequently does. Thus in an important respect the military would appear to be one of the more advanced forms of social institution.

The Aristotelian notion of man as *zoon politicus* is worth some attention if only to contrast with the view of Hobbes mentioned earlier.

Aristotle, and the classical Greeks generally, would not grant Hobbes's view that man's nature is totally egoistic, requiring political arrangements and constraining moral rules to be artificially imposed. The family and the state are in fact viewed as natural to the man who works out his development in the context of these organizations: They are not essentially contrived to hold back man's selfish egoism but rather provide the context and education for each person's growth and contribution to the polis. In this view, political structures are intended to educate individuals for their contributive roles in human societies. Based on the fundamental and unique role of reason in the life of man, the Greek view seeks rational harmony within the individual and in the state; peace and not war would better describe the "natural" state of man. Balance, moderation, development of the intellect—these are the ethical aims appropriate to man and required to be fostered by the state. An ethic based on self-interest, cost-benefit, or the "bottom line" must be totally uncongenial to this perspective of the role of man in society.

It may be necessary to distinguish between self-interest viewed as "selfishness" and self-interest viewed as "self-development." We attribute selfishness to those who seek their own advantage without regard to the consequences of their actions for others or in spite of causing harm to others. To develop one's talents can be viewed as self-interested action, but it need not be selfish. Certainly, some self-interested actions can be morally right and justifiably encouraged (developing one's mind or skills which will be employed for the benefit of all). It is the extreme egoistic sense of self-interested action (selfishness) which gives rise to Hobbesian views of the need for a governmental leviathan. It is also selfishness which characterizes the careerist and his organizational counterpart, militarism.

The root notion of service to the polity seems more accurate and appropriate for understanding the military profession than does the root notion of social contract. William May suggested the possibility that social contract theories remove individuals from active participation in the governing process. "Government is not what one does but what one purchases with taxes." Citizens may, in this view, be active at the founding and dissolution of the state but passive in between. One can easily venture a parallel suggestion when the military function is also viewed as a contractual relationship with the society: "Defense is not what one does but what one purchases with taxes." Thus the average citizen, especially when not under immediate threat of attack, may not feel any obligation to provide anything other than financial support to the military profession; his role is passive. Even when the nation is under immediate attack, if the military function is viewed as contractual only, the nonmilitary citizen remains passive and expects the military professional to protect his client (society) against external enemies.

May had suggested that the extended application of the social contract thesis to the professions in general produces "adversarial" relationships; society as the client of the professions and faced with the threat of the negative (pain, lawsuits, crime, aggression, and the like) is involved only in the formation and dissolution of the relationship which has the professional protecting the client against threats. Analogies in medicine and law are obvious, but perhaps the critical notion to be learned from May is that when governments or professions are dominated by negative motives (formed to suppress evil) rather than positive motives (formed to promote the general good), adversarial relationships are almost certain to be promoted. It is easy to agree with his concern that when professional authority is invoked by fear, it will be difficult to limit and will ultimately generate resentment against the professionals.

Jacques Barzun (1978: 68) observed that for the past decade, the professions have been under fire because the competence and ethical standards displayed by many practitioners in medicine, law, education, and other professions have been exposed and found wanting.

> The message for the professions today is that their one hope of survival with anything like their present freedom is the recovery of mental and moral force. No profession can live and flourish on just one of the two. For its "practical purpose" it requires the best knowledge and its effective use. But since that purpose is to transfer the good of that knowledge from the possessor to another person, the moral element necessarily comes into play. *Moral* here does not mean merely honest; it refers to the nature of any encounter between two human beings.

Like the professions for which Barzun has expressed concern, the military profession has also been "under siege" and needs to reexamine, if not to recover, its "mental and moral force." These reflections contrasting the egoistic foundations of social contract theories with classical Greek notions of man may lead us to fruitful judgments concerning the ethical dimensions of military leadership.

Ethical Implications

The military leader who views his oath of office as merely a contractual arrangement with his government sets the stage for a style of leadership critically different from the leader who views that oath as his pledge to contribute to the common good of his society. For the former, "duty, honor, country" is a slogan adopted temporarily until the contract is completed; for the latter, "duty, honor, country" is a way of life adopted for the good of all and accepted as a moral commitment not subject to contractual negotiations.

If one adopts the contractual view, it is relatively easy to attempt to divorce the military function from moral considerations. War is a dirty business, and the task facing this military leader is to develop armies and weapons systems which can efficiently destroy potential enemies; the body count is the bottom line. This conception is analogous to the adoption of the contractual view in the teaching profession, which envisions the role of the teacher as transmitter of value-free objective knowledge, packaged and distributed; grade-point average is the bottom line. Neither approach accepts responsibility for forming the character of the people being led (to war or to knowledge), and hence there is no predicting the uses to which their weapons or knowledge may be directed. But leadership is not a value-free enterprise; approaches which ignore the critical ethical dimensions of leadership must always be viewed as unsatisfactory. This latter assertion assumes, of course, that the role of the professions, and especially the military profession, is best viewed as more nearly approximating the Aristotelian than the Hobbesian ideal.

In the American context, a leadership committed to the development of character can be on precarious ground. In our pluralistic society, there will always be the question, what kind of character, what virtues can be legitimately taught and inculcated? It seems clear, however, that an ethic for any of the public professions based on a total laissez-faire, egoistic, and self-interested view of man will not do. Professions which do not exercise constraints over their members' standards of competence and over the costs of professional services invite government controls. Professions whose members lose sight of their service function in society and allow the values of the marketplace to become dominant invite unionization. Precarious ground or not, concern for virtue among professionals is critical if the professions are going to survive with anything at all like their past and current status. The medical, legal, and military functions continue to be critical to society, but that is not to be confused with continuing preeminence of the associated professionals.

What every professional should bear in mind is the distinction between a profession and a function. The function may well be eternal; but the profession, which is the cluster of practices and relationships arising from the function at a given time and place, can be destroyed—or can destroy itself—very rapidly [Barzun, 1978: 63].

The function of the military profession (its mission) is relatively well fixed; and it is a noble one whether it is characterized as the management of violence (Huntington), the containment of violence (Hackett), or as constabulary (Janowitz). The latter two characterizations are similar and seem most accurate for the U.S. military profession currently. They do not presume so wide a gulf between war and peace as has been the American predilection prior to the end of World War II, nor do they avoid the essential moral concern that total war, with its potential for the destruction of all humanity, has become an irrational option. Already one sees that the military leader cannot afford the luxury, if luxury is what it is, of viewing his function in some sort of "scientific" or objective value-free way. The uses of military force always involve moral considerations; the decision to go to war is a moral decision; and the judgments on the employment of means are always more than merely military judgments. At least since President Lincoln's acceptance of Lieber's "Instructions for the Government of Armies of the United States in the Field" in 1863, the public position of the United States has been that all is *not* fair in war. This position has been reaffirmed many times through the Hague and Geneva Conventions, in the Army pamphlet, *The Law of Land Warfare,* and through our participation in war crimes tribunals at Nuremberg and Tokyo after World War II. Military leaders are charged with the responsibility of observing the moral positions developed through this tradition, and with educating all members of the profession with regard to the provisions of these "laws of war."

The "military" virtues are virtues in any human society, pluralistic or not; but they are called military virtues because of their essential connection to the specific military function. The end (military mission) is essentially fixed—the choice of means to bring about that end often involves moral considerations and always requires a display of certain virtues in effecting those means. In some professions the most obvious specific virtues are easy to identify; in medicine and law, for example, client confidentiality receives unanimous, clear, dominant, and obvious emphasis. The military virtues are no less obvious: *subordination of the good of the self to the good of the nation and military unit, courage, obedience, loyalty, integrity.* I have argued elsewhere (Wakin, 1979) that integrity is the foundation virtue for military leaders if they wish to successfully develop loyalty and obedience in their subordinates. But the critical thing to notice here is that these virtues are obvious because of their functional necessity; success in battle is impossible without them; preparation for battle requires their inculcation. Please note that these moral virtues are not merely "nice to have," they are functional imperatives in the military profession. Notice also that if the list is a correct one and self-subordination is as crucial as I believe it to be to the military function, then a contractual view of one's role in the profession generated from the Hobbesian view of man cannot adequately serve as the ethical foundation for military leadership.

Superior-Subordinate Relationships

Given the enormous authority over the lives of subordinates that the hierarchical military structure provides to its leaders, what are the moral demands on those to whom subordinates are required to be loyal and obedient? Again the fundamental position on the nature of human relationships is extremely relevant. If the relationship between superior and subordinate is viewed as merely contractual, then each association takes on the dimensions of a transaction.[3] The subordinate expects that the superior will respond to his needs; the superior expects that subordinates will "do their job" in response to his commands. Each has contracted to act in specified fashion. The more Aristotelian view of leadership would have the leader accept responsibility for transforming subordinates with an eye to inculcating the virtues mentioned earlier. The transactional leader places emphasis on objective performance; the transformational leader adds to performance an emphasis on education. The transactional leader is less likely to accept responsibility when his mission fails; in those cases he can easily place the blame on subordinates who did not "fulfill their contract." The transformational leader resembles more the "good leader" depicted by Lao Tzu in the quotation appearing at the beginning of this chapter. The contrast between these two approaches seems authentic when placed in practical context as in the following comments made by officers participating in the Army War College's study of professionalism (1970: 14–16):

> [There is] fear in the subordinate of relief and a bad Officer Effectiveness Report if he admits that his unit is less than perfect or he is presenting a point his superior doesn't want to hear. . . . The subordinate must have the integrity to "tell it like it is" in spite of fear for his career, etc., while the superior owes it to his subordinate to help him as much as possible as opposed to the attitude of "you get it squared away or I'll get someone who will" over a one-time deficiency.

> Across the board the Officer Corps is lacking in their responsibilities of looking out for the welfare of subordinates.

> Everyone is afraid to make a mistake with someone always looking over his shoulder.

They are afraid that if they delegate authority to subordinates . . . they themselves will suffer. . . . . Subordinates are not being properly developed and there is a general feeling among junior officers that seniors are untouchable, unapproachable, unreasonable, and constantly looking for mistakes. . . . A commander who takes a genuine interest in the welfare and training of his subordinates is getting rarer.

It is easy to see from these comments made by officers of different ranks that their perceptions of actual leadership practice in 1970 was that it was transactional (in our terms) when it ought to have been transformational. Is it going too far to attribute many of the moral lapses in the military profession in the United States in recent years to the contractual (transactional) relationship? One of the ethical scandals accompanying the all-volunteer army conception in the middle and late 1970s was the occurrence of recruiting irregularities. Several newspaper articles reported on congressional investigations which revealed that fictitious names were placed on computers to meet recruiting quotas; police records were altered so that those possessing them could be fraudulently enlisted; test scores were altered so that others could be qualified for enlistment. The enlistment quota was viewed by many as a contract, a "bottom line"; and the resulting pressures were seen by some recruiters as reason enough to cheat and lie. Similar pressures, sometimes generated by unrealistic goals or demands for perfection, are frequently adduced as reasons for false reporting of AWOL rates, false readiness reports, cheating on training examinations, false aircraft in-commission reports, and falsification of a host of other quantitative indicators which we have institutionalized and used to evaluate the effectiveness of our leaders at all levels.

Common sense suggests that the "bottom line" ethic most easily accompanies institutionalized overemphasis on *quantitative* measurements of leadership. "When we can't measure the things that are important, we ascribe importance to the things we can measure" (attributed, perhaps erroneously, to Milton). Along with the emphasis on quantitative measurements comes often the requirement to report 100 percent of the quantity measured. Misinterpretation of a "zero-defects" program can lead and has led subordinates to believe that a single mistake or any performance that produces a "bottom line" that is less than 100 percent can lead to career disaster. Professor Flammer (1976: 597) suggested that the institutional pressures generated by exaggerated emphasis on "zero-defects" led to bad superior-subordinate relationships, even to the point of compromised integrity.

[The Zero Defects System], interpreted literally, as some image-conscious and ambitious commanders were inclined to do, automatically moved from the realm of the plausible and desirable to the impossible and impractical. In many instances, the program evolved into a "Zero Error Mentality," that is, the commander felt that his command had to be error free. . . . Yet outlawing risk precludes initiative, which is a basic requisite for modern combat effectiveness. In the end, many errors were made and consequently covered up, for the zero error mentality is automatically wedded to the grotesque philosophy that it is worse to report a mistake than it is to make one.

The transformation leader sets the moral tone for his subordinates by the example of integrity he provides in both his official duties and in his private life. Honesty cannot be instilled by contract—but it may be enhanced by education about its importance to mission accomplishment and by example. Courage cannot be instilled by contractual arrangement, nor should it be expected if the basic mission orientation is merely contractual. It seems clear that selfishness is more generated than sublimated by any contractual/transactional grounding of the military ethic. Army Chief of Staff General Edward C. Meyer (1980: 14) seemed to be summarizing this point of view when he commented recently: "The obligation of service and commitment inherent in the military ethic imposes burdens not customary in the larger society where obligations are normally contractual in nature and limited in degree of personal sacrifice expected. For the soldier, the obligation is complete: to death if necessary."

Is Professional Competence a Moral Obligation?

It is not immoral under normal circumstances to fail a course in school. If a military person is incapable of learning to deal appropriately with a sophisticated weapons system, that is not immoral. But the leader who knowingly assigns the incapable to equipment they cannot operate is not merely foolish; where the stakes are so high in terms of the survival of his society, loss of human life, and use of national treasure, it seems clear he has entered the moral realm. With respect to the development of tactics, weaponry, long-range strategy, and the conditions for employing those weapons systems which pose serious threats to noncombatants, the military leader's competence is a crucial issue. Literally, he has a moral obligation to be competent in these areas. There are analogies in other professions. Judges are morally obliged to research and understand legal precedent relevant to cases over which they have jurisdiction. Incompetence on the judge's part can lead to injustice; and, of course, justice is a very important moral value. Surgeons are morally obliged to develop an understanding of the human organs on which they operate, and they are obliged to study and understand surgical techniques before deciding to employ them. In these areas it seems clear that the obligation to be competent is not merely prudent; where justice and human life are at stake, and where authority to act has been bestowed, the obligation to be competent must be viewed as a moral one. Often in the military context, the authority of the military leader to act is nearly absolute and the stakes at issue are crucial to society. The strength of the moral obligation must be commensurate with that responsibility.

Within the context of the professional ethic, it appears the line between incompetence and immorality is a very thin line, perhaps most obviously so in the military profession. It is obvious that an incompetent physician may, in a lifetime of practicing bad medicine, harm many of his patients, perhaps even cause some deaths. It is also disheartening to contemplate the damage that an incompetent junior high school teacher may do to developing young minds. But the incompetent military leader may bring about needless loss of life and indeed, at the extreme, may have at his fingertips the ability to destroy humanity as we know it. Given this critical uniqueness of the role of military leaders, no nation can afford to have them be intellectually incompetent or morally insensitive. Further, it seems clear that military leaders must extend this concern for competence to all levels of the military hierarchy. It is also quite clear that neither competence nor moral sensitivity are acquired by mere contract; military leadership in these areas must proceed by example and by education. Transformational leadership holds far more promise than transactional leadership where competence and character are at issue.

Perhaps we may lay at the door of advancing technology some of the explanation for our need to connect moral concerns with military leadership in a fashion that was unnecessary for professionals of the past. When there was some possibility that the majority of persons wearing uniforms were likely to confront an enemy in direct combat, the primacy of courage was so obvious as not to require commentary. When unit survival in battle depended on each soldier's fulfilling his assigned task, the need of subordination of self to the common good, conceptions of loyalty and obedience were all so clearly seen as fundamental and functionally imperative that example and encouragement were adequate to guarantee their inculcation. But in the modern U.S. military services, there is great need to call attention to the ultimate purpose of the military profession because technological specialization has brought about a state of affairs that places the majority of uniform wearers in specialized roles remote from anything resembling battle engagements in past wars. Even those in direct control of our most devastating weapons systems will never confront their enemies face-to-face; indeed, their knowledge of the targets of their weapons is frequently restricted to location and numbers.

As early as 1960, Professor Janowitz (1960: Ch. 2) was pointing out that the tasks of military leadership had become segmented into at least three identifiable characterizations: the direct combat roles of the heroic leader, the organizational and administrative functions of the military manager, and the specialized skills of the military technologist. The traditional military virtues and moral considerations are most easily associated with the heroic leader because he most directly employs the instruments of violence and places himself and his men at risk. The moral consequences of incompetence in that role are easiest to discern. Not so with the leader whose essential contribution to the profession is the management of large contracts, or developmental programs, or large numbers of people engaged in support functions. He may see himself in a role analogous to that of a manager in a large business firm or industrial complex and may use analogous measures of successful operation: productivity, cost effectiveness, "bottom line" numbers. In this environment it is remarkably easy to lose sight of the ultimate function of the military profession. What kinds of measurements are the relevant ones to determine if the profession is best prepared to defend our way of life? Productivity is important only if the "product" is contributing to the success of the military function. In a psychological warfare campaign, for example, does the number of sorties flown and the number of leaflets dropped (easily measured and easily increased) provide a measure of the success of the psychological operation?

The military technologist may be the farthest removed from the direct military function. He may spend an entire career in military laboratories, contributing to basic research in optical physics, laser development, analysis of radiation effects, development of computer software, and so on. He may be outnumbered by the civilian researchers participating in the same projects, working the same hours, and differing only in the circumstances of pay and work uniform. How much more like the civilian specialist his daily life appears to be than like the traditional military leader whose principal concerns might have been the inculcation in his subordinates of unity, loyalty, obedience, and the other military virtues. The officer researcher's status in the military profession seems more to resemble that of the military doctor than that of the traditional heroic leader. The military doctor may identify more closely with the medical profession than with the military profession. But both the military technologist and the military doctor may be called upon to place themselves at risk by carrying out their specialized functions in combat zones, while their civilian colleagues are not bound by the same unlimited liability. The danger of diminishing effectiveness of the military profession seems directly proportional to the growing identification of military specialists (technologists or managers) with their specialty at the cost of less identification with the profession of arms.

It is important to notice that often the rewards of daily effort are connected immediately with one's specialized activity and only mediately with the ultimate military function. This is not often true in other professions. The medical doctor who saves a life by timely surgery or relieves pain by curing an illness sees himself fulfilling his function directly and daily. The Air Force major who solves a critical data systems problem leading to more efficient usage of the comptroller's computers gets the immediate fulfillment of the data systems analyst, but may have to extrapolate remarkably well to perceive herself as contributing to the ultimate military mission. The moral dimensions of competence in this environment are easily overlooked, perhaps replaced entirely by prudential considerations. Duty, honor, country; responsibility for the lives of one's subordinates; victory on the battlefield—all seem remote from the many specialized tasks performed in the extremely complex, technologically oriented, modern military structure.

As the distinction between certain military and civilian "jobs" becomes narrower, the relationship between leader and led may have a tendency to become even more contractual and less transformational. It is not sheer coincidence that the standard terminology for civilian assistance to the military has included the phrase "defense contractor." With the word "contract" comes the emphasis on the values of the marketplace, concern for working hours, pay scales, and perhaps even collective bargaining. Charles Moskos (1977) has highlighted perceivable dangers to military effectiveness and legitimacy should the military institution see its traditional professional values replaced by the self-interested values of the contractors who work so closely with the military.

Conclusions

The nature of modern defense policy and the composition of the U.S. defense organization have placed strains on the professional military ethic. Complexity, however much it may conceal the functional importance of the ethical-military virtues, is not an excuse for failure to understand the crucial role these virtues must play. With complicated command, control, and communications networks comes an even more critical need for integrity in reporting. Command decisions are more centralized but depend entirely on honest inputs. There is still need for the heroic leader, but his role must be complemented by the military manager and the military technologist. It is not inconceivable that our most able military professionals will have to demonstrate characteristics of all these roles, sometimes all at the same time.

In an era when miscalculation can lead to tragic consequences for humanity, technological competence takes on an added and crucial moral dimension. If, under the umbrella of a nuclear deterrent posture, future military engagements must be carried out with the intention of containing violence at the lowest possible level, military leaders will have to be totally aware of the political uses of the military instrument. In the context of limited engagements for specific political aims, courageous action and the subordination of self to mission accomplishment become more difficult for the military professional (especially for those immersed in the ethos of "total victory"), but even more important than ever before. Integrity, obedience, loyalty—these qualities take on even more significance in the modern military as it becomes more difficult for military leaders to inculcate them in their people. The military function retains its noble and necessary role of protection of a way of life; the military profession in the United States will be equal to the task of carrying out that function only in proportion to its ability to attract and retain leaders who understand the ethical dimensions of professional competence and who themselves exemplify the highest intellectual and moral qualities.

Notes

1. In July 1980, William May (currently at the Kennedy Center for the Study of Ethics, Georgetown University) read a paper on "Adversarialism in America" at Vassar College as part of a workshop on professional ethics sponsored by The Hastings Center. His paper has caused me to reevaluate formerly held views of social-contract theories, but Professor May should not be held responsible for any distortions of his insights at my hands.

2. These two views are not proposed as the *only* approaches to citizen-state relationships or to leadership-follower relationships. I deal only with these two in this chapter because (1) it seems likely that social-contract theory approaches are most common, and (2) I think they easily lead to harmful practices and should be supplanted by an approach based on the classical conception of the polity.

3. The terms "transactional leadership" and "transformational leadership" are borrowed from William May (Note 1), who in turn credits their usage to James McGregor Burns.

References

Barzun, J., "The Professions Under Siege," *Harper's* 257 (1541), 1978, pp. 61–68.

Flammer, P. M., "Conflicting Loyalties and the American Military Ethic," *American Behavioral Scientist* (May/June), 1976.

Hackett, Sir J. W., Lieutenant General, *The Profession of Arms,* London: Times Publishing, 1962.

Huntington, S. P., *The Soldier and the State,* New York: Random House, 1957.

Janowitz, M., *The Professional Soldier,* New York: Macmillan, 1960.

Lerner, M., "The Shame of the Professions," *Saturday Review* 3:3, 1975, pp. 10–12.

Melden, A. I., *Ethical Theories,* Englewood Cliffs, NJ: Prentice-Hall, 1955.

Meyer, E. C., General, "Professional Ethics is Key to Well-led, Trained Army," *Army* 30:10, 1980, pp. 11–14.

Moskos, C. C., Jr., "From Institution to Occupation," *Armed Forces and Society* 4:1, 1977, pp. 41–50.

U.S. Army War College, *Study on Military Professionalism,* Carlisle Barracks, PA: Author, 1970.

Vagts, A., *A History of Militarism,* New York: Macmillan, 1959.

Wakin, M. M., *War, Morality, and the Military Profession,* Boulder, CO: Westview Press, 1979.

6

Educating Leaders

Admiral JAMES BOND STOCKDALE

In the environment of most educational institutions, the subject of leadership is addressed as part of courses dealing with values, tradition, sociology, management, and so on. In one sense, that's the way it must be, for leadership is not a true discipline. It has no body of distinctive literature, no universally recognized spokesmen or established authorities, no unique assumptions, and even the definition of leadership has raised unanswered questions. Yet the importance of leadership in all sectors of our society has never been greater than now.

Mechanically, teaching leadership is much different from instruction in the sciences where solutions or courses of action can be observed, proved, and repeated in the controlled environment of a laboratory. Some of the humanities can be taught by repetition and feedback. Teaching leadership is a much more complex task, however, particularly when the students are successful men and women at mid-career; there will be disagreements on methodology, qualifications of those teaching, and what should be taught. There is in addition the problem of not being able to settle these arguments once the course is completed. One cannot measure an increase in leadership ability; it's impossible to test before the course and test after it to see how much has been learned or what competence level may have been achieved. Leadership can be tested only in a real life crisis.

Several years in this field have led me to think that the mentality of our military leaders, indeed the mentality of the bulk of both military and civilian mid-level executives in the Pentagon, has become largely that of efficiency-worshiping functionaries. That in itself is a harmless enough state of affairs as long as business-as-usual and riding the bicycle

Reprinted by permission from *The Washington Quarterly, A Review of Strategic and International Issues,* Winter 1983, Vol. 6, No. 1. Copyright © 1983 by the Center for Strategic and International Studies, Georgetown University, Washington, D.C.

of bureaucratic procedure continues to be the order of the day. But my experience—as a fighter pilot operating from aircraft carriers at sea, observing from first hand the unprecedented battle and intelligence scenes of the Vietnam war, and eight years of prison-camp revelations— impressed me with how such mindsets breed disaster when the unexpected occurs, and when it becomes necessary to steer an institution into uncharted waters.

Moreover, I believe that every factor I observed in the pressure cooker of military air combat and prison camp is applicable to first line leadership in the civilian sector. Throughout our society we need people up front who are bored to death with business as usual but are imaginative, classically educated, and yearn to have a chance to be a trail blazer, to confront the unexpected.

In my view, the single most important foundation for any leader is a solid academic background in history. That discipline gives perspective to the problems of the present and drives home the point that there is really very little new under the sun. Whenever a policymaker starts his explication of how he intends to handle a problem with such phrases as "We are at the takeoff point of a new era . . .," you know you are heading for trouble. Starting by ignoring the natural yardstick of 4,000 years of recorded history, busy people, particularly busy opportunists, have a tendency to see their dilemmas as so unique and unprecedented that they deserve to make exceptions to law, custom, or morality in their own favor to get around them. We can all think of several disastrous consequences of this shortsighted dodge within the last decade. Of course, on a day-to-day basis some people get along well enough by leaving considerations of good ends and right actions to their intuitive responses. In the highly structured bureaucratic environments so prevalent today, there is a great temptation to let personal standards go at that. The exponential rise in the flow of communication, particularly of the printed word within organizations—the directives with their endless stream of particularized guidance, programmatic blueprints, acronyms and ever-new buzzwords—tend to deaden the moral sensibilities of the best of us. The way of life on the treadmill, following the horde down the prescribed track by the numbers, gives one the false sense of security that personal philosophies of ordered values will be issued by the system when the need arises.

In the military, the twists and turns of the fortunes of war have a way of throwing operational commanders out into new decisionmaking territory where all previous bets are off, and no one issues philosophical survival kits. One can find himself in a position of not only having to establish law for himself, but of being obliged to write it for others and demand their compliance. This can be a shockingly new ball game—

in which the dishonesty of issuing orders that cannot be obeyed, the willingness to commit oneself to the full consequences implicit in one's policies, the consideration of the possibility that the middle road may lead straight to the bull's-eye of disaster, and the squarely faced realization that one's orders will carry no more authority than the issuer is willing to give them by carrying them out himself, replace the usual considerations of conformity, bureaucratic cover-up and measured "reasonableness."

Philosophy is an equally logical discipline from which to draw insights and inspirations for leadership. The popular and opposite approach of relying on trendy psychological case-study sessions usually rests on a welter of relativism. The social sciences have not yet outgrown an ideology of relativism, an egalitarianism of ideas, a culture-centered positivism, allegedly scientific, that most philosophers have long since called into question. One who leads men into battle or organizations into booby-trapped territory, while committed to the idea that each empirically unverifiable value judgment is just as good as the next, is in for trouble. Thus, I think offerings of a discipline whose founder (Socrates) was committed to the position that there is such a thing as central, objective truth, and that what is "just" transcends self-interest, provide a sensible contrast to much of today's management and leadership literature. Thus, in addition to history, I recommend concentrating on philosophy and high quality "ultimate situation" literature.

By that I mean selections from the Book of Job, the Socratic dialogues of Plato, the ethical writings of Aristotle, Epictetus, Kant, and Mill, as well as readings from Emerson, Dostoyevsky, Melville, Conrad, Koestler, Monod, and Solzhenitsyn. This somewhat intimidating fare can be served up by a teacher who has himself led people under pressure in a way that illuminates the basic principles of right, good, honor, duty, freedom, necessity, law, and justice as they apply to the human predicament generally and to the role of the leader in particular. Not only do these readings lay bare in ways modern management literature seldom does the elements of human nature—pride, envy, courage, fear, nobility, guilt—all of which the leader must understand, by their being framed in an historic context, distanced from the current issues in which mid-career students may already have invested their reputations, they yield more objective seminar discussions.

With these principles digested, what then are indispensable traits of good leaders? First, they need to be moralists—not just poseurs who sententiously exhort men to be good, but thinkers who elucidate what the good is. This requires first and foremost a clear idea of right and wrong and the integrity to stand behind your assessment of any situation.

Integrity is one of those words that many people keep in that desk drawer labeled "too hard." It is not a topic for the dinner table or the cocktail party. When supported with education, one's integrity can give a person something to rely on when perspective seems to blur, when rules and principles seem to waver, and when faced with a hard choice of right and wrong. To urge people to develop it is not a statement of piety but of practical advice. Anyone who has lived in an intense extortion environment realizes that the most potent weapon an adversary can bring to bear is manipulation, the manipulation of a prey's shame. A clear conscience is one's only protection.

When the choices are limited, there is something in all of us that prefers to work with loyal, steadfast plodders rather than devious geniuses. A disciplined life will encourage a commitment to a personal code of conduct, and from good habits a strength of character and resolve will grow. This is the solid foundation by which good is made clear—by action and example. A moralist can raise to the level of consciousness what lies unconscious among his followers, lifting them out of their everyday selves and into their better selves.

Also, there are times when our leaders must be jurists, when decisions will be based solely on their own ideas of fairness, their knowledge of the people who will be affected, and their strength of character. There is often no textbook solution to go by, only hard decisions with seemingly endless complications. As jurists, our leaders must have the courage and wisdom to lay down, that is to say, to "write" the law, and that is a weighty responsibility. Moreover, they need the self-discipline to withstand the inclination to duck a problem or hand it off; they must realize when they must take it head on.

Our leaders will discover also that part of their duty involves teaching. Every great leader I have known has been a great teacher, able to give those around him a sense of perspective and to set the moral, social, and motivational climate among his followers. This takes wisdom and discipline and requires both the sensitivity to perceive philosophical disarray in one's charges and the knowledge of how to put things in order. A leader must aspire to a strength, a compassion, and a conviction several octaves above that held sufficient by the workaday world. He must be at home under pressure and can never settle for the lifestyle or the outlook of that sheltered man on the street whom Joseph Conrad characterized as ". . . skimming over the years of existence to sink gently into a placid grave, ignorant of life to the last, without ever being made to see all it may contain of perfidy, or violence, or of terror."

Glib, cerebral, detached people can get by in positions of authority until the pressure is on. But when the crunch comes, people cling to those they know they can trust—those who are not detached, but involved—those who have consciences, those who can repent, those who do not dodge unpleasantness. Such people can mete out punishment and look their charges in the eye as they do it. In difficult situations, the leader with the heart, not the bleeding heart, not the soft heart, but the Old Testament heart, the hard heart, comes into his own.

Another duty of a leader is to be a steward. This requires tending the flock as well as cracking the whip. It takes compassion to realize that all men are not of the same mold. Stewardship requires knowledge and character and heart to boost others and show them the way. Civil War historian Douglas Southall Freeman described his formula for stewardship when he said that you have to know your stuff, to be a man, and to take care of your men. In John Ruskin's words, such a process is "painful, continual, and difficult . . . to be done by kindness, by waiting, by warning, by precept, by praise, but above all, by example."

One final aspect of leadership is the frequent need to be a philosopher, able to understand and to explain the lack of moral economy in this universe. To say that is not to encourage resignation to fate but to acknowledge the need for forethought about how to cope with undeserved reverses. Just as the leader is expected to handle fear with courage, so also should we expect him to handle failure with emotional stability, or, as Plato might say, with endurance of the soul. He needs the ability to meet personal defeat without succumbing to emotional paralysis and withdrawal, and without lashing out at scapegoats or inventing escapist solutions.

Humans seem to have an inborn need to believe that virtue will be rewarded and evil punished on this earth. When they come face to face with the fact that it is not so, they often become demoralized and erratic. Faced with monstrous ingratitude from his children, King Lear found solace in insanity; the German people, swamped with merciless economic hardship, sought solace in Adolf Hitler. Aristotle had a name for the Greek drama about the good man with a flaw who comes to an unjustified bad end—tragedy. The control of tragedy in this sense is the job of leaders, indeed the job of leadership education.

The only way to handle failure is to gain a historical perspective, to think about men who have lived successfully with failure in our religious and classical past. A verse from the book of Ecclesiastes says it well. It exactly describes the world to which I returned after eight years of isolation in prison: "I returned and saw that the race is not always to the swift nor the battle to the strong, neither yet bread to the wise nor riches to men of understanding, nor favors to men of skill, but time and chance happeneth to them all."

The test of our future leaders' merit may well not lie in perseverance when the light at the end of the tunnel is expected but rather in their persistence and continued performance of duty when there is no possibility that the light will ever show up. The kind of character required to meet such challenges has been all too rarely seen in these United States in the last couple of decades. Simple-minded efficiency and diligence are not sufficient. It is time to discard the illusion of human progress and return to the classics to study human nature where it is accurately portrayed.

7

Mainsprings of Leadership

General S.L.A. MARSHALL

To what has been said just a few things should be added, so that the problem of generating greater powers of leadership among the officers may be seen in full dimension.

The counselor says: "Be forthright! Be articulate! Be confident! Be positive! Possess a commanding appearance!" The young man replies: "All very good, so far as it goes. I will, if I can. But tell me, how do I do these things?" He sees accurately enough the main point, that these manifestations are but derivatives of other inner qualities that must be possessed, if the leader is to travel the decisive mile between wavering capacity and resolute performance.

So the need is to get down to a few governing principles. Finding them, we may be able to resolve finally any argument as to whether leadership is a God-given power or may be acquired through earnest military teaching.

Two learned American commanders have spoken their thoughts on this subject. The weight of their comment is enhanced by the conspicuous success of both men in the field of moral leading.

Said the late Admiral Forrest P. Sherman, when Chief of Naval Operations: "I concur that we can take average good men and, by proper training, develop in them the essential initiative, confidence, and magnetism which are necessary in leadership. I believe that these qualities are present in the average man to a degree that he can be made a good leader if his native qualities are properly developed."

Said General C. B. Cates, when Commandant of the Marine Corps: "Leadership is intangible, hard to measure and difficult to describe. Its qualities would seem to stem from many factors. But certainly they

Reprinted from *The Armed Forces Officer* (Washington D.C.: Government Printing Office, 1975), pp. 58–61.

must include a measure of inherent ability to control and direct, self-confidence based on expert knowledge, initiative, loyalty, pride, and a sense of responsibility. Inherent ability obviously cannot be instilled, but that which is latent or dormant can be developed. The average good man in our Service is and must be considered a potential leader."

There are common denominators in these two quotations that clearly point in one direction. When we accent the importance of extra initiative, expert knowledge, and a sense of responsibility, we are saying, in other words, that out of unusual application to duty comes the power to lead others in the doing of it.

The matter is as simple and as profound as that; if we will consider for a moment, we will see why it could hardly be otherwise.

No normal young person is likely to recognize in himself the qualities that will persuade others to follow him. On the other hand, any individual who can carry out orders in a cheerful spirit, complete his work step by step, use imagination in improving it, and then when the job is done, can face toward his next duty with anticipation, need have no reason to doubt his own capacity for leadership.

But it does not follow that every person can be taught to lead. In most people, success or failure is caused more by mental attitude than by mental capacity. Many are unwilling to face the ordeal of thinking for themselves and of accepting responsibility for others. But the person determined to excel at his own work has already climbed the first rung of the ladder; in that process he perforce learns to think for himself while setting an example to those who are around him. Out of application to work comes capacity for original and creative progress. The personality characteristics, emotional balance, and so forth, which give him excellence in the things he does with his own brain and hand will enable him to command the respect, and in turn, the service of other people.

To this extent, certainly, leadership can be learned. It is a matter of mastering simple techniques that will give more effective expression to the character and natural talents of the individual.

It is therefore not an arbitrary standard for measuring leadership capacity in men and women that puts the ability to excel in assigned work above everything else. The willingness and ability to strive, and to do, are best judged by what we see of them in action. If they are indifferent to assigned responsibilities, they are bad risks for larger ones, no matter how charming their personalities or what the record says about their prior experience and educational advantages. Either that proposition is both reasonable and sound, or Arnold Bennett was singing off key when he said: "I think fine this necessity for the tense bracing of the will before anything worth doing can be done. It is the chief thing that distinguishes me from the cat by the fire."

Love of work is the sheet-anchor of the person who truly aspires to command responsibilities; that means love of it, not for the reward or for the skill exercised, but for the final and successful accomplishment of the work itself. For out of interest in the job comes thoroughness, and it is this quality above all that distinguishes the willing spirit. The willingness to learn, to study, and to try harder are requisite to individual progress and the improvement of opportunity—the process that Thomas Carlyle described as the "unfolding of one's self." Thus it can be taken as an axiom that any person can lead who is determined to become master of that knowledge which an increased responsibility would require of him; and by the same token, that to achieve maximum efficiency at one's own working level, it is necessary to see it as if from the perspective of the next level up. To excel in the management of a squad, the leader must be knowledgeable of all that bears upon the command of a platoon. Otherwise the mechanism lacks something of unity.

Mark Twain said at one point that we should be thankful for the indolent, since but for them the rest of us could not get ahead. That's on target, and it emphasizes that how fast and far each of us travels is largely a matter of free choice.

Personal advancement within any worthwhile system requires some sacrifice of leisure and more careful attention to the better organization of one's working routine. But that does not demand self-sacrifice or the forfeiting of any of life's truly enduring rewards. It means putting the completion of work ahead of golf and bridge. It means rejecting the convenient excuse for postponing solution of the problem until the next time. It means cultivating the mind during hours that would otherwise be spent in idleness. It means concentrating for longer periods on the work at hand without getting up from one's chair. Yet after all, these things do not require any extraordinary faculty. The ability of the normal man to concentrate his thought and effort is mainly the product of a personal conviction that concentration is necessary and desirable. Abbé Dimnet said: "Concentration is supposed to be exceptional only because people do not try and, in this, as in so many things, starve within an inch of plenty." And as to the mien and manner that will develop from firm commitments, another wise Frenchman, Honoré Balzac, gave us this: "Conviction brings a silent, indefinable beauty into faces made of the commonest human clay." Here is a great part of the secret. It is in the exercise of the will that the men are separated from the boys, and that the officer who is merely anxious for advancement is set apart from the one who is truly ambitious to become superior in his life calling. Even a lazy-minded superior, in judging of his subordinates, will rarely mistake the one condition for the other.

When within the Services we hear the highest praise reserved for the man "with character," that is what the term means—application to duty and thoroughness in all undertakings, along with that maturity of spirit and judgment that comes by precept, by kindness, by study, by watching, and above all, by example. The numerous American commanders from all Services who have been accorded special honor because they rose from the ranks have invariably made their careers by the extra work, self-denial, and rigor which the truly good man does not hesitate to undertake. The question facing every young officer is whether he, too, is willing to walk that road for the rewards, material and spiritual, that will sure attend it.

There is always that commonest of excuses for rejecting the difficult and taking life easy. "I haven't time!" But for the man who keeps his mind on the object, there is always time. Figure it out! About us in the Services daily we see busy men who somehow manage to find time for whatever is worth doing, while at the adjoining desks are others with abundant leisure who can't find time for anything. When something important requires doing, it is usually the busy man who gets the call.

Of the many personal decisions that life puts upon the military officer, the main one is whether he chooses to swim upstream. If he says yes to that, and means it, all things then begin to fit into place. Then will develop gradually but surely that well-placed inner confidence that is the foundation of military character. From the knowing of what to do comes the knowing of how to do, which is likewise important. The preeminent quality that all great commanders have owned in common is a positiveness of manner and of viewpoint, the power to concentrate on means to a given end, to the exclusion of exaggerated fears of the obstacles that lie athwart the course. Military service is no place for those who hang back and view through a glass darkly. The man who falls into the vice of thinking negatively must peforce in time become fearful of all action; he lacks the power of decision, because it has been destroyed by his habit of thought, and even when circumstances compel him to say yes, he remains uncommitted in spirit.

But the shadow should not be mistaken for the substance. Positiveness of manner and redoubtable inner conviction stem only from the mastery of superior knowledge, and this last is the fruit of application, preparation, thoroughness, and the willingness to struggle to gain the desired end.

Part Two

THE DILEMMA OF LEADERSHIP AND MANAGEMENT

Are leadership and management the same? Some people believe they are; many others do not. Over the past two decades, an emphasis on budgeting and resource allocation has led to a focus on management tools and techniques throughout the military. Programs like Planning-Programming-Budgeting and Management-by-Objectives come and go, much like they do in industry. Yet the high cost of weapons systems and increased public scrutiny make military efficiency (i.e., good management) a primary concern.

Serious questions have been raised about the limitations created by management and supervisory principles, particularly as they appear to have inhibited the bold, decisive characteristics of many key figures in our military structure. Military education curricula are being rewritten to restore the emphasis on *leader* development. It would seem that management training alone is not enough to develop a cadre of people who can assume and take responsibility for command.

We examine leadership and management in this part with two specific purposes in mind. First, we differentiate what is meant by the two concepts, and having made the distinctions clear, we explore the arguments that separate the two and propose a need for both leadership *and* management in today's military. Second, we offer evidence that leadership is not unique to the military, with management being reserved for business and industry alone. The final two chapters reveal some of the striking similarities that exist between military and non-military organizations.

Part 1 made it clear that leadership is a person-based phenomenon. Dynamic qualities of personality linked with situation and opportunity are expressed in terms of vision, decisiveness, risk-taking, self-confidence, morale, and so on. Leadership is at least partly an influence process, and the personal interactions between leader and followers are a necessary component of leadership. One thing is certain: Leadership comes from the *person*.

Management, on the other hand, is a process that involves tools and techniques. When we think of a manager, we think of specific activities or functions, like planning, organizing, and controlling. Management is concerned with the effective and efficient use of resources—people, money, material, information, and time—in pursuit of the organization's objectives. A widely held belief is that there is a set of universal management skills that can be learned through education and experience. These skills are theoretically transferable from one organization to another and from one situation to another. Central to these universal skills is the ability to formulate optimal solutions to any problem or opportunity. Management, then, is viewed as coming from the *position*.

Is there a dilemma? Not necessarily. Today's military needs both excellent leadership and efficient management. Whether the two rest in a single individual, are mutually exclusive, or are characteristics that emerge depending on the situation we leave for you to decide.

In Chapter 8, General Edward C. Meyer provides a timeless statement on the need to concentrate on the basics to assure continued leadership. As a personal goal, General Meyer sought to create a climate in which every soldier could achieve personal meaning and fulfillment. He cites two important lessons: (1) Techniques appropriate for managing resources may not work on the battlefield; and (2) battlefield techniques may be disastrous when substituted for management in other circumstances. Concern and respect for others are the essentials of leadership, according to General Meyer; a successful leader must possess character, knowledge, and the ability to apply what he knows. This is a simple, powerful statement of the basic tenets of leadership from the unique perspective of the Army Chief of Staff.

Abraham Zaleznik has rewritten his classic 1977 *Harvard Business Review* article for the military in Chapter 9, "The Leadership Gap." He suggests that during periods of stress and change, society feels an inherent tension between the need for leaders and managers. Zaleznik shows how managerial goals are based in the structure of the organization, whereas leadership goals center on the people. Leaders work to bring about change, are willing to take risks, and have great self-confidence; managers are perhaps less willing to take risks, they tend toward careerism, and they emphasize management skills at the expense of good leadership. Both leaders and managers are needed, says Zaleznik, but we need to merge personal and organizational values in order to develop a stronger sense of true leadership. His message applies equally to industry and the military—the need for leaders is evident throughout society.

Charles R. Holloman, in "Leadership and Headship: There Is a Difference" (Chapter 10), takes the structure/people argument one step further. He distinguishes between the static position of "headship" and the dynamic process of leadership. Mere occupancy of a position (rank or grade) of leadership does not make the occupant a true leader. Holloman notes the situational differences between natural and appointed leaders and cites the use of influence and authority. Headship is limiting, he says, and does not insure success; leadership requires a de-emphasis on authority and a commitment to establishing and maintaining strong relationships between the leader and the followers.

To achieve success in today's military, William E. Turcotte says, in Chapter 11, a special combination of leadership qualities and effective management skills is needed. He suggests that leadership development should be the focus in the early years of a military career with emphasis on styles and concepts. Later, executive-level leadership training should be provided to help the leader define goals and to establish an organizational climate. Similarly, basic management skills should be developed early to highlight efficiency, with executive-level management skills honed later to help the manager effectively allocate resources among the competing needs of the organization's various units. Turcotte does an excellent job of acknowledging the differences between leadership and management while providing a logical framework for melding the concepts—a necessary combination for today's complex, technological military.

Because the debate about leadership and management is often equated to a perceived difference between the military and other organizations, we have included Colonel Roy Dale Voorhees' "Comparing Leadership in Academia and the U. S. Military" (Chapter 12). After a thirty-year military career, Colonel Voorhees became a university professor and speaks to us after a decade as a teacher. He quickly points out the inherent problems in measuring performance in the two organizational settings. More important are his observations of the striking similarities between leadership and professionalism in the military and in academia. The similarities hold, he says, when comparing organizational structures and individual motivations. The major difference seems to be in the type of roles one fills in the respective chains of command. His conclusion is that leadership in the military is not a unique phenomenon.

Finally, Chapter 13 examines critical leader behaviors in both the military and industry. David D. Van Fleet looks at six critical leader behaviors: knowledge, decisionmaking, interpersonal interaction, character, organization over person, and policies and records. Comparing populations from industry and the military, Van Fleet concludes that some leadership functions and leader behaviors are of a general nature, while others are specific to either the military or industry. Resolving basic terminology problems between the two organizational settings could make the similarities even greater.

If there is a dilemma between leadership and management, it exists only because we define it as a dilemma. The chapters in this part make clearcut distinctions between the two concepts, but, for military persons and their mission, *both* leadership and management are necessary for success—we cannot afford to emphasize one to the exclusion of the other, particularly in today's world of complex technology, diminished resources, and changing expectations of both leaders and followers.

8

Leadership:
A Return to Basics

General EDWARD C. MEYER

When I became chief of staff, I set two personal goals for myself. The first was to ensure that the Army was continually prepared to go to war, and the second was to create a climate in which each individual member could find personal meaning and fulfillment. It is my belief that only by attainment of the second goal will we ensure the first.

The most modern equipment in the world is useless without motivated individuals, willingly drilled into cohesive unit organizations by sound leadership at all levels. Expert planning, Department of the Army pamphlets, regulations and field manuals will not of themselves rescue the disaffected soldier from apathetic performance of his or her duty. Neither the soldier nor his comrades will survive the first challenge of either the modern world or of the battlefield outside a climate of active and concerned leadership. Because we are a community, a way of life, we cannot isolate our concern to only one of these environments. Our commitment must be complete if we expect dedication returned in kind.

The clear linkage is that our ability to go to war hinges critically on the quality of leadership within the US Army; leadership, what James MacGregor Burns called "one of the most observed and least understood phenomena on earth."[1]

Napoleon listed 115 contributing qualities in trying to define the essentials of leadership. We have no way of knowing if his description was complete at number 115 or if he was otherwise distracted. Some authorities focus on three, five or 10 aspects, while others, perhaps more wisely, begin and end their list with only one, or describe broad theories about leadership. None of these efforts is complete, yet none of them

Reprinted by permission from *Military Review*, LX:7 (July 1980), pp. 4–9.

is useless either, if they assist the professional who already has a firm grasp on fundamentals to better understand and practice leadership.

Need for a Renaissance

Is there a need for a renaissance in the art of military leadership today? I think so. Not because I sense an Army starved for adequate example, but because the circumstances have been such over the past several decades that confusing models vie for attention. Some are woefully deficient and totally inappropriate for tomorrow's battlefield.

We need to discuss openly the fact that we have been lavish in our rewards to those who have demonstrated excellence in sophisticated business and management techniques. These talents are worthwhile to a leader, but, of themselves, they are not leadership. We need to discuss openly the impact that six-month command tours in Vietnam may have had on the perception of a commander's commitment. Under the circumstances of that war, it may have been unavoidable. In the process, have we eroded essential values?

We need to recognize that we have lived through an era in which this country enjoyed massive nuclear superiority. Previously, it was possible to accept less than optimal decisions in the certainty that very few things relating to land forces could be of critical consequence. That is, given our massive, nuclear advantage, only a madman would have challenged us directly. That is no longer the case. Today, we need sensitivity and backbone beyond that which the past several decades have demanded.

We need a renaissance in the art and practice of leadership because this country cannot suffer through the same agonies in a future mobilization which time permitted us to correct the last time around.

The early maneuvers of 1940 turned a harsh spotlight on the then current "training weaknesses of the Army: lack of equipment, poor minor tactics, *lack of basic leadership in many units, and some inept command leadership by officers of high rank.*" [2]

This despite the pre-1940 emphasis of the Regular Army on leadership, administration and technical skills. What was uncovered was a proficient relationship between the leader and the led, rooted in peacetime administration—but insufficiently developed to withstand the rigor of combat.

General George Marshall's strategy was to correct the weakness "by arduous training and by the more drastic solution of eliminating the unfit." [3] We are precisely on that track today. But the climate is somehow different. The leader of the 1940s was training to go to war with his unit for the duration. There was no certainty that at some point he would be plucked out of his situation in adherence to a rigid career development pattern. His career extended only to the bounds of developing his unit so it could survive in combat. He would likely see it through there or at an echelon or two above that unit, still dependent upon its continued excellence.

We would be wrong today to invoke a "for the duration" mentality which excluded preparing the force for its future. That is an essential. But we need to root out those situations where such progression denies full loyalty and devotion to the soldier and the unit.

Despite some of its narrowness, for there was only one way, "the Army way," the Army of World War II was a professional force of immense energy whose traditions were strong and whose values were clear. Service parochialism and narrowness helped to spawn a revolution under Robert McNamara in the early 1960s which sought to rationalize interservice resource demands by the adoption or adaptation of business-oriented management techniques. The intent was that the Department of Defense could and should operate as effectively and efficiently as private enterprise.

Ironically, some of the techniques were ones developed by the military during World War II to achieve high-priority goals in specific sectors of our war machine (strategic bombing, weapons development, antisubmarine warfare).

At no time did anyone say, "Let's have an Army of managers—leaders are passé." However, once the system became firmly entrenched, its power and grasp implied to many that the newly arrived technocrat was an attractive alternative career model. Imperceptibly at first, then with a rush, the traditional focus of leadership slipped for many into the abyss as increasing emphasis was placed on management and specialization. Excellence in its theories and principles became for many an alternative to leadership. Unfortunately forgotten was the fact that employees of Sears Roebuck and Company or General Motors Corporation were not asked to give up their lives for corporate cost-effectiveness!

Leadership and management are neither synonomous nor interchangeable. Clearly, good civilian managers must lead, and good military leaders must manage. Both qualities are essential to success. The size and complexity of today's Army, given no overabundance of resources, requires the use of managerial techniques. Their use is essential if we are to maintain and improve our posture.

Accordingly, such training and practice are important. But the leader must know when and how to apply them, never forgetting that the purpose of an Army is to fight. And, to fight effectively, it must be led. Managers can put the most modern and well-equipped force into the field. They cannot, however, *manage* an infantry unit through training or *manage* it up a hill into enemy fire to seize an objective.

Two Lessons

In this context, two lessons are important—first, techniques which work well for the management of resources may prove disastrous when substituted for leadership on the battlefield. Conversely, techniques which work well for the battlefield may prove disastrous when substituted for management. Management and leadership are coequally important—not substitutes for one another.

Strong personal leadership is as necessary today as at anytime in our history. That which soldiers are willing to sacrifice their lives for—loyalty, team spirit, morale, trust and confidence—cannot be infused by managing. The attention we need to invest in our soldiers far exceeds that which is possible through any centralized management system. To the degree that such systems assist efficient operation, they are good. To the degree that they interfere with essential relationships between the unit and its leader, they are disruptive. Management techniques have limitations which leaders need to identify and curb to preclude destructive side effects.

Just as overmanagement can be the death of an Army, so can undermanagement which deprives units of essential resources. Leaders need to be active to identify either extreme, for either can impact on the ultimate success of comitted forces.

The kind of leadership we need is founded upon consideration and respect for the soldier. That thought is not new. Over 400 years ago, Machiavelli's prince was taught that: "... in order to retain his fidelity [he] ought to think of his minister, honoring and enriching him, doing him kindness, and conferring upon him honors and giving him responsible tasks...."[4]

Repeated through the ages by others, the message—like an overworked popular recording—may have lost its freshness. Societally accustomed as we are to discarding the old for the cleverness of the new, we weary of redundancy and look for the new buzz word, the new turn of phrase: VOLAR (Volunteer Army), DIMES (Defense Integrated Management Engineering Systems), Zero Defects, Management by Objective, Organizational Effectiveness, and so forth. Again, let me remind you, these are all good management-related programs, but not if they replace the essence of leadership essential to an effective Army.

There are no tricks or gimmicks in the watchwords of General John M. Schofield, and I commend them to you:

The one mode or the other of dealing with subordinates springs from a corresponding spirit in the breast of the commander. He who feels the respect which is due to others cannot fail to inspire in them regard for himself, while he who feels, and hence manifests, disrespect toward others, especially his inferiors, cannot fail to inspire hatred against himself.[5]

This summation of leadership leaves the reader to supply his personal "tag line." The premise involves a cultivated feeling by the leader for the attitudes, needs, desires, ambitions and disappointments of the soldier—without which no real communication can exist.

Leaders cannot, must not, bind themselves to a one-answer, one-method scientology. They must discover the method best suited to motivate and employ *each* soldier. Time and one's earnest interest are necessary regardless of method. The end result is an organization which is ready and willing to follow despite hardship or adversity.

In our business, these are much more prevalent than elsewhere in our society. There are the obvious hardships associated with battle; there are also the hardships of peacetime duty—coping economically in a foreign land, coping with old and run-down facilities, coping with constraints on training resources, to name a few. All these will be accepted and creatively overcome by units whose members sense their leader's genuine interest and commitment to their welfare. Abraham Lincoln said that "You can't fool all the people all of the time."[6] To that, I would add that *you cannot fool a soldier anytime!* The leader who tries chooses a hazardous path.

Types of Leadership

How concern and respect are manifested by each of us is the essence of leadership. Just as there are two types of diamonds—gem and industrial quality—there are two types of leadership. The first type, the gem quality, is functional if we only desire our leadership to appear beautiful. The second, or industrial quality, though not cleaved, faceted and polished, is the more functional because its uses are creative. The Army's need is for the industrial quality, the creative quality of leadership.

Just as the diamond requires three properties for its formation—carbon, heat and pressure—successful leaders require the interaction of three properties—character, knowledge and application.

Like carbon to the diamond, character is the basic quality of the leader. It is embodied in the one who, in General Bradley's words, "has high ideals, who stands by them, and who can be trusted absolutely."[7]

Character is an engrained principle expressed consciously and unconsciously to subordinates, superiors and peers alike—honesty, loyalty, courage, self-confidence, humility and self-sacrifice. Its expression to all audiences must ring with authenticity.

But as carbon alone does not create a diamond, neither can character alone create a leader. The diamond needs heat. Man needs knowledge, study and preparation. The novice leader may possess the honesty and decisiveness of a General Marshall or Patton, but, if he or she lacks the requisite knowledge, there is no bench mark from which that character can take form. A leader must be able to choose the harder right instead of the easier wrong, as it says in the Cadet Prayer, but the distinction cannot be made in practice unless the leader possesses knowledge equal to the situation.

General Patton, once accused of making snap decisions, replied: "I've been studying the art of war for forty-odd years. When a surgeon decides in the course of an operation to change its objective ... he is not making a snap decision but one based on knowledge, experience and training. So am I."[8]

To lead, you must know your soldiers, yourself and your profession.

The third property, pressure—acting in conjunction with carbon and heat—forms the diamond. Similarly, one's character, attended by knowledge, blooms through *application* to produce a leader.

Generally, this is expressed through teaching or training—grooming and shaping people and things into smoothly functioning units. It takes many forms. It begins by setting the example and the day-to-day development of subordinates by giving distinct, challenging tasks and allowing free exercise of responsibility to accomplish the task. It extends through tactical drill, weapons operation and maintenance, operational planning, resource management, and so forth. Finally, it is the imparting of knowledge to superiors, for *they* must digest the whole of their organizations and rely increasingly on judgments from below.

Individual Growth

These three properties, brought together, form, like the industrial diamond, a hard, durable creative leader. As the industrial stone is used to cut glass, drill for petroleum products and even for creation of the brilliant gem diamond, leadership works to create cohesive, ready, viable units through a climate which expresses itself in its concern for the growth of the individual.

Growth in a single dimension, that limited to excellence in applied military skills, is only part of the challenge to today's leadership. Alone, it runs the risk of buying single-dimensioned commitment. Full dedication comes by providing a basis for rounded individual development pertinent to survival in life in its broadest aspects.

Today's soldiers seek to become capable citizens across the four critical dimensions of man. The Army, through its leaders, can assist their development mentally, physically, spiritually and socially, equipping them for survival in and out of uniform. Each soldier meaningfully assisted toward development as a whole man, a whole person, is more likely to respond with his or her full commitment.

The leader who chooses to ignore the soldier's search for individual growth may reap a bitter fruit of disillusionment, discontent and listlessness. If we, instead, reach out to touch each soldier—to meet needs and assist in working toward the goal of becoming a "whole person"— we will have bridged the essential needs of the individual to find not only the means of coming together into an effective unit, but the means of "holding together."

Then, we will have effected a tool capable of fulfilling the purpose for which we exist: our ability to go to war. We can then hopefully influence the decision of those who might be tempted to challenge our nation.

As with all scientific and artistic endeavors, one begins with the basics. We must get back to the established basics of leadership. They provide the foundation from which our Army draws its inspiration, its capability and, ultimately, its effectiveness.

Notes

1. James MacGregor Burns, *Leadership,* Harper & Row Publishers Inc., N.Y., 1978, p. 2.

2. Department of the Army Pamphlet 20-212, *History of Military Mobilization in the United States Army, 1775-1945,* by Lieutenant Colonel Marvin A. Kreidberg and First Lieutenant Merton G. Henry, Department of the Army, Washington, D. C., 1956, p. 606.

3. Ibid.

4. Niccolo di Bernardo Machiavelli, *The Prince,* 1513.

5. Speech by General John M. Schofield to the Corps of Cadets, U.S. Military Academy, West Point.

6. Lincoln to a caller at the White House, in Alexander K. McClure, *Lincoln's Yarns and Stories,* J. C. Winston Co., Chicago, Ill., 1904, p. 24.

7. General of the Army Omar N. Bradley, "Leadership," *Parameters,* Winter 1972, p. 7.

8. Edgar F. Puryear, *Nineteen Stars,* Green Publishers Inc., Orange, Va., 1971, p. 382.

9

The Leadership Gap

ABRAHAM ZALEZNIK

Five years ago in the *Harvard Business Review* (*HBR*),[1] I raised the question of whether managers and leaders have distinctly different types of personality. I said that American business had created a new breed called the manager, whose function is to ensure the "competence, control, and the balance-of-power relations among groups with the potential for rivalry." The managerial ethic has fostered a bureaucratic culture that minimizes imaginative capacity and the ability to visualize purposes and to generate values at work, all important attributes of leaders who interact with followers.

The manager was seen as a person with practical responsibilities, who sees that problems are resolved in such a way that people at different levels of responsibility will continue to contribute effectively to the organization. Managerial practice focuses on the decisionmaking process rather than ultimate events, and managers themselves are typically hard working, intelligent, analytical, and tolerant of others. Individuals who are usually thought of as leaders, on the other hand—more dramatic in style and unpredictable in behavior—seem to dominate the swirl of power and politics with an authority that stems from personal magnetism and commitment to their own undertakings and destinies.

During periods of stress and change, society feels an inherent tension between its need for both managers and leaders, for both stability and innovation, and shows symptoms of the deficiency it may have created by stimulating an adequate supply of one type at the expense of the other.

Managerial goals are deeply embedded in the structure of the organization, in contrast to entrepreneurial or individual leadership goals,

Reprinted by permission from *The Washington Quarterly, A Review of Strategic and International Issues,* Winter 1983, Vol. 6, No. 1. Copyright © 1983 by the Center for Strategic and International Studies, Georgetown University, Washington, D.C.

which actively attempt to shape public ideas and tastes. Instead of boldly adopting technical innovation or taking risks with untested ideas, managers tend to survey constituents' needs and build their goals on a rational anticipation of the response. They tend to avoid direct confrontation or solutions that could stir up strong feelings of support or opposition. To reconcile differences among people they often seek ways to convert win-lose situations into win-win situations. They focus subordinates' attention on procedures rather than on the substance of decisions, communicate in signals rather than in clearly stated messages, and play for time to take the sting out of win-lose. These tactics frequently create a climate of bureaucratic intrigue and control, which may account for subordinates often viewing managers as inscrutable, detached, and manipulative.

A leader is more interested in what events and decisions mean to people than in his own role in getting things accomplished. The atmosphere leaders create is often one of ferment, which intensifies individual motivation and often results in unanticipated outcomes. Risk is involved in the uncertainty of whether this intensity produces innovation and high performance, or is just wasted energy.

A sense of belonging, of being part of a group or organization, is important to a manager. Perpetuating and strengthening existing institutions enhances his sense of self-worth: he is performing in a role that harmonizes with the ideals of duty and responsibility. Leaders tend to feel somewhat apart from their environment and other people; their relationship toward individuals in a group and their own approach to work are more important to them than group membership and work roles. It is this separate sense of self that makes leaders agents of change, whether technological, political, or ideological.

Even great talent will not guarantee that a potential leader can achieve his ambitions, or that what he achieves will benefit the world. Leaders, like artists, are inconsistent in their ability to function well, and some may give up the struggle.

Is the Distinction Valid?

Our recent concern over declining U.S. productivity, declining standards of quality, and the low state of our work ethos testifies to some missing element in the way we organize economic activity in our society. I think this is directly related to the failure of modern bureaucracies to make use of one kind of leadership talent. If managers and leaders are both needed—one to maintain order by controlling the processes of strategy and operations, the other to effect necessary change by raising standards and defining future goals—we now face the serious challenge of how to build alliances or coalitions not merely between people who work at different jobs but between different kinds of personality types. Leadership involves the personal effect of the leader as an instrument of change on the thinking and behavior of other people.

In my *HBR* article, I used the example of Alfred P. Sloan, whose genius for management was responsible for introducing such new concepts as marketing programs related to product line segmentation, a new kind of distribution organization, and a balanced program of centralization and decentralization that is still a classic model of formal organizational structure. I showed how he handled a conflict between the heads of the manufacturing companies in General Motors, who wanted to go ahead with production of a water-cooled engine that they could make easily and take to market, and Charles Kettering, who was the head of research and development (R&D) and wanted more time and resources to develop an air-cooled engine. Sloan needed a solution that would not alienate Kettering or his ally, Pierre S. du Pont. Instead of exercising his authority to make the practical decision in favor of the manufacturing heads, he threaded his way through the problem by creating a new structure, a mythical organization called the air-cooled engine company, with Kettering in charge. Sloan knew that Kettering was an inventor and not a manager and that the air-cooled engine would probably not materialize, but his maneuver was brilliant because it solved the problem so everyone concerned accepted the process rather than saw it as a win-lose situation.

Such manipulations are useful to managers when the only apparent alternative solutions would hurt the organization or interfere with its output. A leader might have plunged headlong into the conflict, relying on his own powers to steer things through to what he saw as a sound long-range solution, but he might only have aggravated the problem by holding the manufacturers at bay and blocking production in the waiting factories.

Most American managers would probably take umbrage at the notion their profession overlooks any important element. To understand why effective management is not enough, I would like to point out four management assumptions that seem to me mistaken.

One assumption is that the goals of the organization are inherently sound. Managers do not think of themselves as having responsibility for rapid changes in orientation and attitudes, but instead they perpetuate existing goals. One of the elements missing in management, as well as in our economic institutions, is a willingness to question the goals inherent in organizations.

A second assumption is that setting up structures and forms to solve problems involves no cost to the organization. There is in fact a cost that should be calculated for every structural innovation, and if we were able to calculate these, managers would less frequently manipulate structures and think more directly about the nature of the problem they are trying to solve.

A third assumption that may be wrong is that the motivations, beliefs, needs, and desires of human beings are constants and will automatically support the structures that managers try to implement. I think this assumption should be questioned very seriously. There is ample evidence that human motivations vary not only according to incentives and rewards, but also with the social setting and culture of the organization.

The fourth and weakest link in the whole foundation of ideas that supports the management ethos is the assumption that behavior is predictable. We do not yet know enough about behavior, and I do not think we ever will. If behavior could be predicted, organizations could be run with a great deal more assurance than is actually possible simply by calculating the likely effects of doing certain things.

Leadership involves more of the personal effect of the leader as an instrument of change in raising the aspirations and values of other people. Leaders center their assumptions on people—why they act as they do, what they think, what is important to them—rather than on structures.

Leaders assume they can and will be responsible for directing and bringing about any appropriate change. Their primary job is to work persuasively on the values, beliefs, and ideas of people who are going to be part of this change. James MacGregor Burns, in his impressive synthesis drawn from a broad range of disciplines that have tackled the subject of leadership, shows how this "transforming" process worked in the lives of dominant world figures who changed the course of events.[2] During periods of upheaval the leaders tapped the immediate needs and desires of constituencies and transformed them into a higher stage of aspiration and expectation that led to effective action. Burns distinguished this transforming from a transactional kind of leadership, which is kept within contractual boundaries and is based on exchange of one thing for another, such as services rendered in return for money or responsibility accepted in exchange for tenured rank. This corresponds more to the work of managers and their concern with the orderly processes and getting things done through contractual relationships in a structure with a minimum of emotional engagement.

In his book *Leadership* Professor Burns points out that in the past there have been two approaches to the subject: leaders are viewed either as heroic and famous figures, which is essentially an elitist and exclusive point of view, or as agents from the perspective of followers. He proposes a more realistic concept for the twentieth century, uniting these two views in which the processes and interplay of leadership are seen as part of the dynamics of conflict and power, with leadership as something more than power holding. In the more complex and potent form of transformational leadership, a leader's power is based on an inherent sensitivity to followers' latent ideas, and his ability to raise them toward higher goals. Interaction between leader and followers is mutually stimulating and elevating, and the change in motives and goals of both has a direct effect on social relations—and morale—ranging from the small and hardly noticed to the creative and historic.

Leadership also involves risk. In contrast to the manager's reliance on structure, the leader risks losing his authority or an erosion of his power base by putting his personal desires on the line. Nothing is as perishable as power if it is used unwisely, or held without being used. The conservatism of managers may well be based on the necessity of guarding the extent to which they risk erosion of their power base. But leaders assume, more often than not, that the impetus for action comes from within themselves rather than from an imposed structure, and accept this inner challenge.

Probably the most important characteristic of leaders is that they must understand themselves before they can work on others. Because they view themselves as instruments of action, Socrates' maxim "Know thyself" is fundamental to leadership. Whereas the burden of responsibility for managers is basically on the structural network of people contributing to output, the essential responsibility of a leader is to himself and to effective interaction with his constituents. Leadership is meaningless without values. An organization or hierarchy can set its values and hope to develop leaders who will articulate them, but values cannot be imposed. They must correspond to the values latent in leaders and followers that can mesh with those of the organization.

The only values that can be relied on are those that are deeply felt and have been absorbed from experience. The styles and standards that evolve from the experience of a functioning relationship between leader and followers will survive even though they may be diverse and occasionally conflicting. The healthy expression of a loyal opposition strengthens the development of durable policies in well-run governments and institutions. There is no reason why democratic institutions, including corporations, cannot thrive by accepting the positive value of different attitudes, expressions, styles, opinions, and personalities.

Is There a Leadership Gap?

The increasing imbalance in our society weighted toward management has created a shortage of leaders in American institutions. One prevalent symptom of this gap is the loss of confidence in authority. Without the bond of confidence between those in authority and those responsive to it, achieving unity of purpose or any common understanding of what a business enterprise, university, or government is trying to accomplish becomes difficult.

Simultaneous with a decline in confidence, a dangerous trend toward careerism has developed. More often than not, people think of their own advancement or personal goals in terms of salary and status rather than the long-range effects of their work on others or on larger organizational objectives. Nothing destroys mutual confidence between a person in authority and the subordinates more than an awareness that the supervisor, executive, or officer is fundamentally looking out for his own self-interest. We must find ways to counteract careerism. I think it is a dangerous symptom—at least as destructive at middle and lower levels as at the top—reflecting deterioration in a culture that does not adequately recognize the importance of personal or human values. If we respect power and money above personality, intelligence, and ideas, we establish careerist incentives and rewards that blur the significance of personal accomplishment or of higher social goals.

Executives often reject my view that managers and leaders are different. Because complexity makes their jobs so extremely demanding, they feel that being a top manager takes more talent and ability than I appreciate. Others contend that real managers have to *be* leaders to cope with elaborate, accumulated layers of hierarchies, especially in the defense area where the structure has been described as "just there." Layers of management and review and the anonymity of upper echelon staffs make it difficult to run a sprawling enterprise encompassing a tremendous range of personnel, operations, equipment, and supplies and seem to require leadership in managers as well as managerial expertise in leaders. I certainly would not minimize the burdens of responsibility at these levels, or the need for talent. The anonymity so keenly felt even by top officials in the defense organization is, however, the product of a managerial culture that has restricted the development of networks of individual leaders as an integral force in the organization.

Does not the mobility of people in responsible positions—the general lack of anchors—again indicate that our institutions have encouraged management at the expense of leadership? We find an illustration of this in the army's attempt to encourage unit cohesion by introducing a cohort system to keep enlisted men committed to their units and to the goals of the military organization. A military sociologist's observation that the new system has promoted positive mentor relationships between unit leaders and soldiers demonstrates again that a leadership gap has had its demoralizing causal effects.

The application of systems analysis and econometric models to the All-Volunteer Force is, of course, another structural attempt at solving the problems of efficiency in a large multiunit organization. That it is a civilian-imposed change, a deviation from the long-time military tradition, makes it no less a characteristically managerial structural solution, stressing skills over rank but neglecting to incorporate subjective, qualitative factors like cohesion and commitment on the very mechanistic ground that such factors don't lend themselves to quantitative analysis.

Looking closely at the issues of leadership in organizations, I come back to the concept that it is essential and possible to underline the necessity for a coherent structure of authority in which individuals view themselves as major agents of action, without readily shifting responsibility on to structures over which they have no feeling of control or personal investment. We could enhance our work ethos and our quality of production if organizations emphatically adopted the point of view that to direct people and communicate policy you must believe what you say and say only what you believe. Production indicators might rise dramatically when supervisors are encouraged to probe problems, propose improvements, and stimulate those working under them to adopt new attitudes and practices. It could reasonably be expected that through more widespread use of individual example and engagement the transformational process would prove far more efficient than consultants' surveys or organizational directives.

We all know by now that the American automobile industry, for instance, cannot be turned around by cautious piecemeal solutions or structural adjustments. Not only will bold decisions have to be made, but many risks will have to be taken in adopting technical innovations. The kind of initiative needed may be outside the experience of U.S. managers, but it can be found in the personality pattern of leaders whose self-reliance and ties with their followers give them the power to steer through problems toward the decisions that must be made for long-range solutions.

The complaint is made that Americans will not become followers because they have lost a sense of values. It has even been proposed that we should organize followers first around a set of goals or programs before leaders step forward to attach themselves to the appropriate cause. But as I have said, these proposals fail to consider the overriding aspect of leadership: the leader's intuitive abilities and personal qualities are essential in eliciting a response from followers in order to extend their energies and attitudes toward larger goals and values. Organizational attempts to prefabricate scenarios or instill prescribed values are futile, because they dodge the issue of personal influence and engagement by leaders and draw one more veil of anonymity between people and programs.

Can We Educate for Leadership?

Historians note that leaders emerge in times of crisis, as if the crisis itself had brought them forth to satisfy a public yearning for one individual to symbolize people's hopes, desires, ambitions, and determination. Apart from the disadvantages of waiting for crises to produce leaders, we can in our own time wonder whether the apparent phenomenon of crisis leadership is as dependable as it seems to have been in the past. The opposing influence of man-made bureaucratic structures may have been too effective. Our institutions will have to reassess their needs and determine not only how they can encourage and develop leaders at many different levels, but where the particular gaps are that leaders could most effectively fill.

"How do we recognize leadership? And do we understand it?" managers ask. It is true that we cannot pinpoint potential leaders in advance, but we can give them opportunities. Mentors can test the willingness of younger people to shape and mediate conflict and to step forward with their own criticisms and proposals for work problems—especially where structural solutions have not worked.

In the early days of the American republic an astonishing number of great men were prominently active in public life. Before schools of law, medicine, science, and technology had been established, the political arena was virtually the only field open to men of talent, so they concentrated there and shone brilliantly. The talent they represented is widely diffused today through many specialties in the arts, sciences, and professions, but it is far less conspicuous in the bureaucracies of those institutions that shape our social standards: business, education, government.

It is a mistake to assume that people have changed from one generation to another and can no longer respond to initiative. Our system of training and educating people has denied a certain kind of leadership talent enough significant participation in the life of the organization. Managers, teachers, and people in responsible positions in the society can recognize potential leaders more easily when they understand that freely developed personal relationships between supervisors and subordinates can benefit the culture of the group, that questions and challenges can yield results, and that encouraging experimentation can produce a more dynamic environment where talent can grow.

Is it an elitist concept to train selected individuals to become leaders because of talent, personality, and potential influence over followers?

Americans have always felt a tension between the polarized ideals of looking up to a select group of leaders and participation in a democracy.

The fundamental tension in our society between elitist and populist viewpoints tends to focus on a version of leadership representing either extreme. As a result we do not think much about the many effective leaders who have functioned importantly in their own time and place, but who have not captured headlines or appeared in history books. I think it is time to separate the term "charisma" from the concept of leadership. Charisma leads but can also mislead followers. It is not a necessary ingredient of leadership and certainly inclines toward elitist and mystical conceptions, as well as singling out certain leaders and diminishing others whose influence on followers may have been as enduring and significant.

Above all, charismatic leadership as a concept diverts attention from the important educational function of leadership. The energy and time expended in trying to bring out a talent for management in leaders, or leadership traits in good managers, could be allocated more realistically to teaching managers and leaders to understand their different approaches to work relationships without becoming destructively competitive, and for each to see the need for the other. This would also focus more attention on how to overcome the many obstacles to early identification of leaders.

Manager and Leader Orientations— Both Have Value

Our management culture is based on the rational principle of contract, which binds individuals to terms covering an exchange of something for something else without further infringements on their freedom. Contractual relationships are the key to a democratic economy and the free enterprise system, although extending the principle of contract into all family or community relationships tends to leave people deprived of the benefits of important human relationships.

The leader-manager distinction has been viewed by the sociologist Charles Moskos as a contrast between commitment to the institution, whose purpose and values transcend self-interest, and to occupational categories, where responsibilities are purely contractual, exchanging work for cash. I think this may miss the important potential synergistic effects of leadership and management in improving the ways in which people approach work and the solution of problems. Although executives' personal goals, according to this proposed theory, are more explicitly linked to institutional goals, the relationships with followers that leaders can develop in the professional and occupational categories could be at least as significant to the character and quality of the organization.

A more useful analogy might compare the effects of leaders and managers to those of strategy and operations, with strategists staking out the direction, relative position, and objectives of the organization in its competitive setting, and operations managers dealing with current applications and implementation of specifications and programs. Strategy is the job of projecting into the future: surveying a company's situation and deciding between alternative courses of action with many possible consequences. Operations coordinates the work of implementing decisions that have been made and getting the job done. Strategy corresponds to leadership in making decisions and taking actions that affect others, while operations corresponds to the many interrelating responsibilities of management.

This analogy suggests how the synergistic relationship between strategy and operations would apply also in a fully functioning relationship of mutual respect between leaders and managers in large organizations. To view the distinction as one between ideals and commitment, on one hand, and occupations and material self-interest, on the other, seems to oversimplify and even distort the real difference.

The notion that managers deal with things and leaders deal with people is another oversimplification. Managers deal with a great many people and have to be aware of their needs. The difference I would stress is that managers deal with people in interacting groups, aiming at consensus agreement and on the whole minimizing the one-to-one relationship that is essential to a leader's makeup and development. Both managers and leaders can contribute to a society and its institutions. The art of business management has obscured the importance of personal initiative and leadership by its emphasis on structural arrangements, processes, and order, to the point where personal leadership needs to be retrieved and drawn out in individuals whose talents predispose them in that direction.

Experimenting with one-to-one relationships, such as apprenticing junior executives to senior mentors, could inject a healthy elixir into the managerial culture. Peer alliances, through which corporations attempt to differentiate responsibilities equally among persons of equal status, theoretically promote learning uninhibited by the restraints of authority or criticisms of superiors, but I believe such alliances consistently develop team players rather than the kind of individual who might become a leader. In a one-to-one relationship with a superior, a junior executive can learn first hand about power, performance, and integrity. These relationships could teach senior executives that a direct exchange of ideas, open challenges, and the competitive impulses of subordinates can be creative and stimulating without shattering their own authority. Furthermore, apprenticeships prepare individuals to move more rapidly into strategy-related positions where they can put their ideas to work.

To undergo the necessary transformation in this decade, management will have to accept the feasibility of working alliances with leaders who question old practices and propose new solutions, and to think of the link between them as essential as the link between strategy and operations. While guarding against the cult of elitism, managers must nevertheless lean toward a culture of individualism. Only when the values of an organization also can be expressed as the personal values of those within the organization can they have any real meaning.

Notes

1. Abraham Zaleznik, "Managers and Leaders: Are They Different?" *Harvard Business Review,* May–June 1977, pp. 67–68.

2. James MacGregor Burns, *Leadership* (New York: Harper & Row, 1978), chapters 1, 3, 6, 7, 9, and 11.

10

Leadership and Headship: There Is a Difference

CHARLES R. HOLLOMAN

It is a common notion that persons appointed to managerial or supervisory positions display leadership by virtue of their position in the hierarchy.[1] Industrial managers and military commanders, for example, have traditionally been referred to as leaders for no other reason than their position and title. Not only have they been described as leaders, but it has been presumed that they always exercised leadership behavior in directing the activities of their subordinates. The major shortcoming of this assumption is its failure to distinguish clearly between the static position of *headship* and the dynamic process of *leadership*.[2]

Mere occupancy of an office or position from which leadership behavior is expected does not automatically make the occupant a true leader. Such appointments can result in headship but not necessarily in leadership. While appointive positions of high status and authority are related to leadership, they are not the same thing. What is properly considered leadership is much more comprehensive than headship because leadership may or may not be exercised by persons appointed to formal positions of authority.

This paper focuses on the differences between headship and leadership in the hierarchical organization. The objective is to provide the supervisor with some useful leads for viewing and better understanding his relationships with his subordinates. In making this distinction between headship and leadership, the intent is to establish the idea that leadership is more a function of the group or situation than a quality which adheres to a person appointed to a formal position of headship.[3]

Reprinted by permission from *Personnel Administration,* 31:4 (July–August 1968), pp. 38–44.

Leadership: Natural and Appointed

Leadership is more than a position in an organization or the personal qualities of the person in that position. While position or personal qualities may enhance a person's chances of being accepted as a true leader, these factors alone do not constitute leadership. Leadership is a characteristic of the functioning of groups resulting from the interaction of leader, group, and situation. One of the more useful definitions of leadership has been offered by Stogdill. He has defined leadership as "... the process of influencing the activities of an organized group in its efforts toward goal setting and goal achievement."[4] Implied in this definition are three essential conditions which must exist before leadership can be presumed to take place. These are (1) the presence of a group, (2) a common task or objective, and (3) a differentiation of responsibility.

The last of these three conditions is perhaps in need of further clarification. In any group or organization, the persons who constitute the membership are usually differentiated as to the role they will play or the contribution they will make. This is necessary because of the many kinds of activity which are necessary for goal accomplishment. It is this distinction between roles that makes leadership both possible and necessary. Without it there is no opportunity or need for the would-be leader to supervise or coordinate the efforts of the group members toward goal accomplishment.

In voluntary organizations the elected leader is usually a natural leader who has emerged. According to Stogdill's definition of leadership, he is usually that person who most effectively influences group activities toward goal setting and goal achievement. He represents and articulates group goals and values to others, both within and outside the group. This is not the case in hierarchical organizations. Appointed supervisors in these organizations are not always natural leaders nor are they always able to function as such. Andrews has noted that "... a supervisor can be appointed to his organizational position by management, but he cannot, through appointment, be made the natural leader."[5] Appointments to these supervisory positions are based upon and supported by formal authority. They result in supervisory headship but not necessarily in leadership behavior by the appointee. Sometimes, as a consequence, the appointed supervisor is an individual who does not have group acceptance.

There are a number of theories of how the natural leader emerges into the leadership role. According to one theory, he may be elected or in some other way chosen by the group; or, according to another, he may purposefully take over the leadership role and be spontaneously accepted by the group. However he emerges into the leadership role, he must be perceived by the group as a means to the achievement of some recognized, desired goal. Group members willingly accept his direction because they believe that through following him they can satisfy their own personal needs as they achieve group goals. Regardless of the validity of their judgment, the person in the leadership role derives influence because the group believes that he can help them.

The natural leader in a voluntary organization is usually able to maintain his position as long as he is able to satisfy the members' needs for affiliation. He is responsible only to the membership of his group. The responsibility of the appointed leader, however, is two-directional. He is, in the first instance, responsible to a higher level of management for the achievement of specified organizational goals. At the same time, he is responsible to the group or activity of which he is a member. While he has obligations outside the group, he must also attempt to satisfy needs within the group.

Leadership Is Influence

In order to define the leader as that group member who is able to influence his followers to willingly cooperate in certain ways in working toward group goals, it is necessary to restrict the term leadership to situations in which the relationship between the leader and followers is voluntarily accepted by the members of the group. In a hierarchical organization the appointed head may rule, or dominate, or command; but unless those in the subordinate role have some choice to follow or not follow, there is no leadership. Where there is no choice, there is domination, the antithesis of leadership.[6] Thus, leadership results when the appointed head causes the members of his group to accept his directives without any apparent exertion of authority or force on his part. Through his ability to influence group action, he is able to create and use the power within the group; and his authority is received from the group.

The real problem facing the appointed supervisor is finding a pattern of leadership which recognizes the need for understanding and motivation without causing him to feel that his authority and control are being diluted.[7] Possible patterns of behavior range from authoritarian control on the one hand to true democratic leadership on the other. Under certain emergency conditions, it is sometimes necessary to employ the former means. When this is done, the relationship between the supervisor and his subordinates is an authority relationship. When, on the other hand, the mission is accomplished by the collective, integrated efforts and desires of all members of his work group, leadership is said to exist. The superior-subordinate relationship becomes a leader-follower relationship, and the authority of headship is replaced by the influence of the leader upon the group.

While the natural leader in a voluntary organization leads his followers, they exert a reciprocal influence upon him. The leader must always be aware of the needs and expectations of his followers and provide a reasonable measure of satisfaction of them. If he fails to do this, his followers will cease to support him and turn to another. Without followship, there can be no true leadership. It is the follower who accepts or rejects leadership acts on the part of the would-be leader. Thus, in a sense, followers are also leaders—they lead their leaders, select their leaders, and sometimes reject their leaders because they do not meet expectations.

Even though the appointed supervisor possesses formal authority, it usually remains within the discretion of the group members to choose the more decisive factor in their acceptance of his directives. That is, a subordinate can say, "I accept his direction of my activities because he is my legal supervisor. I have no choice but to obey." Or, he can say, "I accept his direction of my activities because I believe that he is best qualified to deal with our particular problems. Following him will help me to satisfy some of my own personal needs and wants." Whether the subordinate offers the former or the latter reason will depend upon the degree to which the supervisor has gained acceptance as the true leader of the group.

Headship, Leadership, and Authority

Within hierarchical organizations, a supervisor may be regarded as a person who has been designated to take charge of a specified number of persons, activities, or organizational elements. Used in this manner, the term supervisor refers not only to first-line supervisors and foremen, but also to managers and staff officers at higher levels. Supervisors are responsible for directing and coordinating the activities of others and are expected to carry out a specific part of the organization mission by getting subordinates to work toward specified goals.

There is evidence that the act of creating a supervisory position also creates a predisposition on the part of subordinates to accept the authority and directives of the occupant of that position. But it cannot be assumed that occupancy alone endows the supervisor with the ability to use that authority in a manner that will ensure the willing cooperation of subordinates. There are significant differences between achieving a headship position and the exercise of true leadership behavior. The appointed supervisor may very well be no more than what has been called the "headman."[8] Before the person in the appointed supervisory position can learn to function in a true leadership manner, he must be able to see the differences between his headship position and the leadership process.

In almost all hierarchical organization, the person in the headship or supervisory position is not selected by the group he is to lead, but is appointed by a higher level of the organization. He is placed in the supervisory position for the purpose of achieving the objectives of those who appointed him—objectives which may or may not be compatible with the personal goals of those persons whose activities he is supposed to direct. His authority is formal authority, and it comes not from the group being led but from those who appointed him to the position. This authority gives him the legal right to direct the activities of his subordinates, and they comply with his directives under threat of sanction.

The Limitations of Headship

When the supervisor is chosen by someone external to the group being led, there are special problems not usually felt by the natural leader in the voluntary organization. Most important of these problems is the fact that the appointed leader is not always free to choose his own methods of dealing with subordinates. When the conditions of the relationship between the appointed head and his subordinates are prescribed by the organization, the supervisor is prevented from functioning in a true leadership role. He is expected to succeed as a leader even though he does not always have the freedom to control the functional relationship between himself and his subordinates.

To view supervisors in hierarchical organizations as natural leaders is to overlook the organizational setting in which they work. The leadership function in these organizations is more limited than that of the natural leader. Every supervisory position is clothed with an expressed delegation of authority. It is exercised by virtue of rank and position and incorporates the idea that the person appointed as supervisor has the legal right to direct and that the subordinate has an enforceable duty to obey. The decisions of the superior guide the actions of the subordinate, and these decisions are made with the expectation that they will be accepted by the subordinate.

Persons appointed to these positions do occupy positions of *nominal* leadership; and if they possess sufficient status and power, they can secure obedience to their directives through the processes of domination. But status and power are not the same as leadership. This is not to say that appointed leaders do not have status and power; rather, it means that persons may have status and power without being true leaders. Conversely, it is also possible that certain persons will be able to exhibit true leadership even though they occupy a role in the organization other than that of the designated head. Headship can enforce compliance even though attempts to do so introduce resistance among subordinates. Leadership, on the other hand, is dependent upon voluntary followership; and without it there can be no leadership, though there may be obedience. While headship is imposed upon the group, leadership is generally accorded by the group being led.

Supervisors are appointed because of their technical or administrative qualifications more often than because of their leadership abilities or the fact that they have group acceptance. Appointments made on this basis usually reflect management's thinking about the relative importance of technical skills as compared to leadership attitudes and abilities. It is true that in planning and organizing work it is important for the supervisor to have sufficient knowledge of the job to make wise decisions. Without this knowledge the supervisor cannot be fully effective, and there is always the possibility that his subordinates would fail to respect him for not having it. The real danger of this situation, however, is in overlooking the fact that the basic responsibility of the supervisor is to supervise and direct the activities of others. When the technical aspects of the job are disproportionately emphasized, the problem of providing supervisory leadership receives correspondingly less attention.

At the present time, there appears to be little possibility of changing the traditional bases for appointing supervisors in hierarchical organizations. It is possible, however, and necessary, that the potential shortcomings of imposed headship be recognized.

The question remains as to the possible outcome of a situation in which an effective leader is appointed to a headship position. In this kind of situation, as it often happens, the two elements of headship and leadership are successfully fused. The appointed head is able to gain group acceptance and to establish within his work group those characteristics usually found only within voluntary groups. While many persons appointed to headship positions do function effectively in true leadership roles, it cannot be assumed that followership develops automatically. An appointed head cannot be regarded as a true leader unless his subordinates voluntarily accord him a measure of influence and power greater than formal authority alone permits.[9]

From Headship to Leadership

Although it has always been tempered by the necessities of human nature, formal supervision has traditionally been based upon authoritarian control. But there is today some evidence of a gradual shift being made in the authority systems of hierarchical organizations from domination to more indirect forms of control such as positive leadership and group consensus. Within military organizations, for example, there is emerging a new philosophy of leadership based more upon loyalty than upon military custom.[10] Loyalty presupposes obedience, but it indicates a wider latitude of initiative and freedom of action within the limitations of the situation.

Within both military and nonmilitary organizations there are two factors which can be identified as contributing to this shift in leadership emphasis and philosophy. First, there is the necessity for supervisors to consult and share authority with staff specialists on technological matters. They are not able to work as autonomously as they once were, and the fact that they must interact with others to get the job done means that they must consider the opinions and actions of others. Second, there is the increasing recognition that successful leadership depends more upon the supervisor developing and using the skills of motivation and understanding than upon delegating to him increased amounts of formal authority.

The appointed supervisor who aspires to be accepted as the true leader of his work group must establish and maintain relationships with his subordinates which approximate those found within voluntary groups. To do this he must be able to relate to them in terms of his being aware of and responsive to their personal needs and desires. Not only must he be able to perceive their needs and wants, but he must contribute something that will bring the group closer to its goals. He must be able to have his subordinates accept his directives for reasons other than the formal authority he possesses. To put it another way, he must be accepted by the group as a person they would have chosen had they been given the right to decide. A group free to choose its own leadership will tend to choose the person seen as being most capable of fulfilling their needs. Through their acceptance of him as their leader, they agree to follow him.

Leadership is always directed toward achieving goals desired by both the leader and the group being led, and control is exercised by all.[11] Under any other condition leadership becomes headship. To the extent that the appointed supervisor recognizes these differences between headship and leadership, the door is open for him to gain acceptance as a true leader.

Summary

This paper has presented an operational distinction between supervisory headship (authority relations or control by virtue of position) and leadership (leader-follower relations or personal influence). Headship is maintained by a system of formal institutional authority and directives; leadership is accorded from the members of the group being led and depends upon the acceptance of the appointed head by the group. In order to emphasize leadership behavior, the use of formal authority needs to be deemphasized. Appointed heads who aspire to acceptance as true leaders must establish and maintain relationships with subordinates which approximate those found within voluntary groups.

Notes

1. The views expressed herein are those of the author and do not necessarily reflect the views of the United States Air Force or the Department of Defense.
2. See Cecil A. Gibb, "Leadership," in Gardner Lindzey (Ed.), *Handbook of Social Psychology* (Reading, Mass.: Addison-Wesley, 1954), Vol. II, and Eugene L. Hartley and Ruth E. Hartley, *Fundamentals of Social Psychology* (New York: Alfred A. Knopf, 1961), Chap. XIX.
3. The term "group" is used here to refer to a congregation of persons who (1) interact with or are affected by the actions of others, (2) are psychologically aware of this interaction or effect, and (3) perceive themselves to be a group. Business and military organizations are special kinds of groups.
4. Ralph M. Stogdill, "Leadership, Membership, and Organization," *Psychological Bulletin*, 47:1–14, January 1950, p. 4.
5. Richard E. Andrews, *Leadership and Supervision* (Washington, D.C.: U.S. Civil Service Commission, Personnel Management Series No. 9, 1955), p. 23.
6. Paul Pigors, *Leadership or Domination* (Boston: Houghton Mifflin Co., 1935), p. 20.
7. For a comprehensive discussion of this problem, see Robert Tannenbaum and Warren H. Schmidt, "How To Choose a Leadership Pattern," *Harvard Business Review*, 36:95–101, March–April 1958.
8. W. H. Cowley, "Three Distinctions in the Study of Leadership," *Journal of Abnormal and Social Psychology*, 23:144–157, July–September 1928.
9. Peter M. Blau and W. R. Scott, *Formal Organizations* (San Francisco: Chandler Publishing Co., 1962), p. 141.
10. See Morris Janowitz, "Changing Patterns of Organizational Authority: The Military Establishment," *Administrative Science Quarterly*, 3:473–493, March 1959, and Brig. General Cecil E. Combs, "Loyalty: The Military Touch-Stone," *Air University Quarterly Review*, 7:30–36, Spring 1955.
11. Hubert Bonner, *Group Dynamics* (New York: The Ronald Press Co., 1959), p. 174.

11

Leadership Versus Management

WILLIAM E. TURCOTTE

Many observe that leadership and management are mutually exclusive, or at least conflicting, areas of study. Concern is regularly expressed that inappropriate applications of human relations management theories have resulted in overdemocratization of the military. In addition, quantitative measures are blamed for dysfunctionally influencing judgment, ranging from combat action to obtaining recruit quotas. These observations have led some to the conclusion that a military managerial mind is emerging, which is harmful to the image of the heroic leader and successful warrior.

At one extreme, some regard leadership as a near mystical and charismatic capability to motivate followers toward desired goals, utilizing practices suitable to particular situations. Others say that management is the application of suspicious quantitative techniques involving systems analysts putting forth unwise planning and employment alternatives. Participatory decisionmaking, body-count-like measurements and cost-benefit techniques are most frequently cited as illustrative of the dangers stemming from a managerial point of view. With such concepts and perceptions in mind, a heated debate emerges demanding that more leadership (whatever that is) and less management (whatever that is) is the obvious remedy.

Of course, what we really need is more of both, because they are inexorably intertwined. First, however, we need some agreement as to what we mean by each. Some might say that leadership is the energizing of human resources to move willingly and coherently toward organizational goals, despite the potential hardship of those goals. Management, on the other hand, might reasonably be regarded as the effective and efficient allocation of resources—human and material—toward desired goals. This definition can be enriched further to include the selection of those goals and the exercise of controls to measure progress toward achievement.

In this regard, management might tend to dominate success variables in preparing for warfare and providing resources for leaders to employ. I think it important to note that in most, if not all, of the management literature leadership is treated as a subset of the so-called managerial process, while the military community takes the opposite view.

For much of their careers, military officers seek to master at least two major activities calling for different types of skills. The first activity is war-fighting proficiency. The second is choosing and supporting forces for possible war. The mastery of increasingly complex war-fighting skills dominates perhaps the first 16 years of an officer's career. Indeed this complexity tends toward an ever-narrowing understanding of the way all forms of military power and resources can be integrated into what might be referred to as a balanced choice of forces. As officers become more senior, their efforts increasingly involve major resource allocation decisions. Much of their time is involved in choosing, acquiring, and then supporting military force.

The summit of many senior officers' careers occurs when they must balance the competing demands within and between services for desired weapons, manpower, and material. In a come-as-you-are war era, brilliant prewar performance in planning, choosing, and allocating resources rivals the role of the brilliant war-fighter. No matter how courageous and artful the fighter, his task will be most difficult should the tools provided be inadequate or inappropriate.

Many types of service schools are dedicated to training and educating officers in performing or directing war-fighting tasks. Fewer of these institutions focus in adequate depth on the process of wisely allocating major resources for integrated future forces. Indeed, many officers first learn this activity when they become responsible for it. At this point in their careers, they are asked to integrate many types of choices, often outside their career experiences. In these assignments they are asked to reflect balance and to forsake at times, rather than to advocate, the war-fighting experience that dominates their knowledge.

I want to strongly emphasize that I am not thinking here of the structure and process of planning, programming, and budgeting, nor the memorization of multiyear defense programs. I am rather referring to the development of an integrated thought process and point of view regarding the choice of future military forces, along with supporting structures and material.

Is this management? Yes, certainly. It is executive-level management and quite different from the objectives and content of undergraduate and postgraduate management education. Moreover, it can be taught successfully only when an officer is well along in his career. Executive-level management education unique to the national security resource transformation process will become even more important in the future as technical complexity continues to narrow war-fighting expertise and thus experience-based perspectives.

Leadership training and education is a natural and immediately acceptable part of professional military education programs. Leadership can be categorized broadly into two distinct applications independent of the styles and concepts used. The first categorization is one-on-one or small group leadership, most often associated with combat units. This category of leadership represents our most persistent frame of reference when the subject is discussed. It invokes images of a personal impact on an immediate circle of associates—subordinates and superiors—and is most appropriately taught and discussed in early and lower intermediate professional military education programs.

A second and far less appreciated category—executive-level leadership—is necessary for larger organizations. Many differences separate these two leadership types, but the major one is that in larger organizations, the leader must project the required goals and organizational climate for their attainment through several hierarchical levels. These organizational structures and behaviors are less well-defined; indeed they are often ambiguous. Most members of these organizations rarely are in personal touch with the executive. The leader/executive must take into account the various organizational filters, the communication leakages and misinterpretations, sometimes deliberate, of desired policy, goals and priorities. He initiates the structure and process, projecting the desired goals in a congruent way. This structure and process resembles management control and *comes close to defining the point at which executive leadership and management practices become inexorably intertwined.*

The concept of executive leadership is associated with power strategies and management control theory. The study of this rather subtle skill, especially as it applies to major national resource allocation problems, is unique and nontraditional. It cannot be extracted from conventional management literature and practices. It is properly a study requirement for upper levels of professional military education and is probably best referred to as military executive development. The areas essential for such education, which I like to call defense economics and decision-making, are as follows:

- First, an executive and integrative viewpoint must be taken, challenging the tendency to think only along past career experiences and preferences when major allocation decisions or studies are to be made.
- Second, the characteristics must be identified of the unique structure of the national security resources allocation decisionmaking environment.
- Third, the capacity of the national economy to generate and support military forces among other conflicting demands must be studied, especially detailing potential international economic provocations and risks for conflict. Our adversary's economic capacity and related problems in supporting forces and meeting domestic needs must also be examined.
- Fourth, the unique influences of organizational and individual behavior on decisionmaking must be squarely, sometimes brutally, studied.
- Fifth, all of the above must be related to the major long-range national security resource allocation issues, especially those involving the choice of forces.
- Sixth, these five areas must be integrated into a coherent curriculum.

Three general and interrelated conceptual frameworks should be evolved by the student officer. The first involves the many and sometimes competing variables related to major resource allocation issues, especially choosing and supporting future military forces. The second is an analytical, not necessarily quantitative, and systematic approach to choosing among competing alternatives that seek to achieve similar war-fighting outputs. The third includes all of the elements of a personal strategy of executive leadership and management for integrating the activities of and exerting management control over a significantly sized and complex national security organizational entity.

Many officers will have an implicit and partial framework from past experiences. The task is to integrate these frameworks to expand and balance the officer's point of view, while making the framework an explicit part of the officer's skill base.

The effective military executive blends indivisibly a special type of leadership and management in the wise acquisition and allocation of resources. Senior officers spend much of their time in that activity, and its most important application is in the choosing of future forces and supporting force structure. In most situations this allocation is far removed from the process and decisionmaking tools of profit-making organizations and, therefore, demands a very specialized military executive development curriculum.

12

Comparing Leadership in Academia and the U.S. Military

Colonel ROY DALE VOORHEES

After 30 years in the United States Air Force—11 of them in the Pentagon—followed by 11 years as an associate professor at a large Midwestern state university, I sometimes—particularly after an intense committee meeting or problem-solving session—have trouble remembering which organization I am serving. If one is not paying close attention, the same organizational rules, personalities, and behavior patterns become strikingly similar and seem to take over with a sort of timeless indifference. As experience at the university continues, I am haunted by the uneasy feeling that I have observed this organizational scenario before and know how it will end. I had assumed that the academic and military professions and organizations were very different, but continuing experience tends to temper that conclusion.

"Aren't the products or services of academia and the military entirely different, that is, doesn't one make war on people and the other educate people?" The products are different, of course, but both organizations have similar problems measuring and evaluating their products. For example, the military perceives its product to be a vital, intangible service called national security. It is epitomized by many terms and slogans such as "strategic deterrence" or "Peace is our Profession." How does one measure success or failure for such a product? How does one know when there is enough, too much, or too little?[1] Suppose, for example, too little investment is made in the military. By the time the

---

Reprinted by permission from *Air University Review,* XXXIV:1 (November–December 1982), pp. 84–90.

deficiency was detected, a holocaust could be on a nation, and it would be much too late for corrective measures. On the other hand, if the military is successful and manages to postpone or avoid conflict, the community will probably be unwilling to recognize a job well done.*[2]

The education community, on the other hand, perceives its task to be "academic excellence," although there is some dichotomy as to the priority ranking of how to achieve or identify it. In general, the task is perceived to be teaching (and counseling), scholarship (and publication), and service to the university and community. The participant observer has found this task as intangible and difficult to measure in terms of success, failure, or adequacy of investment as does the military. In general, the education community is also spring-loaded for accountability with the same open-ended responsibility as the military. In the event of failure, academia is directly responsible; but success for the most part goes unrecognized and unrewarded.

Thus, responsibility for the products of the two communities is similar. This similarity derives mainly from the intangible nature of the products, the difficulty of measuring success or failure, and the fact that both ᵈ˗ᵖend largely on public support. In both instances, the producᵗ˒ₛ are vital to community interests, and failure in either can have the most serious consequences for the future of the community. In both situations, the community provides most of the financial support, then delegates most of its responsibility to the leaders of each profession, and ultimately relies, with little faith and much hope, on the leaders' professionalism.

Leadership and Professionalism in the Two Communities

The selection of leaders, generally achieved through the promotion process, poses difficult problems for both communities. These problems derive from the intangible nature of the products and the difficulty of measuring the productivity of the participants. Yet although each of the communities has separate procedures to deal with this measurement problem, the final results are similar.

The military community traditionally has used rating procedures administered by the senior management to judge performance. To be

---

*In the Department of Defense, one becomes accustomed to living with this loaded situation. If the holocaust were avoided, society never extended any recognition for success, but if a deficiency or failure developed in national security policy or in military operations, society was quick to recognize it and look squarely at the defense establishment for the direct identification of culpability.

promoted and selected for leadership positions, one must be judged to be an excellent or outstanding performer by practically all of one's raters—as many as 50-75 over a 30-year career. Each military rater has the potential to destroy or severely limit a career by submitting one mediocre or poor rating, but he does not possess the corollary authority to promote or make a career. This situation gives rise to the axiom, "Everybody can break you, but no one can make you!" Failure to be selected for leadership can result in either early retirement at a rank usually no higher than lieutenant colonel (05) or to be passed over and compulsorily separated from the service.[3]

The education community traditionally has used the granting of tenure as the selection method to distinguish personnel capable of professional growth, promotion, and retention. Those not selected for tenure are usually separated from the university. In academia, the critical component of the selection procedure is peer evaluation, i.e., judgment by one's peers as to one's professional capability and potential for continued growth and service. Peer authority does cause a perceived difference between academia and the military. It is the foundation for the collegial organization, wherein all the faculty have at least a nominal responsibility, from the bottom up, for the welfare and effectiveness of the university. However, this perceived difference is in reality little different from the service or unit loyalty that is such an important part of military service. It is important to note that in both communities the selection and promotion procedures are focused as much on identifying and excluding the least competent as to identifying and promoting the truly outstanding leaders. The effect is that both communities end up with a large group of basic competents, which also includes some potentially outstanding leaders.[4]

In spite of some perceived differences, the ultimate responsibilities of faculty and military managers are broadly similar. Both institutions are staffed by serious professionals dedicated to their tasks. Both are self-policing, albeit with different procedures, with the objectives of developing leadership from within their own professions and organizations. Public trust and hope for effective performance, then, is placed ultimately in the professionalism of the members. Both professions have a serious responsibility to inform society as to their needs and conditions. Interaction with the public does reluctantly take place in both communities but not always with enlightened enthusiasm.

Organizational Structures

Education, as a whole, may not have the same rational and detailed organizational order as the Department of Defense, but most universities have organizational structures with pronounced similarities. The university president may be compared to the Army division commanding general or the numbered Air Force commander—on approximately a two-star level. The president usually is served by a staff of vice-presidents (mostly colonel status) with perhaps one senior (one-star) vice-president of academic affairs who would be "more equal" than his fellow vice-presidents. Subordinate to the university president are individual colleges, which compare with USAF operational wings or Army brigades. Most colleges are headed by deans, who correlate closely to many one-star commanders of similar subordinate line organizations. In both communities, I have found that the deans (generals) are usually either basically competent or highly qualified, distinguished leaders. One usually does not find incompetents.

Among the basically competent, there are the young and ambitious persons, believed by higher leaders to have potential for future excellence but lacking direct experience; or older persons who have fewer observable ambitions yet who have had much professional experience but perhaps have had little opportunity to demonstrate excellence and leadership. For the most part, the young and ambitious deans (generals) are, organizationally speaking, "on the make." Each is seeking security in his new position, and each is seeking to show that he has great potential for growth and promotion. In his first assignment, he will usually set out to enlarge his immediate staff by adding quasi-clones who share similar philosophic viewpoints and ambitions. Such a move usually requires releasing older staff personnel with diverse viewpoints because diverse views are inconvenient at best and detract from the appearance of unity and teamwork. Above all, the young deans (generals) must make their mark on the organization. This, they believe, is accomplished by action and not by quietly managing the new office and encouraging the subordinate units to cooperate.[5]

The distinctive motivation of the young ambitious dean (general) is upward mobility.[6] Such mobility is made possible by staff enlargement, physical facility enlargement, and other signs of progress. Such progress requires notice as much, if not more, than performance. Notice means—"to be seen being successful."[7] "Being successful" is the impression in an observer's mind as to how the young dean (general) would look in another upwardly oriented position. Therefore, it is important that the young upwardly mobile dean (general) create the impression of accomplishment, action, and personal involvement in the fast-moving management scenario in which he plays the central role of the bright, innovative, involved, busy, responsible, and brilliant leader. This posture and impression need not, and frequently does not, need to be rooted in reality. Indeed, it has been observed that the higher one moves, the more isolated one becomes from reality.[8] This would appear to be true of both communities.

The older and more experienced dean (general) may have different motivation. He probably has been seasoned by long years of working and socializing within familiar organizational guidelines. Therefore, he is more apt to make fewer changes at the top or within his own office. Emphasis may be more on continuity and resisting change. In many ways, the older dean (general) has organizational security and does not have the same intense need to establish himself on an upward career path as his younger colleagues. Usually he is not as ambitious. As a result, younger members of his organization may become restless because of the lack of progress or change. The basically competent older dean (general) may aspire to be recognized as a "solid professional" who values dependability and reliability and may view change with suspicion.

Those operating organizations that have received a new basically competent dean (general), young or old, frequently continue to operate and produce with the same systematic, phlegmatic rhythm and schedule as they did prior to the executive change. Thus, the changes, or lack thereof, taking place in the front offices by the new actors fortunately have little real effect—for better or worse—in either academia or the military. The staff reorganizations, changed methodologies, the new meetings, new directions, new personnel groupings, and new enlarged office arrangements are simply the price both communities must pay for progress—or is it simply change?

Fortunately, in both communities, outstanding leaders, young and old, occasionally emerge from the large group of basically competent professionals. These outstanding deans (generals) make fundamental improvements and progress, not just change. Progress is felt from "tail-end Charlie" in the military to the newest instructor in the academic setting—perhaps the same leadership capability in different settings. It can be quickly recognized and differentiated from cosmetic changes in the front offices. The dominant common characteristic of these outstanding leaders is that, above all, they have a sense of the direction in which they want the organization to move. Whether this direction is appreciation of the role the military unit plays in a larger scenario or whether it is educational philosophy for faculty, outstanding deans (generals) have a similar sense of direction.

Operating Organizations

Operating organizations responsive to the deans and generals are academic departments and operational groups, respectively. Academic departments, organizationally speaking, center around a discrete discipline such as history, English, or economics. These line departments are managed by chairmen and heads, who compare to colonels as line commanders of operating groups. In the educational community, the difference between chairmen and heads is the duration of their appointment. Chairmen are appointed for fixed periods, such as three, four, or five years in much the same manner as officers are assigned to command positions. Unlike the military, however, heads are theoretically appointed for life. This difference prompted one very wise dean to observe that chairmen rotate and heads fall!

Operations take place within departments (groups). Each department has a specific task or mission and the personnel and other resources to carry out that task. In the academic community, the "troops who march" on the "order" of the chairmen are the professors, associate and assistant professors, and instructors. They teach classes and perform other scholarly work in their areas of expertise. In an organizational sense, their work compares to the scheduled and nonscheduled responsibilities of operational group officers and staff who fly or perform operational assignments as scheduled by the group commander. There are differences in the content of the assignments, but in both communities, it is at these levels where real productivity and performance take place.

In both communities, real productivity is enhanced by truly successful senior professors and colonels who for one reason or another are no longer on an upward career course. In the military, such colonels are sometimes referred to as "beyond their professional menopause" although some in this group are considered to be the most valuable members of the profession.[9] Likewise, in academia, some senior professors not involved in administration frequently become the most valuable teachers, researchers, and leaders in their profession.

Motivations and Conflicts

One may be surprised at how similar one's professional dilemmas and motivations can become in both communities. In each there is motivation for peer or service acceptance and approval. There is also the ever-present urge to identify oneself with the goals of the organization—instead of the classical motivation for maximum private gain—and the companion hope that by appropriate effort, and perhaps by self-negotiation, one can accommodate the organizational goals to one's own.

Persons in both communities tend to be assimilated into their individual organizations, and their movitations are then molded to the unique imperatives of these organizations. Such a situation is not new. In the past, men (today one would say persons) joined the Marine

Corps, became Air Force pilots, or joined the Army not for financial gain but because they were proud to become identified with those organizations and their goals. They chose to join the service not for self-enrichment but because they believed, or were easily convinced, that their service was enhancing and for high and noble causes, i.e., democracy, national security, or world peace.[10]

Likewise, no one becomes a faculty member in search of gold. Faculty members should be motivated by higher purposes symbolized by the objectives of the university, i.e., search for knowledge, academic excellence, the rewards of teaching, etc. The faculty member who identifies with these objectives feels enhanced and satisfied, perhaps even noble and proud.

In both communities, then, there are strong drives for peer approval and for organizational acceptance. Indeed, in both communities, organizational objectives are substituted for personal goals.[11] The exception is the person who leaves the service or the university for what both communities term "the real world" for private gain. Those who stay must recognize that the *truly* successful military or university professional must, as a top priority, be trusted, respected, and accepted as an honest, competent person by one's colleagues. In both communities there is the problem of identifying the *truly* successful professional and separating him from those who have simply been promoted and, therefore, appear successful. The success of the latter is based on "a careerist ethic," which holds that it is more important to be promoted and identified as successful than to be honorable, honest, and, of course, competent. In either community, the models of success become self-perpetuating. When certain kinds of people get ahead, they teach others on the way up to act the same way, or quit. Both communities share the dilemma over this conflict and should maintain close watch over their models for success.[12]

Dissimilarities: Commissars and Yogis

One must also note the dissimilarities. Most important and noteworthy is the proclivity of the typical military representative to be, in the words of Anthony Jay, a commissar. He defines the commissar as a man of action. Put him in charge of something and he will sort it out, keep everyone on his mark, and make the system work efficiently. He has had few innovative ideas and rarely questions the assumptions on which his orders are based. If there is an iceberg ahead, he will run straight into it. Commissars do not need to be prodded. They have sufficient drive and enjoy the work of doing—not the contemplation of a thing. They are the engines that pull an organization along, but the tracks need to be planned and laid down by someone else. Action is the commissar's God, and his *Weltanschauung* is that old military axiom, "Do something even if it is wrong."[13]

On the other hand, many in the academic community tend to be yogis. The yogi is a contemplative person, a thinker. In business or industry, such a person would be in the research and development labs or in the design and planning office where he performs in a remarkably innovative manner. In the academic community, this person is found in the trenches—teaching his classes, doing research, publishing, debating endlessly with his colleagues, and enjoying the pure intellectual acts of examining and discarding every possible idea or hypothesis. But a yogi cannot organize or run anything. Put him in charge of an office or organization and disaster ensues. Further, the yogi hates such an assignment because contemplation is his forte; action is his bane.[14]

Few are pure commissar or pure yogi, but most people tend to polarize around one or the other. Although there are certainly yogis in the military community (who are sometimes brilliant when properly assigned as staff officers), success in the military more often is based on emulation of the commissar. Within the educational community, on the other hand, the model to be followed for career success is the yogi. Indeed, the commissar is frequently viewed as an inferior being.

Often both communities make the tragic mistake of selecting yogis for commissars and vice versa. For example, the university community frequently selects one of its outstanding professors, a well-published research-oriented yogi, for administrative responsibilities. The results are predictably disastrous for the organization and the individual. The organization becomes chaotic, and the individual becomes devastated and unhappy. Usually he cannot wait to get back to the laboratory or his classroom. On the other hand, the military community frequently selects an outstanding young commissar for assignment to a choice staff and planning assignment. Generally, this commissar cannot wait to get back to the field or his favorite organization where "the real action is." The staff duties in which he is engaged may really be much more important, may be laying the tracks for that favorite organization in the field, but the contemplation needed in that process results in no enjoyment or satisfaction for him.

Both communities are hierarchic organizations and attempt to perpetuate organizational arrangements that have brought success in the past. The training, indoctrination, and selection process for role models are also geared toward what has worked in the past. Each community perceives its role models for success to be dissimilar—indeed opposites. It may well be that within both communities there is that rare person who is a combination of yogi and commissar, who is both a brilliant original thinker and a vigorous, decisive man of action. But the hierarchies of both organizations have been reinforcing their own prejudices for so long that they would rarely believe it even if it were true. To quote Professor Hugh Trevor-Roper:

> Any society, so long as it is, or feels itself to be, a working society, tends to invest in itself: a military society tends to become more military, a bureaucratic society more bureaucratic, an academic society more academic, as the status and profits of war or office or education are enhanced by success, and institutions are framed to forward it. Therefore, when such a society is hit by a general crisis, it finds itself partly paralyzed by the structural weight of increased social investment. The dominant military official or commercial classes cannot easily change their orientation: and their social dominance, and the institutions through which it is exercised, prevent other classes from securing power or changing policy.[15]

There are similarities and dissimilarities in the academic and military communities. The similarities in the two professions surprised me because of my initial assumption that the two professions are really very different. Players who have been in both communities need to be ever mindful of which field they are playing on. The turfs and one's teammates can look alike in many ways.

Notes

1. Alain C. Enthoven and K. Wayne Smith. *How Much is Enough? Shaping the Defense Program 1961–1969* (New York, 1971), p. 160.

2. Robert S. McNamara. *The Essence of Security: Reflections in Office* (New York, 1968), pp. 90–99.

3. William L. Hauser. "The Army Career Officer System: A Continuing Need for Professional and Managerial Reform," *The Bureaucrat,* Fall 1979, p. 8.

4. Jeffrey Pfeffer. "The Ambiguity of Leadership," *Academy of Management Review,* January 1977, p. 106.

5. S. G. Green and T. R. Mitchell. "Attributional Processes of Leaders in Leader-Member Interactions," *Organizational Behavior and Human Performance,* 1979.

6. James D. Thompson. *Organizations in Action* (New York, 1967), pp. 140–41.

7. Maureen Mylander. *The Generals: Making it Military Style* (New York, 1974), p. 45.

8. Albert Speer. *Inside the Third Reich* (New York, 1970), p. 309.

9. James Fallows. *National Defense* (New York, 1981), p. 150.

10. Cincinnatus. *Self-Destruction: The Disintegration and Decay of the United States Army during the Vietnam Era* (New York, 1981), p. 84.

11. Fallows, pp. 170–72.

12. Charles C. Moskos. "Making the All-Volunteer Force Work: A National Service Approach," *Foreign Affairs,* Fall 1981, p. 34.

13. Anthony Jay. *Management and Machiavelli: An Inquiry into the Policies of Corporate Life* (New York, 1967), pp. 114–30.

14. Ibid., p. 149.

15. Hugh Trevor-Roper. *The Rise of Christian Europe* (London, 1965), p. 184.

13

Organizational Differences in Critical Leader Behaviors: Industrial and Military

DAVID D. VAN FLEET

Are the specific behaviors identified as critical leader behaviors different in industrial and military organizations? Whether or not the specific behaviors are different, are the relative proportions of behaviors in particular categories different? In general terms, by comparing critical elements of leader behavior in differing organizations, what can we learn regarding the impact of organizations or environmental contingencies on leadership?

While the literature is replete with studies of both industrial and military organizations, seldom have comparisons been made between them. [For industrial examples—4; 9; 15; 18; 22. For military examples— 2; 10; 11; 12; 13; 14; 16.] Fleishman [7] compared indices of performance between military officers and industrial managers but did not examine the nature of any differences in specific leader behaviors. In another study, some comparisons were made which suggest that military cadets score higher on "Initiating Structure" and lower on "Consideration" than do industrial foremen (based on weighted averages of means from Table 8 of Fleishman [8]). Other comparative studies are rare indeed. However, the relative dearth of such studies suggests the need for investigation.

But how shall such specific behaviors be obtained and how shall they be studied? Campbell, Dunnette, Lawler, and Weick [3] suggest that the critical incident technique be used to develop examples of such specific behaviors. Generally, that technique includes a step in which subjects

Reprinted and edited with permission from *Journal of Management*, 2:1 (Spring 1976), pp. 27–36.

classify or categorize behaviors; those classifications, along with the specific behaviors themselves, could provide the basis for comparisons. The purpose of this paper is to provide the results of such a comparative study.

Early Work—Functions

Flanagan [5], using the approach which would come to be known as the critical incident technique [6], analyzed nearly 3,000 incidents for a military organization. Those incidents led to the development of six broad categories for classifying or describing military leader behavior. Williams [21] used the same technique to obtain over 3,500 incidents for business executives. He, too, used six broad categories to describe industrial leader behavior. Those two separate categorizations are very similar and can be "matched" rather well, as shown in Table 1.

Additionally, Williams reported eighty critical requirements distributed over the six categories while Flanagan reported fifty-four job essentials also distributed over his six categories. An examination of these data reveals that Relations with Associates accounts for more of the incidents in industrial situations than Supervising Personnel does

TABLE 1

Williams (Industrial)	Flanagan (Military)
Knowledge	Technical competence
	Proficiency in military occupational specialty
Decision-making	Planning, organization, and execution of policy
	Planning and direct action
Interpersonal interaction	Relations with associates
	Supervising personnel
Character	Work habits
	Acceptance of personal responsibility
Organization over person	Adjustment to the job
	Acceptance of organizational responsibility
Policies and records	Coordination and integration of activities
	Handling administrative details

in military ones. On the other hand, Handling Administrative Details accounts for more of the incidents in military situations than Coordination and Integration of Activities does in industrial ones. A chi-square test of the hypothesis that there are no differences between the distributions of incidents for military and industrial situations leads to accepting the hypothesis at the 95 percent level. The Spearman rank coefficient of 0.589 (n=6) suggests a non-significant relation between these two distributions. Thus, while no firm conclusions may be drawn on the basis of this early work, a tentative one is suggested. While some differences exist between military and industrial leader behavior, those differences are more likely to be in specific behaviors than in the manner in which such behaviors are distributed over functions of leadership.

More Recent Work—Functions

In an effort to test that tentative conclusion, two recent studies are compared. One was primarily an industrial study [19] while the other was essentially military [20]. Each study used the critical incident technique; hence, this comparison should be satisfactory as a replication of the previous ones.

Industrial

The industrial study was conducted over a two-year period and involved nearly 50 subjects from over twenty companies. These subjects reported over 500 incidents of which 268 were usable. The incidents were condensed and those with substantial means along two scales— importance and effective/ineffective—were retained. This procedure resulted in 75 specimens of critical leader behavior for industrial situations.

The 75 specimens were then classified by the subjects according to the six requirements of Williams. The striking similarity of the distributions suggests that while specific behaviors might vary, the functional distribution of those behaviors may be relatively stable, at least within a given general organizational context such as "industrial."

Military

The military study involved nearly a thousand cadets from a college military program which has had over 100 of its graduates reach general officer rank, including two admirals. These subjects reported over 3,000 incidents of which 520 were finally usable. The incidents were separated by "drill" and "non-drill" as well as by effective and ineffective. They were also checked for substantial means along the two scales—importance and effective/ineffective. This procedure resulted in 159 (83 "drill"; 76

"non-drill") specimens of critical leader behavior for military cadet organizations. These specimens were then classified by the subjects according to the six requirements of Williams. The resulting distributions are, however, each different from the distribution of Flanagan. This could mean that military leader behavior is not as stable, in terms of its distribution over functions, as is industrial leader behavior or that "cadet" military organizations are not comparable to "regular" military organizations.

One check of which of these may be more nearly correct can be found by examining the distributions between "drill" and "non-drill" leader behavior. A statistical test of these two distributions indicates that they are significantly different. The three functional distributions within this one organization are related and not significantly different. This would appear to suggest that the functional distribution of leader behavior within the general organization context, "military," may not be stable. For differing situations within the same organization, however, some stability may exist.

Industrial Compared With Military

Since no significant difference exists between the two industrial distributions, either could be used for comparison with the several military distributions. Statistical tests were conducted for both, however, to insure that contradictory results would not be obtained. Since the results conform to one another, only those comparisons based on the more recent industrial study are useful.

In every instance, the industrial distribution of critical leader behaviors by function is different from the military distribution. The function most concerned with interpersonal interaction (Supervising Personnel or Relations with Associates) is in every case the dominant function of leadership. The function most concerned with the leader's knowledge (Proficiency in Military Occupational Specialty or Technical Competence) is low in industrial leader behavior but higher in military leader behavior. The "regular" military distribution was, in this respect, however, more nearly like that of industry than were the "cadet" military distributions.

The decision function is substantially less evident in military situations than in industrial ones. Once again, though, the "regular" military study was more nearly parallel to the industrial ones. Finally, the "paper work" function dealing with Policies and Records is rather low in all but the "regular" military situation. Apparently in most circumstances, this function is something which must be done and may be descriptive of a good deal of "managerial activity" but is apparently little involved in leadership.

Styles

These findings are not directly comparable to many previous studies of leadership. Most studies tend to structure leader behavior by a set of categories ("Initiating Structure" and "Consideration") more descriptive of styles of behavior than functions of leaders. Hence, the relation of styles both within and between these two organizational contexts needs to be examined.

The two early studies did not deal with this issue and therefore are not used further in this study. The two more recent studies, however, did ask the subjects to classify critical leader behaviors in terms which are more similar to types than functions. The particular categories used were the four "factors" developed by Bowers and Seashore [1].

Industry and Military

Since only one distribution was developed for the industrial situation, no "internal" comparison by "aspects of style" can be made; however, such a comparison can be made for the military situation since three distributions were developed there. A cursory examination of the distributions for the three military situations suggests that no real differences exist. Hence, here too one finds reasonable stability within the military organizational context.

Industrial Compared with Military

The percentage distributions of critical leader behaviors by Aspects of Style reveal that, just as with functions, the industrial distribution is different from each of the military ones. Not only do they appear to be different from one another, the statistics suggest the possibility that they may be inversely related.

A direct examination of the data bears this out. The category Work Facilitation contains the largest proportion of behaviors in the industrial study but the smallest in each of the military situations. Goal Emphasis is much more nearly alike in all four circumstances while Support tends to be much higher in the military than it is in the industrial situation.

The "style" comparisons, then, would appear to support the findings of the "function" comparisons. Within the organizational contexts, industry and military, reasonable stability exists in terms of the relative proportions of both functional and style distributions of critical leader behaviors.

Functions and Styles

Does the similarity of these results indicate that perhaps "functions" and "styles" are related in some way? Certainly, for example, "knowledge" is different from "decision-making"; but it is also most certainly related to decision-making. What is the degree of relation, if any, between "functions" and "styles"?

Some "collapsing" was necessary. In every case, the "style" categories could remain and only the "functions" categories necessitated some combinations. For comparative purposes, the combinations employed were used for both the industrial and the military situations.

One combination used was to collapse the Knowledge, the Decision-Making, and the Policies and Records functions into a single category. Another combination involved collapsing Organization Over Person with Character. Finally, a third combination involved collapsing Interpersonal Interaction with the second combination just referred to above.

The results of the analysis confirm the hypothesis that there is a relation between these two sets of attributes. Or to state it another way, this analysis reflects the hypothesis that functions and styles are independent attributes. Are they, however, separate but related attributes, or are they merely the same attribute classified two different ways? Perhaps these two categorizations are simply two different ways of "slicing the same piece of pie." Apparently, functions and styles are not merely two different yet related attributes of leaders.

Specific Behaviors

One further question remains: Are the specific behaviors identified as critical behaviors different in industrial and military organizations? The answer is that some are and some are not.

Comparing exact behaviors [19] involves some judgment as to the meaning of words. For instance, is the behavior "Is willing to listen to others' ideas" (industrial) the same as "Listens to subordinate's suggestions" (military)? For practical purposes most would say that they are essentially the same. But how about "Ridicules someone" (industrial) and "Mistreats subordinates" (military)? Here agreement would probably be less. Thus, to compare behaviors, a range was determined.

The military list contains more specimens of behavior than does the industrial list. However, in several cases one specimen from the industrial list might be similar to several on the military list. While less true, the reverse also holds. The military behaviors overlap the industrial ones from 31.5 to 44.8 percent, while the industrial behaviors overlap the military ones from 44.0 to 48.4 percent. These data seem to suggest that just under half of all critical leader behaviors are essentially the same across these two organizational contexts while slightly over half are specific to the particular situation.

Summary and Conclusions

The analysis made here indicates that within the organizational contexts of industry and military, distributions of critical leader behaviors by both leadership function and leadership style are reasonably similar. Across these organizational contexts, no such similarity exists. These findings suggest that other organizational contexts would display internal similarity or stability yet be different from these two.

This study also suggests that while leadership functions and leadership styles are related, they are two different attributes and not merely two different ways of expressing the same thing. Particular behaviors appear to be classifiable by one or both sets of attributes, and such classification may well yield a greater understanding of the situational contexts of leadership.

Finally, this study suggests that from one-third to one-half of critical leader behaviors may be of a general nature while one-half to two-thirds may be specific to particular situations. This would mean, of course, that a single measure of leadership might not be readily recognizable or obtainable.

A measure of leadership containing only items related to the general regularity would be deficient by the amount of the specific regularity, and the predictive or descriptive power of such a measure would be less than it could be. Likewise, an instrument attempting to measure both general and specific aspects of leadership might be too long to serve as a useful instrument or might contain sufficient contamination to weaken its value. This problem may well account for much of the inability of previous research to be replicable without rewording or reworking the instruments used. It could also help account for some of the contradictory nature of much of the research on leadership. Hopefully, future research will consider this dual nature of leadership.

References

1. Bowers, D. G. and Seashore, S. E. "Predicting Organizational Effectiveness With a Four-Factor Theory of Leadership." *Administrative Science Quarterly,* 1966, 11, 238–263.
2. Campbell, D. T. and Damarin, F. L. "Measuring Leadership Attitudes Through an Information Test." *Journal of Social Psychology,* 1961, 55, 159–176.
3. Campbell, J. P., Dunnette, M. D., Lawler, E. E., and Weick, K. E. *Managerial Behavior, Performance, and Effectiveness.* New York: McGraw-Hill, 1970.
4. Evans, M. G. "The Effects of Supervisory Behavior on the Path-Goal Relationship." *Organizational Behavior and Human Performance,* 1970, 5, 277–298.

5. Flanagan, J. C. "Defining the Requirements of the Executive's Job." *Personnel,* 1951, 28, 28–35.
6. Flanagan, J. C. "The Critical Incident Technique." *Psychological Bulletin,* 1954, 51, 327–358.
7. Fleishman, E. A. "Differences Between Military and Industrial Organizations," In R. M. Stogdill and C. L. Shartle (Eds.), *Patterns of Administrative Performance.* Columbus: Ohio State University Bureau of Business Research, 1956. (a)
8. Fleishman, E. A. "The Leadership Opinion Questionnaire." In R. M. Stogdill and A. E. Coons, *Leader Behavior: Its Description and Measurement.* Columbus: Ohio State University Bureau of Business Research, 1956. (b)
9. Fleishman, E. A. and Harris, E. F. "Patterns of Leadership Behavior Related to Employee Grievances and Turnover." *Personnel Psychology,* 1962, 15, 43–56.
10. Halpin, A. W. "The Leadership Behavior and Combat Performance of Airplane Commanders." *Journal of Abnormal and Social Psychology,* 1954, 49, 19–22.
11. Halpin, A. W. "The Leadership Ideology of Aircraft Commanders." *Journal of Psychology,* 1955, 39, 82–84. (a)
12. Halpin, A. W. "The Leader Behavior and Leadership Ideology of Educational Administrators and Aircraft Commanders." *Harvard Education Review,* 1955, 25, 18–32. (b)
13. Holloman, C. R. "The Perceived Leadership Role of Military and Civilian Supervisors in a Military Setting." *Personnel Psychology,* 1967, 20, 199–210.
14. Hood, P. D. *Leadership Climate for Trainee Leaders: The Army AIT Platoon.* Washington, D.C.: George Washington University, 1967.
15. House, R. J., Filley, A. C., and Kerr, S. "Relation of Leader Consideration and Initiating Structure to R and D Subordinates' Satisfaction." *Administrative Science Quarterly,* 1971, 16, 19–30.
16. Newport, G. "A Study of Attitudes and Leader Behavior." *Personnel Administration,* 1962, 25, 42–46.
17. Siegel, S. *Nonparametric Statistics for the Behavioral Sciences.* New York: McGraw-Hill, 1956.
18. Stogdill, R. M. *Managers, Employees, Organizations.* Columbus: Ohio State University Bureau of Business Research, 1965.
19. Van Fleet, D. D. "Toward Identifying Critical Elements in a Behavioral Description of Leadership." *Public Personnel Management,* 1974, 3, 70–82.
20. Van Fleet, D. D., Chamberlain, H., and Gass, W. K. "Some Critical Elements of Leader Behavior in a Military Cadet Organization." *Organization and Administrative Sciences,* 1975, 5, 73–94.
21. Williams, R. E. "A Description of Some Executive Abilities by Means of the Critical Incident Technique." Unpublished Doctoral Dissertation, Columbia University, 1956.
22. Yukl, G. "Toward a Behavioral Theory of Leadership." *Organizational Behavior and Human Performance,* 1971, 6, 414–440.

Part Three

LEADERSHIP
IN TRANSITION

Leadership cannot be static. As the world about us changes, so must we change our concept of leadership. Are historical perspectives on leadership relevant to our world of tomorrow or, for that matter, today? Clearly, our technological, economic, social, and political environments are changing at a rapid pace; so are the education and experience levels of leaders and followers. The military is more complex in both form and substance than ever before, but despite increasing dependence on advanced technology, we still rely on the men and women of the military to serve with commitment and honor.

There is a narrowing gap between leaders and followers. Where military leaders were once elite in terms of economic and social background as well as education, our society now endorses educational development for everyone while diminishing the importance of economic and social backgrounds. With the elimination of inherent differences between leader and follower, there seems to be an increased emphasis on human skills, on understanding the strategic implications of decisions, developing a common purpose, and providing direction as key elements of leader success. No longer is the leader always the most skilled soldier; today the technical skills of followers may well exceed those of the leader. It simply is not possible to keep up with the rapid rate of technological change while coping with the incessant demands of command. A leader's self-confidence is, therefore, perhaps based more on intuition than on specific knowledge.

Nonetheless, followers seem to expect more from their leaders today. This is partly due to the access they now have to the leader—communication technologies can give everyone instant reports of a leader's successes and failures. Computers and information systems also provide exhaustive data to help leaders make decisions. But can any one person possibly assimilate all of the data available on all issues and still react as a leader? Although leaders in the past often made decisions despite a lack of information, the leaders of tomorrow may be forced to deal with too much information. In crises, will leaders study the computer printouts or will they still act on "gut feel" or intuition?

Leadership today may be supported by a degree of technological sophistication, but that technology is not without a price. The education and training that give us sophistication also run counter to developing the elements of leadership described in the earlier chapters. The perspectives that follow represent alternative futures for leadership. Your task is to identify those elements that will impact on the development of continued excellence in our military leadership.

In "The Ambiguity of Leadership" (Chapter 14) Jeffrey Pfeffer questions whether leaders have any substantive influence on the performance of their organization. Clearly, he contradicts the generally held notion that leaders are major determinants of organizational success or failure. He argues that leaders are given too much credit for organizational success, on one hand, and too much blame when things go wrong, on the other. Pfeffer suggests that in selecting leaders we are using organizationally irrelevant criteria; he sees leadership as a process of attributing causal relationships to social actors. In essence, he asks the uncomfortable question, "Do leaders really make a difference today?"

Robert K. Mueller takes an action orientation in his "Leading-Edge Leadership" (Chapter 15). His underlying postulate for the future is that a leader must influence an institution more than it influences him or her. Balancing artful leadership attributes against management science capabilities calls for new organizational structures, policies, processes, and styles. More flexible organizations are needed to respond to the leadership issues continually sprouting from the leading scientific, technological, political, economic, social, and cultural developments. Mueller suggests a framework for identifying the teleological-ideological, instinctive, spiritual, and charismatic attributes of a leader. His framework goes beyond the logical, rational, sequential, and quantitative framework of human functioning. As the environment changes, so must our leaders.

In Chapter 16, Warren G. Bennis poses the question, "Where Have All the Leaders Gone?" They are around, says Bennis, but it is hard to recognize them. They're consulting, pleading, trotting, temporizing, putting out fires, avoiding or taking too much heat—and spending too much energy doing these things. They are difficult to spot because their authority and autonomy are, more and more, being whittled away by forces over which they have little or no control—they resign or they burn out. At a time when the trust and credibility of our leaders is at an all-time low and when survivors in leadership feel inhibited in the amount of power they dare exercise, our need for individuals who can lead is stronger than ever. The solution is not simple—leaders must develop vision, conceptualize with continuity and significance, and be willing to take risks. They must learn to lead despite the ambiguities and inconsistencies that confront them. And, most of all, the test of today's leader is whether he or she can define and direct the process of change and, by so doing, build new strengths. If we agree with Bennis, then we must examine whether a traditional military structure can facilitate the development of the leadership he describes.

One of the most significant chapters in this volume is John W. Gardner's essay from 1965, "The Antileadership Vaccine" (Chapter 17). His concerns are with the dispersion of power and our failure to cope with the "Big Question." In his opinion, the antileadership vaccine is administered by our educational system and by the structure of our society, causing people to lose the confidence they must have in order to assume a leadership role. In training people for leadership, we have neglected the broader moral view of shared values, thus inhibiting vision, creativity, and risk-taking. As a result, we appear to be approaching a point at which everyone will value the technical expert who advises the leader, or the intellectual who stands off and criticizes the leader, but no one will be concerned with the development of leadership itself.

In Chapter 18, "Thinking About Leadership," Thomas E. Cronin suggests that situational and contextual factors are of enormous importance, and that military leaders are not always effective when they make the transition to business and industry. Cronin also notes that leaders are not the same as managers—managers are concerned with doing things the right way, while leaders are concerned with doing the right thing. Although both groups start out as trained specialists, only those who are creative generalists emerge as leaders. Among the key ingredients necessary for successful leadership, he includes the ability to identify important problems, risk-taking and vision, sense of humor and proportion, positive self-concept, and integrity.

Interestingly, the personal qualities necessary for successful leadership in the future are quite similar to those attributes embodied by leaders of the past. The theme of this section is that our culture, with its large bureaucratic organizational structures and our followers' increased expectations from their leaders, is acting to inhibit the development of desired leader behaviors. It's almost as if we have unconsciously shifted our attention to other areas—in the military as well as in society at large—while assuming that leadership development will continue on its own as a natural phenomenon. But we cannot take leadership for granted; individually and organizationally we must work at it, addressing the leadership issues of today and tomorrow, or there will be no leaders when we need them most.

14

The Ambiguity of Leadership

JEFFREY PFEFFER

Leadership has for some time been a major topic in social and organizational psychology. Underlying much of this research has been the assumption that leadership is causally related to organizational performance. Through an analysis of leadership styles, behaviors, or characteristics (depending on the theoretical perspective chosen), the argument has been made that more effective leaders can be selected or trained or, alternatively, the situation can be configured to provide for enhanced leader and organizational effectiveness.

Three problems with emphasis on leadership as a concept can be posed: (a) ambiguity in definition and measurement of the concept itself; (b) the question of whether leadership has discernible effects on organizational outcomes; and (c) the selection process in succession to leadership positions, which frequently uses organizationally irrelevant criteria and which has implications for normative theories of leadership. The argument here is that leadership is of interest primarily as a phenomenological construct. Leaders serve as symbols for representing personal causation of social events. How and why are such attributions of personal effects made? Instead of focusing on leadership and its effects, how do people make inferences about and react to phenomena labelled as leadership (5)?

The Ambiguity of the Concept

While there have been many studies of leadership, the dimensions and definition of the concept remain unclear. To treat leadership as a

Reprinted by permission from *Academy of Management Review*, 2:1 (January 1977), pp. 104–112.

separate concept, it must be distinguished from other social influence phenomena. Hollander and Julian (24) and Bavelas (2) did not draw distinctions between leadership and other processes of social influence. A major point of the Hollander and Julian review was that leadership research might develop more rapidly if more general theories of social influence were incorporated. Calder (5) also argued that there is no unique content to the construct of leadership that is not subsumed under other, more general models of behavior.

Kochan, Schmidt, and DeCotiis (33) attempted to distinguish leadership from related concepts of authority and social power. In leadership, influence rights are voluntarily conferred. Power does not require goal compatibility—merely dependence—but leadership implies some congruence between the objectives of the leader and the led. These distinctions depend on the ability to distinguish voluntary from involuntary compliance and to assess goal compatibility. Goal statements may be retrospective inferences from action (46,53) and problems of distinguishing voluntary from involuntary compliance also exist (32). Apparently there are few meaningful distinctions between leadership and other concepts of social influence. Thus, an understanding of the phenomena subsumed under the rubric of leadership may not require the construct of leadership (5).

While there is some agreement that leadership is related to social influence, more disagreement concerns the basic dimensions of leader behavior. Some have argued that there are two tasks to be accomplished in groups—maintenance of the group and performance of some task or activity—and thus leader behavior might be described along these two dimensions (1, 6, 8, 25). The dimensions emerging from the Ohio State leadership studies—consideration and initiating structure—may be seen as similar to the two components of group maintenance and task accomplishment (18).

Other dimensions of leadership behavior have also been proposed (4). Day and Hamblin (10) analyzed leadership in terms of the closeness and punitiveness of the supervision. Several authors have conceptualized leadership behavior in terms of the authority and discretion subordinates are permitted (23, 36, 51). Fiedler (14) analyzed leadership in terms of the least-preferred-co-worker scale (LPC), but the meaning and behavioral attributes of this dimension of leadership behavior remain controversial.

The proliferation of dimensions is partly a function of research strategies frequently employed. Factor analysis on a large number of items describing behavior has frequently been used. This procedure tends to produce as many factors as the analyst decides to find, and permits the development of a large number of possible factor structures. The resultant factors must be named and further imprecision is introduced. Deciding on a summative concept to represent a factor is inevitably a partly subjective process.

Literature assessing the effects of leadership tends to be equivocal. Sales (45) summarized leadership literature employing the authoritarian-democratic typology and concluded that effects on performance were small and inconsistent. Reviewing the literature on consideration and initiating structure dimensions, Korman (34) reported relatively small and inconsistent results, and Kerr and Schriesheim (30) reported more consistent effects of the two dimensions. Better results apparently emerge when moderating factors are taken into account, including subordinate personalities (50), and situational characteristics (23,51). Kerr, et al. (31) list many moderating effects grouped under the headings of subordinate considerations, supervisor considerations, and task considerations. Even if each set of considerations consisted of only one factor (which it does not), an attempt to account for the effects of leader behavior would necessitate considering four-way interactions. While social reality is complex and contingent, it seems desirable to attempt to find more parsimonious explanations for the phenomena under study.

The Effects of Leaders

Hall asked a basic question about leadership: is there any evidence on the magnitude of the effects of leadership (17, p. 248)? Surprisingly, he could find little evidence. Given the resources that have been spent studying, selecting, and training leaders, one might expect that the question of whether or not leaders matter would have been addressed earlier (12).

There are at least three reasons why it might be argued that the observed effects of leaders on organizational outcomes would be small. First, those obtaining leadership positions are selected, and perhaps only certain, limited styles of behavior may be chosen. Second, once in the leadership position, the discretion and behavior of the leader are constrained. And third, leaders can typically affect only a few of the variables that may impact organizational performance.

Homogeneity of Leaders

Persons are selected to leadership positions. As a consequence of this selection process, the range of behaviors or characteristics exhibited by leaders is reduced, making it more problematic to empirically discover an effect of leadership. There are many types of constraints on the selection process. The attraction literature suggests that there is a tendency for persons to like those they perceive as similar (3). In critical decisions such as the selections of persons for leadership positions, compatible styles of behavior probably will be chosen. Selection of persons is also constrained by the internal system of influence in the organization. As Zald (56) noted, succession is a critical decision, affected by political influence and by environmental contingencies faced by the organization. As Thompson (49) noted, leaders may be selected for their capacity to deal with various organizational contingencies. In a study of characteristics of hospital administrators, Pfeffer and Salancik (42) found a relationship between the hospital's context and the characteristics and tenure of the administrators. To the extent that the contingencies and power distribution within the organization remain stable, the abilities and behaviors of those selected into leadership positions will also remain stable.

Finally, the selection of persons to leadership positions is affected by a self-selection process. Organizations and roles have images, providing information about their character. Persons are likely to select themselves into organizations and roles based upon their preferences for the dimensions of the organizational and role characteristics as perceived through these images. The self-selection of persons would tend to work along with organizational selection to limit the range of abilities and behaviors in a given organizational role.

Such selection processes would tend to increase homogeneity more within a single organization than across organizations. Yet many studies of leadership effect at the work group level have compared groups within a single organization. If there comes to be a widely shared, socially constructed definition of leadership behaviors or characteristics which guides the selection process, then leadership activity may come to be defined similarly in various organizations, leading to the selection of only those who match the constructed image of a leader.

Constraints on Leader Behavior

Analyses of leadership have frequently presumed that leadership style or leader behavior was an independent variable that could be selected or trained at will to conform to what research would find to be optimal. Even theorists who took a more contingent view of appropriate leadership behavior generally assumed that with proper training, appropriate behavior could be produced (51). Fiedler (13), noting how hard it was to change behavior, suggested changing the situational characteristics rather than the person, but this was an unusual suggestion in the context of prevailing literature which suggested that leadership style was something to be strategically selected according to the variables of the particular leadership theory.

But the leader is embedded in a social system, which constrains behavior. The leader has a role set (27), in which members have expectations for appropriate behavior and persons make efforts to modify the leader's behavior. Pressures to conform to the expectations of peers, subordinates, and superiors are all relevant in determining actual behavior.

Leaders, even in high-level positions, have unilateral control over fewer resources and fewer policies than might be expected. Investment decisions may require approval of others, while hiring and promotion decisions may be accomplished by committees. Leader behavior is constrained by both the demands of others in the role set and by organizationally prescribed limitations on the sphere of activity and influence.

External Factors

Many factors that may affect organizational performance are outside a leader's control, even if he or she were to have complete discretion over major areas of organizational decisions. For example, consider the executive in a construction firm. Costs are largely determined by operation of commodities and labor markets; and demand is largely affected by interest rates, availability of mortgage money, and economic conditions which are affected by governmental policies over which the executive has little control. School superintendents have little control over birth rates and community economic development, both of which profoundly affect school system budgets. While the leader may react to contingencies as they arise, or may be a better or worse forecaster, in accounting for variation in organizational outcomes, he or she may account for relatively little compared to external factors.

Second, the leader's success or failure may be partly due to circumstances unique to the organization but still outside his or her control. Leader positions in organizations vary in terms of the strength and position of the organization. The choice of a new executive does not fundamentally alter a market and financial position that has developed over years and affects the leader's ability to make strategic changes and the likelihood that the organization will do well or poorly. Organizations have relatively enduring strengths and weaknesses. The choice of a particular leader for a particular position has limited impact on these capabilities.

Empirical Evidence

Two studies have assessed the effects of leadership changes in major positions in organizations. Lieberson and O'Connor (35) examined 167 business firms in 13 industries over a 20 year period, allocating variance in sales, profits, and profit margins to one of four sources: year (general economic conditions), industry, company effects, and effects of changes in the top executive position. They concluded that compared to other factors, administration had a limited effect on organizational outcomes.

Using a similar analytical procedure, Salancik and Pfeffer (44) examined the effects of mayors on city budgets for 30 U.S. cities. Data on expenditures by budget category were collected for 1951–1968. Variance in amount and proportion of expenditures was apportioned to the year, the city, or the mayor. The mayoral effect was relatively small, with the city accounting for most of the variance, although the mayor effect was larger for expenditure categories that were not as directly connected to important interest groups. Salancik and Pfeffer argued that the effects of the mayor were limited both by absence of power to control many of the expenditures and tax sources, and by construction of policies in response to demands from interests in the environment.

If leadership is defined as a strictly interpersonal phenomenon, the relevance of these two studies for the issue of leadership effects becomes problematic. But such a conceptualization seems unduly restrictive, and is certainly inconsistent with Selznick's (47) conceptualization of leadership as strategic management and decision making. If one cannot observe differences when leaders change, then what does it matter who occupies the positions or how they behave?

Pfeffer and Salancik (41) investigated the extent to which behaviors selected by first-line supervisors were constrained by expectations of others in their role set. Variance in task and social behaviors could be accounted for by role-set expectations, with adherence to various demands made by role-set participants a function of similarity and relative power. Lowin and Craig (37) experimentally demonstrated that leader behavior was determined by the subordinate's own behavior. Both studies illustrate that leader behaviors are responses to the demands of the social context.

The effect of leadership may vary depending upon level in the organizational hierarchy, while the appropriate activities and behaviors may also vary with organizational level (26, 40). For the most part, empirical studies of leadership have dealt with first-line supervisors or leaders with relatively low organizational status (17). If leadership has any impact, it should be more evident at higher organizational levels or where there is more discretion in decisions and activities.

The Process of Selecting Leaders

Along with the suggestion that leadership may not account for much variance in organizational outcomes, it can be argued that merit or ability may not account for much variation in hiring and advancement of organizational personnel. These two ideas are related. If competence is hard to judge, or if leadership competence does not greatly affect organizational outcomes, then other, person-dependent criteria may be sufficient. Effective leadership styles may not predict career success when other variables such as social background are controlled.

Belief in the importance of leadership is frequently accompanied by belief that persons occupying leadership positions are selected and trained according to how well they can enhance the organization's performance. Belief in a leadership effect leads to development of a set of activities oriented toward enhancing leadership effectiveness. Simultaneously, persons managing their own careers are likely to place emphasis on activities and developing behaviors that will enhance their own leadership skills, assuming that such a strategy will facilitate advancement.

Research on the bases for hiring and promotion has been concentrated in examination of academic positions (e.g., 7, 19, 20). This is possibly the result of availability of relatively precise and unambiguous measures of performance, such as number of publications or citations. Evidence on criteria used in selecting and advancing personnel in industry is more indirect.

Studies have attempted to predict either the compensation or the attainment of general management positions of MBA students, using personality and other background information (21, 22, 54). There is some evidence that managerial success can be predicted by indicators of ability and motivation such as test scores and grades, but the amount of variance explained is typically quite small.

A second line of research has investigated characteristics and backgrounds of persons attaining leadership positions in major organizations in society. Domhoff (11), Mills (38), and Warner and Abbeglin (52) found a strong preponderance of persons with upper-class backgrounds occupying leadership positions. The implication of these findings is that studies of graduate success, including the success of MBA's, would explain more variance if the family background of the person were included.

A third line of inquiry uses a tracking model. The dynamic model developed is one in which access to elite universities is affected by social status (28) and, in turn, social status and attendance at elite universities affect later career outcomes (9, 43, 48, 55).

Unless one is willing to make the argument that attendance at elite universities or coming from an upper class background is perfectly correlated with merit, the evidence suggests that succession to leadership positions is not strictly based on meritocratic criteria. Such a conclusion is consistent with the inability of studies attempting to predict the success of MBA graduates to account for much variance, even when a variety of personality and ability factors are used.

Beliefs about the bases for social mobility are important for social stability. As long as persons believe that positions are allocated on meritocratic grounds, they are more likely to be satisfied with the social order and with their position in it. This satisfaction derives from the belief that occupational position results from application of fair and reasonable criteria, and that the opportunity exists for mobility if the person improves skills and performance.

If succession to leadership positions is determined by person-based criteria such as social origins or social connections (16), then efforts to enhance managerial effectiveness with the expectation that this will lead to career success divert attention from the processes of stratification actually operating within organizations. Leadership literature has been implicitly aimed at two audiences. Organizations were told how to become more effective, and persons were told what behaviors to acquire in order to become effective, and hence, advance in their careers. The possibility that neither organizational outcomes nor career success are related to leadership behaviors leaves leadership research facing issues of relevance and importance.

The Attribution of Leadership

Kelley conceptualized the layman as: "an applied scientist, that is, as a person concerned about applying his knowledge of causal relationships in order to *exercise control* of his world" (29, p. 2). Reviewing a series of studies dealing with the attributional process, he concluded that persons were not only interested in understanding their world correctly, but also in controlling it.

> The view here proposed is that attribution processes are to be understood not only as a means of providing the individual with a veridical view of his world, but as a means of encouraging and maintaining his effective exercise of control in that world (29, p. 22).

Controllable factors will have high salience as candidates for causal explanation, while a bias toward the more important causes may shift the attributional emphasis toward causes that are not controllable (29, p. 23). The study of attribution is a study of naive psychology—an examination of how persons make sense out of the events taking place around them.

If Kelley is correct that individuals will tend to develop attributions that give them a feeling of control, then emphasis on leadership may derive partially from a desire to believe in the effectiveness and importance of individual action, since individual action is more controllable than contextual variables. Lieberson and O'Connor (35) made essentially the same point in introducing their paper on the effects of top management changes on organizational performance. Given the desire for control and a feeling of personal effectiveness, organizational outcomes are more likely to be attributed to individual actions, regardless of their actual causes.

Leadership is attributed by observers. Social action has meaning only through a phenomenological process (46). The identification of certain organizational roles as leadership positions guides the construction of meaning in the direction of attributing effects to the actions of those positions. While Bavelas (2) argued that the functions of leadership, such as task accomplishment and group maintenance, are shared throughout the group, this fact provides no simple and potentially controllable focus for attributing causality. Rather, the identification of leadership positions provides a simpler and more readily changeable model of reality. When causality is lodged in one or a few persons rather than being a function of a complex set of interactions among all group members, changes can be made by replacing or influencing the occupant of the leadership position. Causes of organizational actions are readily identified in this simple causal structure.

Even if, empirically, leadership has little effect, and even if succession to leadership positions is not predicated on ability or performance, the belief in leadership effects and meritocratic succession provides a simple causal framework and a justification for the structure of the social collectivity. More importantly, the beliefs interpret social actions in terms that indicate potential for effective individual intervention or control. The personification of social causality serves too many uses to be easily overcome. Whether or not leader behavior actually influences performance or effectiveness, it is important because people believe it does.

One consequence of the attribution of causality to leaders and leadership is that leaders come to be symbols. Mintzberg (39), in his discussion of the roles of managers, wrote of the symbolic role, but more in terms of attendance at formal events and formally representing the organization. The symbolic role of leadership is more important than implied in such a description. The leader as a symbol provides a target for action when difficulties occur, serving as a scapegoat when things go wrong. Gamson and Scotch (15) noted that in baseball, the firing of the manager served a scapegoating purpose. One cannot fire the whole team, yet when performance is poor, something must be done. The firing of the manager conveys to the world and to the actors involved that success is the result of personal actions, and that steps can and will be taken to enhance organizational performance.

The attribution of causality to leadership may be reinforced by organizational actions, such as the inauguration process, the choice process, and providing the leader with symbols and ceremony. If leaders are chosen by using a random number table, persons are less likely to believe in their effects than if there is an elaborate search or selection process followed by an elaborate ceremony signifying the changing of control, and if the leader then has a variety of perquisites and symbols that distinguish him or her from the rest of the organization. Construction of the importance of leadership in a given social context is the outcome of various social processes, which can be empirically examined.

Since belief in the leadership effect provides a feeling of personal control, one might argue that efforts to increase the attribution of causality to leaders would occur more when it is more necessary and more problematic to attribute causality to controllable factors. Such an argument would lead to the hypothesis that the more the *context* actually effects organizational outcomes, the more efforts will be made to ensure attribution to *leadership*. When leaders really do have effects, it is less necessary to engage in rituals indicating their effects. Such rituals are more likely when there is uncertainty and unpredictability associated with the organization's operations. This results both from the desire to feel control in uncertain situations and from the fact that in ambiguous contexts, it is easier to attribute consequences to leadership without facing possible disconfirmation.

The leader is, in part, an actor. Through statements and actions, the leader attempts to reinforce the operation of an attribution process which tends to vest causality in that position in the social structure. Successful leaders, as perceived by members of the social system, are those who can separate themselves from organizational failures and associate themselves with organizational successes. Since the meaning of action is socially constructed, this involves manipulation of symbols to reinforce the desired process of attribution. For instance, if a manager knows that business in his or her division is about to improve because of the economic cycle, the leader may, nevertheless, write recommendations and undertake actions and changes that are highly visible and that will tend to identify his or her behavior closely with the division. A manager who perceives impending failure will attempt to associate the division and its policies and decisions with others, particularly persons in higher organizational positions, and to disassociate himself or herself from the division's performance, occasionally even transferring or moving to another organization.

Conclusion

The theme of this article has been that analysis of leadership and leadership processes must be contingent on the intent of the researcher. If the interest is in understanding the causality of social phenomena as realiably and accurately as possible, then the concept of leadership may be a poor place to begin. The issue of the effects of leadership is open to question. But examination of situational variables that accompany more or less leadership effect is a worthwhile task.

The more phenomenological analysis of leadership directs attention to the process by which social causality is attributed, and focuses on the distinction between causality as perceived by group members and causality as assessed by an outside observer. Leadership is associated with a set of myths reinforcing a social construction of meaning which legitimates leadership role occupants, provides belief in potential mobility for those not in leadership roles, and attributes social causality to leadership roles, thereby providing a belief in the effectiveness of individual control. In analyzing leadership, this mythology and the process by which such mythology is created and supported should be separated from analysis of leadership as a social influence process, operating within constraints.

References

1. Bales, R. F. *Interaction Process Analysis: A Method for the Study of Small Groups* (Reading, Mass.: Addison-Wesley, 1950).
2. Bavelas, Alex. "Leadership: Man and Function," *Administrative Science Quarterly*, Vol. 4 (1960), 491–498.
3. Berscheid, Ellen, and Elaine Walster. *Interpersonal Attraction* (Reading, Mass.: Addison-Wesley, 1969).
4. Bowers, David G., and Stanley E. Seashore. "Predicting Organizational Effectiveness with a Four-Factor Theory of Leadership," *Administrative Science Quarterly*, Vol. 11 (1966), 238–263.
5. Calder, Bobby J. "An Attribution Theory of Leadership," in B. Staw and G. Salancik (Eds.), *New Directions in Organizational Behavior* (Chicago: St. Clair Press, 1976), in press.
6. Cartwright, Dorwin C., and Alvin Zander. *Group Dynamics: Research and Theory*, 3rd ed. (Evanston, Ill.: Row, Peterson, 1960).
7. Cole, Jonathan R., and Stephen Cole. *Social Stratification in Science* (Chicago: University of Chicago Press, 1973).
8. Collins, Barry E., and Harold Guetzkow. *A Social Psychology of Group Processes for Decision-Making* (New York: Wiley, 1964).
9. Collins, Randall. "Functional and Conflict Theories of Stratification," *American Sociological Review*, Vol. 36 (1971), 1002–1019.

10. Day, R. C., and R. L. Hamblin. "Some Effects of Close and Punitive Styles of Supervision," *American Journal of Sociology,* Vol. 69 (1964), 499–510.
11. Domhoff, G. William. *Who Rules America?* (Englewood Cliffs, N.J.: Prentice-Hall, 1967).
12. Dubin, Robert. "Supervision and Productivity: Empirical Findings and Theoretical Considerations," in R. Dubin, G. C. Homans, F. C. Mann, and D. C. Miller (Eds.), *Leadership and Productivity* (San Francisco: Chandler Publishing Co., 1965), pp. 1–50.
13. Fiedler, Fred E. "Engineering the Job to Fit the Manager," *Harvard Business Review,* Vol. 43 (1965), 115–122.
14. Fiedler, Fred E. *A Theory of Leadership Effectiveness* (New York: McGraw-Hill, 1967).
15. Gamson, William A., and Norman A. Scotch. "Scapegoating in Baseball," *American Journal of Sociology,* Vol. 70 (1964), 69–72.
16. Granovetter, Mark. *Getting a Job* (Cambridge, Mass.: Harvard University Press, 1974).
17. Hall, Richard H. *Organizations: Structure and Process* (Englewood Cliffs, N.J.: Prentice-Hall, 1972).
18. Halpin, A. W., and J. Winer. "A Factorial Study of the Leader Behavior Description Questionnaire," in R. M. Stogdill and A. E. Coons (Eds.), *Leader Behavior: Its Description and Measurement* (Columbus, Ohio: Bureau of Business Research, Ohio State University, 1957), pp. 39–51.
19. Hargens, L. L. "Patterns of Mobility of New Ph.D.'s Among American Academic Institutions," *Sociology of Education,* Vol. 42 (1969), 18–37.
20. Hargens, L. L., and W. O. Hagstrom. "Sponsored and Contest Mobility of American Academic Scientists," *Sociology of Education,* Vol. 40 (1967), 24–38.
21. Harrell, Thomas W. "High Earning MBA's," *Personnel Psychology,* Vol. 25 (1972), 523–530.
22. Harrell, Thomas W., and Margaret S. Harrell. "Predictors of Management Success." *Stanford University Graduate School of Business, Technical Report No. 3 to the Office of Naval Research.*
23. Heller, Frank, and Gary Yukl. "Participation, Managerial Decision-Making, and Situational Variables," *Organizational Behavior and Human Performance,* Vol. 4 (1969), 227–241.
24. Hollander, Edwin P., and James W. Julian. "Contemporary Trends in the Analysis of Leadership Processes," *Psychological Bulletin,* Vol. 71 (1969), 387–397.
25. House, Robert J. "A Path Goal Theory of Leader Effectiveness," *Administrative Science Quarterly,* Vol. 16 (1971), 321–338.
26. Hunt, J. G. "Leadership-Style Effects at Two Managerial Levels in a Simulated Organization," *Administrative Science Quarterly,* Vol. 16 (1971), 476–485.
27. Kahn, R. L., D. M. Wolfe, R. P. Quinn, and J. D. Snoek. *Organizational Stress: Studies in Role Conflict and Ambiguity* (New York: Wiley, 1964).
28. Karabel, J., and A. W. Astin, "Social Class, Academic Ability, and College 'Quality'," *Social Forces,* Vol. 53 (1975), 381–398.

29. Kelley, Harold H. *Attribution in Social Interaction* (Morristown, N.J.: General Learning Press, 1971).
30. Kerr, Steven, and Chester Schriesheim. "Consideration, Initiating Structure and Organizational Criteria—An Update of Korman's 1966 Review," *Personnel Psychology*, Vol. 27 (1974), 555–568.
31. Kerr, S., C. Schriesheim, C. J. Murphy, and R. M. Stogdill. "Toward A Contingency Theory of Leadership Based Upon the Consideration and Initiating Structure Literature," *Organizational Behavior and Human Performance*, Vol. 12 (1974), 62–82.
32. Kiesler, C., and S. Kiesler. *Conformity* (Reading, Mass.: Addison-Wesley, 1969).
33. Kochan, T. A., S. M. Schmidt, and T. A. DeCotiis. "Superior-Subordinate Relations: Leadership and Headship," *Human Relations*, Vol. 28 (1975), 279–294.
34. Korman, A. K. "Consideration, Initiating Structure, and Organizational Criteria—A Review," *Personnel Psychology*, Vol. 19 (1966), 349–362.
35. Lieberson, Stanley, and James F. O'Connor. "Leadership and Organizational Performance: A Study of Large Corporations," *American Sociological Review*, Vol. 37 (1972), 117–130.
36. Lippitt, Ronald. "An Experimental Study of the Effect of Democratic and Authoritarian Group Atmospheres," *University of Iowa Studies in Child Welfare*, Vol. 16 (1940), 43–195.
37. Lowin, A., and J. R. Craig. "The Influence of Level of Performance on Managerial Style: An Experimental Object-Lesson in the Ambiguity of Correlational Data," *Organizational Behavior and Human Performance*, Vol. 3 (1968), 440–458.
38. Mills, C. Wright. "The American Business Elite: A Collective Portrait," in C. W. Mills, *Power, Politics, and People* (New York: Oxford University Press, 1963), pp. 110–139.
39. Mintzberg, Henry. *The Nature of Managerial Work* (New York: Harper and Row, 1973).
40. Nealey, Stanley M., and Milton R. Blood. "Leadership Performance of Nursing Supervisors at Two Organizational Levels," *Journal of Applied Psychology*, Vol. 52 (1968), 414–442.
41. Pfeffer, Jeffrey, and Gerald R. Salancik. "Determinants of Supervisory Behavior: A Role Set Analysis," *Human Relations*, Vol. 28 (1975), 139–154.
42. Pfeffer, Jeffrey, and Gerald R. Salancik. "Organizational Context and the Characteristics and Tenure of Hospital Administrators," *Academy of Management Journal*, Vol. 20 (1977), in press.
43. Reed, R. H., and H. P. Miller. "Some Determinants of the Variation in Earnings for College Men," *Journal of Human Resources*, Vol. 5 (1970), 117–190.
44. Salancik, Gerald R., and Jeffrey Pfeffer. "Constraints on Administrator Discretion: The Limited Influence of Mayors on City Budgets," *Urban Affairs Quarterly*, in press.
45. Sales, Stephen M. "Supervisory Style and Productivity: Review and Theory," *Personnel Psychology*, Vol. 19 (1966), 275–286.

46. Schutz, Alfred. *The Phenomenology of the Social World* (Evanston, Ill.: Northwestern University Press, 1967).
47. Selznick, P. *Leadership in Administration* (Evanston, Ill.: Row, Peterson, 1957).
48. Spaeth, J. L., and A. M. Greeley, *Recent Alumni and Higher Education* (New York: McGraw-Hill, 1970).
49. Thompson, James D. *Organizations in Action* (New York: McGraw-Hill, 1967).
50. Vroom, Victor H. "Some Personality Determinants of the Effects of Participation," *Journal of Abnormal and Social Pscyhology,* Vol. 59 (1959), 322–327.
51. Vroom, Victor H., and Phillip W. Yetton. *Leadership and Decision-Making* (Pittsburgh: University of Pittsburgh Press, 1973).
52. Warner, W. L., and J. C. Abbeglin. *Big Business Leaders in America* (New York: Harper and Brothers, 1955).
53. Weick, Karl E. *The Social Psychology of Organizing* (Reading, Mass.: Addison-Wesley, 1969).
54. Weinstein, Alan G., and V. Srinivasan. "Predicting Managerial Success of Master of Business Administration (MBA) Graduates," *Journal of Applied Psychology,* Vol. 59 (1974), 207–212.
55. Wolfle, Dael. *The Uses of Talent* (Princeton: Princeton University Press, 1971).
56. Zald, Mayer N. "Who Shall Rule? A Political Analysis of Succession in a Large Welfare Organization," *Pacific Sociological Review,* Vol. 8 (1965), 52–60.

15

Leading-Edge Leadership

ROBERT K. MUELLER

1. Introduction

About the year 1800, the word *leadership* entered the English language. It was and is a sophisticated concept with multiple definitions. Leadership defined as the initiation and maintenance of structure in expectation and interaction may be the meaning best suited for the future manager. New structures can often create new expectations and interactions in group goal attainment and problem solution.

How can a person prepare for such a leadership role? What are the attributes of a 21st century leader? These are elegant questions posed for a fuzzy future. They are important questions for these leaders are just now entering our schools and colleges.

Theories of leadership are many. Future leadership calls for more than logic. Theories run the gamut of great man theories, environmental theories, person-situation theories, interaction-expectation theories, humanistic and exchange theories. Research has shown that effective leaders score high in social service, persuasive, business and intellectual values.

An underlying postulate for the future is that a leader must influence an institution more than it influences him or her. Certainly this activist perspective is the core challenge of leading-edge-leadership. No longer can the leader be only the "wave pushed ahead by the ship" as Tolstoy wrote. Instead, he must become the force behind the movement and the navigator. Sections 2 and 3 describe the turbulent situation and the key issues to be faced in the future.

The true leader is a trumpet that does not give an uncertain sound. He or she tends to be a revolutionist, an innovator and not an evolutionist or traditionalist. This role is distinct from what sociologists call an

Reprinted by permission from *Human Systems Management,* 1 (1980), pp. 17–27. Copyright © 1980 by North-Holland Publishing Company.

executive, manager or administrator. Three key components of leadership thought, beliefs and behavior required to cope with the leading management issues of the future are proposed later in this discussion.

Many years ago Bishop Gore of Oxford, whose total life had been dedicated to education, was asked to make some generalization about students. He said the most striking and unexpected discovery he had made was that, although the natural gifts of people varied enormously, he was convinced that such differences in talent were of little or no value compared with the issue of how a person uses the talent he possesses.

Without strong individual determination, the executive or manager's role is likely to be determined by the organization or by the environment in which the institution finds itself. The challenge is to reverse this equation.

The future leader will need some sense of purpose, an ability to make trade-offs amongst emergent factors and an understanding of the broader aspects of institutional governance.

2. Leading Where and How?

2.1. The Fuzzy Future

Futurology, a newly fledged discipline, is having as much trouble establishing itself as fuzzy set theory. None of the three Hellenic coinages for the study of the future have caught on. Jedrzejewski's *stoxology*—the science of conjecture—; the anonymously minted *mellology*—the science of the future—; and Wescott's *alleotics*—the study of change—haven't made it any better. The only purely Latin term for this field was dubbed *futuribles* by Bertrand de Jouvenel. This term has more currency in Europe.

Flechtheim's *futurology* or the slightly less Hellenic *futuristics* focuses mainly on techniques of prediction: determinative, normative and random. The intellectual freemasonry of futurists consists of members who are open to new ideas and often noncompetitive in their relationship to one another.

The purpose of this discussion is not to attempt to forecast or predict a future end-state for managers but rather to identify certain trends and patterns now; the driving forces, impacts, possible swings, events and alternative end-state characterizations. Their implications for the manager 20 to 30 years ahead are profound.

Some basic hypotheses have been made in connection with some recent research at Arthur D. Little, Inc. These identify certain global trends affecting the probable end-state environment for institutions. The requirement, both for more leadership and more management ability is clear. Some of the trends which call for new capabilities are:

(a) The internationalization of political and economic institutions in other than the large industrialized nations.

(b) A growing dependence of developed nations on the availability of key external resources obtainable mainly in less developed countries. The balance of physical survival and economic health versus political relationships is shifting to redress this interdependence.

(c) As developing countries reach a more advanced state, different patterns of government and business relationships enter the international competitive area. This causes increased uncertainty in the conduct of international business and a strong sense that there will be a transition to new patterns of institutions, business, government and international relationships.

(d) A political explosion in the formation and reformation of new nations increases the number of actors on the global stage. A rapid increase in sophistication of these participants is occurring whether they are new governments, political aggregations, culture groups, new private enterprises, new suppliers or consumers.

(e) Basic value systems are changing. There is a strong drive toward egalitarianism resulting from the growth and affluence of developed nations. There is a growth in interdependence among nations. There is also a search by individuals and institutions for a stronger sense of identity.

(f) All of this calls for more clarity (legal, strategic nature, social, political) in the interrelationships of institutions and presages a change in the relative aging of industries and societies.

(g) Relationships and conflicts between fundamental driving forces and systems will gradually develop to provide special incentives and some differentiation. These will be based on self value, egalitarianism and of course market values in free world areas.

(h) The impacts of technology will affect industries, social-economic maturity and the balances between nations and social force systems. These will be a continuing cause for future turbulence.

The presumption that if government, activists, communities, unions and shareowners will only leave the corporation alone, everyone's welfare will be served just doesn't fit the prospective future complex society anymore than it does today.

In recent years, the Faraday type force-fields of hard-science technology occupied man's interest persistently and more effectively than similar force-fields in the softer sciences of sociology, anthropology, political science and psychology. The creations of technology have pushed institutions of the developed world to where different governance concepts and systems are required if corporations are to be effectively managed. This is taking place in the social-political jungle and ambiguous situations in which managers and leaders now find themselves. These situations will become progressively more complex in the future. The leading edges of these force-fields are where the management action must occur.

It seems appropriate that a systems view of such force-fields will continue to be useful. This means an understanding of an orderly arrangement of interdependent activities and related processes. The task of the executive and of the leader is to identify the dominant force-fields, to watch and assess them in an experimental frame of mind. The storm watch of the weather bureau comes to mind as a metaphor. Especially equipped aircraft and crews seek and interact with impending storms, pierce hurricane vortices to size up the forces at work and assess probable impacts for warning purposes.

Suffice it to say, there is a Sargasso Sea of problems ahead for the leading-edge-leader. I suggest that he must be a student of at least six different perspectives. We refer to these as the shifts and trends at the leading edge of the force-fields currently at work in the world. These emergent factors are the subject of Section 3 of this set of notions about leading-edge-leadership.

2.2 Wanted: More Leaders, Fewer Executives

What this prospective future suggests—certainly the need exists today—is the need for more leaders and fewer executives. We need persons who can initiate structure in group expectation and show us how to master and motivate institutions and individuals within a complex environment experiencing excessive internal and external stresses and changes.

The interactions, conflicts and increasing rates of change with which we must coexist require the use of new (or venerable) insights and tools of the psychologists and anthropologists [8]. No longer can a "yellow pages manager" pick out from a conventional inventory list, the theme or strategy which is most effective for leadership of an institution.

Balancing artful leadership attributes along with management science will be necessary to achieve useful results in practice. This will occur in the future through many processes which may lack adequate experimental verification today. Whether a leader can also be a manager, a governor, an administrator, an executive, and a professional is doubtful given the turbulence ahead. Political effectiveness, managerial effectiveness and charismatic leadership is an unusual combination of attributes to find in any one individual. Hence the recent trend toward plural management organizational structures.

Walter Lippman once said that "the genius of a good leader is to leave behind him a situation which common sense without the grace of genius can deal with successfully." The 21st century leader will have to first develop a core team of unusually qualified persons who can jointly cope with the problems and uncertainties in the future.

(1) *Eclectic traits and behavior.* Certain leadership and management characteristics have no impact on, or are dysfunctional with respect to, group performance and follower satisfaction. Recognition of these is vital. Determination of leader characteristics and their interaction with followers and with the environment requires an understanding of the leader's and follower's values, judgments, behavioral patterns, personality and vision. Recruitment, development and educational programs will have to recognize these factors.

(2) *Style.* Leadership style can be developed so that it has a favorable impact on groups or followers in terms of adequate satisfaction, group cohesion and group drive. Patterns of behavior and expectation should be flexible with respect to the expected future managerial environment. Oversensitivity developed by such techniques as T-Group training often incapacitate a leader in coping with this job. Experimental work is required to determine specifically what style will strengthen or weaken the retention of a leadership position for each individual and each encountered circumstance.

I visited Yugoslavia about a year after the major political shakeup of the ruling League of Communists of Yugoslavia to try to fathom the contradictory trends in economic reform and attractiveness of the country for foreign investment. At that time, there occurred a striking example of the psychological dominance style of a leader in dealing with the matter of respective roles and mutual trust as we know them in Western industrial countries.

The group of foreign European, American and Asian businessmen with whom I was associated in the visit were deeply impressed with the off-record discussions with President Tito, his ministers and leading figures in the financial, government and business communities. Their complex—to us—concept of free enterprise with stateowned facilities bugged our group for almost a week of free wheeling interrogation and exchange of views.

The authority of the management to reserve funds for growth, for example, rather than to raise the year-end bonus, always bowed officially to a Worker's Council which, it appeared, attempted to act as a board of directors on the one hand and a union group on the other hand. In questioning one of the industrial leaders, we were unable to get to the nub of how he made a basic business decision. The chief manager of one of the largest stateowned enterprises said (with the translator's tailoring of this into three languages) what may be paraphrased as "I just tell the council that's the way it's got to be!"

As a 230 pound, direct-mannered Yugoslavian type of executive-leader that he appeared to be, it was obvious his dynamic personality and personal prestige transcended any artificial, ideological network of constraints. He did not permit these abstract constraints to inhibit a clear resolution of an action in the best interest of the enterprise as might be judged by any Western value system.

(3) *Interpersonal reinforcement of leadership.* This involves consolidating the position with careful use of personal style and attitude characteristics. Techniques vary for large or small companies, for different types of organizations. The interpersonal space factors, commitments of persons to the corporation or profession, the status factors, the management hierarchy, the identity, certain social norms, reference groups and value systems all fit into reinforcement of a leadership position.

The future leader will be aware of these elements and deal with them accordingly. Frequent reorganization of central versus decentral units, ad hoc task force formation, spin-off of separate business enterprise and use of non-uniform incentive schemes are among the obvious variants.

(4) *Political power.* Leadership behavior, personality and the interaction with power are affected differently according to whether a task-pattern or a person-oriented-pattern is involved and whether it provides a low or high powered influence. Seeking power equalization and leader legitimacy with those involved, and resolving role conflicts which occur are important factors in coping with political power.

Organizations have been characterized with respect to the nature of their primary power that often is used to control their lowest ranking participants. Coercive organizations, such as a prison, keep order through threat of physical force. Utilitarian organizations, such as manufacturing or service entities, keep order primarily through monetary rewards. Normative organizations, e.g., churches, professional organizations, learned societies and schools elicit compliance through allocation and manipulation of symbolic awards, e.g., diplomas, licenses, titles and membership status.

Normative organizations tend to demand higher degrees of commitment and allegiance from the members. Charisma is ascribed to the officers or senior participants of the elite group. Use of charismatic power by personal contact, symbols, rituals and the gift of grace may parallel the formal organizational chart as means to relieve the political strain of challenges to organizational hegemony, integration and competition for resources. Charismatic power however cannot be routinized as a source of political power.

(5) *Contingency management.* In recent years, there has been growing acceptance of what is an eclectic use of various theories of comparative organization.

There has been a growing acceptance of contingency management which is also called situational management. This states that the optimum management strategy or practice is contingent upon the real world situation. It has become clear that the classical bureaucratic design, the neoclassical or decentralized design, or even modern structural design such as free-form systems and matrix-setups do not hold up under all organizational situations. In effect, bureaucracy was found unable to cope with dynamic situations. Matrix or free-form designs are not adequately adaptable to situations which require cutbacks and stability. Fred E. Fiedler [1,2] and his associates did early research in the situational approach to leadership. They found that a task-oriented leader is more successful in extreme situations when he has a great deal of influence: i.e., position power is high and the task is highly structured, or alternatively when he has very little influence: i.e., position power is low, and the task is unstructured.

(6) Group survival is dependent upon leader behavior and this has direct but unquantifiable effects on group arousal, group drive, group cohesiveness and productivity. The future leader will be conscious of this dependency and modify his behavior to enhance his own survival and effectiveness. He will employ, inter alia, what has been called the "helicopter factor." This is the ability to rise above the particulars of a situation and perceive it as a whole, in its relation to the overall environment.

Given these attributes of a 21st century leader we can expect to see an emerging change in management style.

2.3. Future Management Style

The biologists teach that inefficiency is an extremely important element in the survival of the species. A species will not expand to the limit of its environment if it is to survive. Otherwise the environment would worsen and the opportunity for continued existence is jeopardized. The efficient species simply collapses into extinction whereas the inefficient species possesses reserves. Redundancy and some irrelevance are the sort of elements that a governance system requires in order to survive.

We can look at an institution as such a "repository of redundance in society" to use the phrase of Kenneth Boulding, Professor at the University of Colorado. The task of the leader is to get out of an institution's action as much in terms of human values as he possibly can in proportion to whatever values are put in. Redundancy and vagueness are important reserves in this regard. They are obviously of great value in time of crisis.

One of the outstanding properties of a fuzzy future is its irreducible uncertainty. The ability to make decisions under these conditions is limited. While our techniques could produce projections of the future, we cannot totally trust them. Data needs to be treated as evidence in the same form that a physician treats symptoms and protocol checks when examining a patient. A way to approach the fuzzy future is through adaptability and use of the heuristic process.

In looking at the societal network in which the leader finds himself, we see a finite number of states undergoing transition at discrete instances of time. A societal network will undergo an evolution of its states and may be thought of as a dynamic process. The long-term behavior of the societal network indicates it will either reach a stable state or a periodic pattern of state transitions in which the leader may find himself. An effective leader will be sensitive to these states in the chain-of-being. Instinct and intuitive powers will be vital in this situation.

That instinct plays an important part in leadership is asserted by many experienced persons. The adjective *instinctive* connotes innate, impulsive or spontaneous attitude as a result of behavioral patterns which are mediated by reactions below the conscious level and are conditioned by environment.

The adjective *intuitive* implies direct perception of apprehension without apparent reasoning, or evolutionary behavior patterns. Such "reason in a hurry" is a significant trait in successful leadership. In some instances it may be the result of protracted, long and agonizing groping.

From my observation, a good leader is one who is able to simplify problems. Validation of this is obscure or absent in most studies of leadership and management. The ability to intuitively select significant factors of a situation, without going through the rigor of reducing it through a logical chain of reasoning, identifies leadership talent in a practicing world. This insight apprehends the inner nature of problem situations and is a powerful ability of a leader.

The skill to jump to the crux of a complex matter while the rest of the crowd are still trying to identify the problem is a rare gift of leaders albeit sometimes a risky one. Only exceptional leaders, and few executives or managers, possess this ability to a degree that results in a good batting average for their decisions. Certainly this is an area for future leadership research. First we need to identify the nature of means by which *rapid reification* can be developed. Secondly, we need to integrate and relate a charismatic component with the logical and intuitive attributes which we suggest are vital to leading-edge leadership. This integration is both the key and challenge and is the subject of Section 4.

There is increasing interaction, interdependency and proliferation of institutional units occurring in this sea of socio-technical-cultural-political-individual forces. A free-form organizational style is probably the most likely to survive. Attributes of such a type and the style involved may be characterized by the following:

(1) Organizational fluidity. Work engagements and pursuits of objectives are often carried out in the task force mode spawned from core resource groups.

(2) The center of gravity of the professional or economic cutting edge is placed in a core group of individuals. Beyond this center extends a group of satellite organizations placed in pattern form reminiscent of Buddhists' graphic symbols. This Buddhist concept of a mandala configuration includes certain primary components; a core and an enclosing boundary with a complex of satellites around a center. Some components will have a permanent nature, some exist as interim task forces and others are transient imperatives around the compass of far-flung organizations.

(3) A climate of encouragement of individual priority-setting needs to be present with an increasing degree of freedom in such choices. Appropriate incentives will be available for leading-edge leaders.

(4) More employee mobility will occur between institutions as a more acceptable way of life. The one-company-one-career-one-job ethos will be replaced by professional career changes at all stages of a working life. Increased attention will be given to optimal time for retirement or "repotting" in another career setting.

(5) Peer systems of management with minimum hierarchical structure are more likely to retain the leading-edge leader. He will have to be comfortable and be able to survive within this type management context. Organizational policies will employ more collegial style as distinct from directive style common to most institutional managements.

(6) Increase in service and software activity as distinct from fixed assets and hardware. This will extensively alter the management of resources. Individuals may have to be willing to invest their own time in research and development in the softer socio-cultural areas of corporate activity.

(7) Consciousness of the concept of intellectual property will be raised as a key element in management. In addition to conventional industrial property rights, this concept also involves intangibles such as statutory

and moral rights associated with education, art, and literature which are so important in the further world development.

The bulwark concept of intellectual property in the early 17th century was first set forth in Anglo-Saxon terms in the United Kingdom. The rationale for including incorporeal property under a broad juridicial-trust concept rested on the premise that the main ingredients to progress were the theoretical scientists, the inventors and entrepreneurs. The legal principles say that a society intending to progress must enter into a compact with the inventive and creative members of that society through a legal structure for protecting intellectual property rights.

A future analogy will be society entering into a compact with institutional leaders in order to deal with socio-cultural and techno-economic inventions. Those in responsible charge will need certain political and interpersonal sensitivities, professional talents, visions and experience to apply throughout the development process [6]. As these skills produce socio-technical-economic inventions, their value can be enormous.

(8) An entreprencurial climate fostered by special incentives will become more common and will encourage innovation. Future organizations will need to allow relative freedom to their staff to spend time on individual entrepreneurial pursuits and projects. Many companies are now struggling with revised compensation schemes to nurture the entrepreneur [7].

(9) There will be more carefully controlled security systems where need-to-know criteria would be strictly observed in order to retain intellectual property values in an enterprise and to keep a competitive edge. Future managers will be skilled in techniques, policies and appropriate communications in order to manage these improved security systems.

(10) Those persons engaged in the governance of institutions will have to permit unusual degrees of freedom and encouragement to leaders, professional staff and administrative managers. This will allow staff to pursue non-conflicting non-sensitive interests on their own time or even part-time. This freedom will help to retain outstanding persons who need to extend their perspectives; continually sharpen intellectual, academic and business capabilities. It will further reduce the dependency on the central-life interest factor for a balanced career.

Given the ten attributes of the future free-form style organizations, the intellectual focus of the leader is likely to be like the Brownian movement, always in motion. Some philosophical arrangement may help to cluster the problems, opportunities, concepts and leading ideas with which a leader must cope.

3. Edge or Hedge?—Emergent Factors

3.1. Shifts and Trends

The work at the Center for Social Policy at Stanford Research Institute (among other organizations) has outlined certain consciousness-raising trends for the future [3]. These are not unlike my own postulates for the environment in which leaders will have to manage.

These shifts and trends are popularized in the form of:

(1) *Alternative futures or options.* This includes awareness of the Faustian powers of technological manipulation in shaping the future. New dimensions of human responsibility are emerging for the future in which our managers will function. Job rights, human rights, social cost accounting are examples. Futurism, one of the significant recent intellectual developments along with the systems theory, has provoked a shift from the discipline of the factory and Weberian bureaucracy to more flexible, knowledge-based organizations and a decline in traditional sources of authority.

(2) *Spaceship earth system.* Concern for environment, ecological systems, resource control, an awareness of the biosphere as a life support system. This has been called a revolution in lowering expectations. The expectations are a complex of concerns over limits to growth, the energy crisis, pollution, exhaustion of non-renewable resources. This "revolution" is in direct conflict with the revolution of rising expectations of millions of persons in the developing nations for a higher standard of living.

(3) *Growing international awareness of inequities.* These are caused partly by the rapid advances in transport, communications and the mobility of a managerial elite in taking up residence in non-native environs. People are becoming aware of the need to redress the balance between the less developed areas and those in a greater state of development with a better standard of living.

(4) *Shift towards humanistic and spiritual values.* This includes the movement towards egalitarianism. The shift is manifest in forms of employee discontent, new political and social emphasis on self-determination and in the new styles of management for coping with these trends. The movement to upgrade opportunities for qualified females and minorities is yet another symptom.

(5) *Shortage of meaningful social roles.* Automation, specialization of work to the detriment of personal satisfaction has reduced the meaningfulness of work opportunities. Increase in leisure time and the recent change in retirement age are not the answer to this problem. A world job-shortage by the year 2000 despite a declining birth rate is

predicted by the Population Reference Bureau in Washington. The pressure will be mainly in the developing countries where the search for jobs is already desperate. Between 300 and 500 million persons are already unemployed worldwide with the labor force expected to rise from the current 1.7 billion to 2.5 billion by the end of this century. Research is needed to illuminate solutions for these human needs through meaningful socially responsible work and for self-service new industrial patterns.

(6) *Shift towards a new transcendentalism.* This is manifested by the emergence of widespread interest in new naturalism, religious and spiritual concerns, psychic phenomena and other self-exploratory techniques.

The future leader will have to be aware of the potential impacts of these shifts which are due to cause future problems. The issues include overpopulation, problems of the aged, biological and nuclear hazards, environmental integrity, unemployment, urbanization, excessive energy consumption, rising expectations and rebellion against nonmeaningful work, egalitariansim, and the anticipated consequences of technological applications further widening the gap between the have and have-not regions of the world.

The 21st century leader will be acutely aware of these trade-off equations. Resolution can directly or indirectly impact most enterprises through the changes in life expectancy, geriatric costs, further technical breakthroughs, incentive-motivation changes, work-leisure patterns, health care and other economic and social issues. Sophistication on the part of the leader will be needed in exercising his powers of human choice given this array of today's decisions to make about the future.

3.2. New Leadership Issues

The 21st century leader will be confronted with a large variety of issues as he is today. These sprout from the leading edge of scientific, technological, political, economic, social and cultural forces already at work. The issues seem to fall into five general categories.

(1) *Intellectual operations* involving the acquisition, development and retention of new ideas and concepts including:

(a) The formation of ideas—situations of creativity, invention, discovery, insight, intuition and experience.

(b) Communication of ideas. We often deal in communications with the ambiguous, the unexplained, the unexpected, the unknown, the random event and the entrepreneurial dimension.

(c) Innovation. This embraces societal, personal or market acceptance of new developments which may threaten, enhance or be neutral to the recipient. Institutional rejection of new implants of intellectual variety is as common as in biological transplants.

(2) *Phenomenon of power.* This means the ideas derived from the exercise of volition on the part of power holders. It involves issues of choice, intersocial and group relationships, and decision making:

(a) Power use concerns individuals' trade-off strategies, tactics, authority, risk, change, growth, development, antagonism, discord, conflict, crisis, dilemma, instability, disorganization and behavior. Examples of these problems abound: Arthur D. Little's proprietary studies of government loans to farmers in the Philippines to motivate individuals to develop the agricultural sector, or the personal-social issues involved in the mass distribution strategy and techniques created for introducing contraceptives in India. Determination of private enterprise conflict factors in New Zealand rested on many of the power issues cited above.

(b) Intersocial and group relations. These embrace, along with other things, the classical conflicts of social order. This concerns the use of force by the stronger, guile and fraud by the weaker in a competition for the scarce resources and rewards. Relationships relevant here include alienation, tension, risk, interracial problems and opportunities.

(3) *Abstract relationships,* particularly:

(a) The phenomenon of change. This concerns growth, innovation, development, crises, diversification, discontinuity, instability and mutations. Arthur D. Little's recent study of public policy, tax, legal, financial issues affecting technological innovations in the United States is a prime example of this category. Administration attitudes, regulatory trends and legal constraints were found to be in need of change [4].

(b) Causation. These are the phenomena caused by force, power, perturbation, disorder, tension, conflict and creativity. A private diagnostic study of industrial problems and root causes in financial, production and manpower areas of Argentina involved a critical analysis of the industrial sector. Detailed evaluation of problems and analysis of government policies with their effect on industry produced recommendations on changes in tax, tariff and financial policies.

(c) Order and disorder. The problem situations derive from form, structure, instability, confusion, discontinuity, diversity, discord, tradeoffs and conflict. They afford a particular arena of managerial challenge.

(4) *Materials world.* This concerns the inorganic and organic matter of nature, the physical sciences, energy, and the domains of engineering and technology. Technoeconomic forces are key factors in the future.

(5) *Ethical, legal, religious spheres* of sentient and moral powers. This involves work in many cultures and value systems around the world. An example of constructive work in this category was the impact

and linking of cultural change in economic development conducted by Arthur D. Little for the Dominican Republic.

In ancient Greece, a custom prevailed for a time in which a man proposing a law in the popular assembly did so on a platform with a rope around his neck. If his law passed, they removed the rope; if it failed, they removed the platform. In early American Indian tribes, the man who dared represent himself as a rainmaker lived a similar go-no-go existence. If the rainmaker's prognostications failed to come true with at least reasonable accuracy, he was buried alive. The leader today runs a similar risk in maintaining his position and in structuring expectations. It is likely that opinions rather than events would unseat him in times of trouble in the future.

From a pragmatic viewpoint, the keys appear to be personal equilibrium, reasonable goal development, recognition of potential limitations, realism, interest level, self realization and personal fulfillment. What the leading-edge leader needs, however, is some sense of protocol which provides him with a balanced grasp of reasonable knowledge of logical science and humanistic arts. Our conventional education and training programs do not address this need now. Check and balance in making use of logic, emotion and drive is a process little understood by most leaders.

An appreciation of purpose and respect for our place in the scheme of things is the key issue to leading-edge leadership. This will be most challenging. It is a sophisticated component of the mental and emotional baggage the future leader will carry into the 21st century.

4. Leadership and Governance

4.1. Threeness in Governance

Threeness appears in many religious systems as the Holy Trinity of God. The Brahma, Vishnu and Shiva in the Hindu traditions is a triune example. As it seems with all threes, there is an intrinsic movement that shifts the reference point as soon as one tries to pin it down. However, we can at least distinguish a temporal succession. In the trinity of thinker, manager and leader, the thinker tends to be the antecedent to any situation even though often dealing with unreal time. The manager is the successor struggling to administer the present, often without thinking about the future. The leader is the visionary providing immanence to the present and a transcendental drive into the future.

The thinker is usually termed a "professional" in this governance threesome of the future. Most often the manager is the action-oriented producer and the leader is a charismatic visionary providing the expectation and structure. These three components are not necessarily tightly bound together but they exist in a rather relaxed form, often in several persons and in a fuzzy type of relationship.

The asset of ambiguity and the virtue of vagueness surrounding such a future tripartite grouping presents us with the option of three separate roles for governance in the 21st century. One person may aspire to provide all three components. Perhaps more realistically and in the mode of situational management, an individual must select only one (or two) of the three roles since future complexity and dynamics make a triple approach unrealistic in most anticipated circumstances and for most available persons. Like a golfer, the chief executive officer has a bag of clubs. He uses the one most appropriate for the shot he has to make. To be a winner he must:

(a) choose the right club,
(b) be skillful in the use of most of the clubs in the bag,
(c) be better than the others.

Inquiry into the management of such plural human systems requires a transdisciplinary study of principles and methods. Such principles should seek to enhance both the analytical and intuitive faculties of management practitioners. An abstract construct can be helpful to the future practitioner for advancing from simple, well-structured, statistical and deterministic concepts towards the more complex, fuzzy, dynamic and stochastic problems of managing. This process is of course reversible and could go from the complex to the well-structured, simpler state if a leader is capable of reifying the situation.

It has been proposed by Professor Milan Zeleny that the optimal working framework of the human mind changes from the logical, rational, sequential and quantitative (LRSQ) framework to the perceptive, intuitive, simultaneous and qualitative (PISQ) mental framework for approaching managerial problems. The concept is useful both in the present and for the future. This issue is as old as the conflict between Aristotle and The Rhetoricians. In full complexity, Professor Zeleny's framework calls for an inseparable unity between the LRSQ and PISQ ends of an ever shifting continuum of thought [10].

However, with respect to *leadership,* either in the present and certainly more in the future, a third framework of the human mind and soul, *TISC,* could be suggested. This concerns the teleological-ideological, instinctive, spiritual and charismatic attributes of a leader. These may or may not exist in the managerial or the professional affective framework to the same degree.

There is a surprising lack of experimentation, other than rhetoric and opinion, regarding the importance of this dharmic framework in leadership. For example, in the ancient institution of divine kingship, charisma was often gained by special initiation, regalia of office, sumptuary privileges, ascetic practices or auspicious birth. These were recognized signs of merit and power accumulated in previous lives. The modern version of corporate practice, power flow concepts, perquisites, democratic canons and professional management are often antithetical to these charismatic concepts, even though some institutions attempt to recapture their symbolism.

Another ancient notion, the group-soul concept, has always been a part of the tradition of primitive people. It has been demonstrated in the animal kingdom by Marais that the same species have the same instincts (Marais, 1939). The group-soul concept however has been studied and found inadequate for man because of his peculiar individuality in the evolutionary sense. More of such experimentation is needed in the TISC framework of man.

Traits of charisma, instinct, intuition, inspiration, ideology, emotion and will are elusive but key components of mind and soul. They are seminal to our leading-edge leadership postulate and we hypothesize will be the cachet of the 21st century leader. This will not be a new set of attributes. While these traits are vital to leadership today, they will be needed to an even greater extent in the future.

Oliver Wendell Holmes, Jr., once said, "There are one story intellects, two story intellects, three story intellects with skylights. All fact collectors who have no aim behind their facts are one story men; two story men compare, reason, generalize, using the labors of the fact collectors as well as their own. Three story men idealize, imagine, predict. Their best illumination comes from above through the skylight." Leading-edge-leaders will be Holmesian third story persons aided and abetted in their work by one story colleagues and their management subsystems.

Robert A. Smith, III, Organizational Behavior Analyst, NASA ret., has suggested how this holistic integration can take place in his "trichotomy of complex organizations" setting forth three components, institutional, functional and programmatic in overlapping fields [9]. These are interconnected and revitalized constantly. The programmatic component corresponds to Zeleny's LRSQ component. The functional component representing multiple systems, heterostasis and skills in the professional sense is represented by the PISQ collect of mental processes.

The institutional open system rests on normative principles. According to Smith, it embraces such processes as decision, judication, membership, turnover of elite, program selections, sanctions, awards and objectives. However, it does not capture the TISC transcendental notion suggested previously in this section. This notion is that inspiration, ideology, vision, purpose and design form a balance with the LRSQ and PISQ factors and that certain ends are preordained in nature. Those who deal with leading-edge forces must grasp these notions in a triad of mental frameworks. This is a key to shaping activities towards a worthy purpose, ideological in content, and perhaps religio-philosophical in nature.

Very few persons possess all three sets of attributes as inherited mental equipment. By my definition, the leading-edge-leader will certainly have the TISC component. He may join forces with those who have special logic or intuitive talents for coping with the complex area of conflicts which face institutions in the future. The power struggle deals with survival and immortality of the institution which is being led which endeavors to perpetuate itself through normative principles or canons. These principles can include a pluralistic overview, social transformation, transcendental vision or a capability for continuous self-renewal.

Future leadership will need to include the ability of enhancing an institution or society's capability for such self-renewal on a continuous basis. Thus, the effort becomes a political creation with the orientation in the corporate sense being toward a socio-technological-economic system of purposeful work. In this, the purpose is the long-range outcome and orientation versus focusing on short-term outputs to the system.

The function of managing human systems, then, is the management of conflict by avoidance, dissolution, removal or resolution usually between short-term and long-term needs while at the same time pursuing a process of continuous self-renewal.

4.2. The Challenge

Requirements for effective leadership of corporations are changing rapidly. The complexities surrounding our institutions introduce more legal, strategic, economic, social and political interrelationships than in the past.

New patterns of government and business relations are developing as interactivity and interdependence increase internally.

Value systems of societies and individuals are changing. These are intensified social pressures and confrontations with challenges that most present-day managers have not been trained to meet. The challenge is to deal with the questions in a manner that serves society without compromising the legitimate corporate objectives. This is fast becoming a major requirement for effective leadership and management. Leaders in the future will have to be multi-talented and well-trained. Ability to manage with flexible, plural type hierarchical structures will require new, creative organizational development thinking and planning.

There is also a focus toward egalitarianism in compensation as well as opportunity. All of these forces will call for a new generation of managerial elite to lead our enterprises.

The expectation that our corporations, because they have proven effective in the economic sphere, can bear the responsibility or even be effective instruments for accomplishing new, broader social goals, demands a new set of leadership attributes which have to be developed.

Executives and managers, as persons in positions of leadership and power, must take up part of the responsibility to articulate and move toward social goals. This should be a strategic decision and a positive one. Business corporations cannot be made to adequately approach this challenge in an atmosphere of social guilt and adversary proceedings.

Given this complex situation in which to govern, leadership talent will become an even more valued attribute in the executive suite. A new breed of leaders conscious of the changing forces, conflicts, values and uncertainties will emerge from the ranks well-trained in schools of education and experience. The concept of a triple framework (LRSQ, PISQ, TISC) for conceptual thinking about management and leadership described previously may be a helpful trait to seek in a new managerial elite. Without some special talents, understandings, an enlightened style and philosophy about governance, it will be difficult to initiate and maintain structure in expectation and interaction. Such is the challenge for the leading-edge-leader of the future.

References

1. F. E. Fiedler, A contingency model of leadership effectiveness, in: L. Berkowitz, Ed., Advances in Experimental Social Psychology (Academic Press, New York, 1964).
2. F. E. Fiedler, Personality and situational determinants of leader behavior, Technical Report, Department of Psychology, University of Washington, Seattle (1971).
3. Willis W. Harman, The coming transformation in our view of knowledge, The Futurist (June 1974) 126–128.
4. Arthur D. Little, Inc. and Industrial Research Institute, Inc., Barriers to innovation in industry: Opportunities for public policy changes, prepared for the National Science Foundation (Contracts NSF-C725) (September 1973).
5. Eugene Marais, The Soul of the White Ant, translated by Winifred Dekok (Methuen and Company, London, 1939).
6. Robert Kirk Mueller, Metadevelopment: Beyond the Bottom Line (Lexington Books, Lexington, MA, 1977) Ch. 9.
7. Robert Kirk Mueller, The Innovation Ethic (AMACOM, New York, 1971).
8. R. K. Mueller, The managementality gap in IEEE Transactions on Systems and Cybernetics, IEEE Trans. Systems, Man Cybernet. 3(1) (1979). Published

also in: Robert Kirk Mueller, Ed., Risk, Survival and Power (AMACOM, New York, 1970) Ch. 4.

9. Robert A. Smith, III, National goals, planning and human potential, HSM Human Systems Management 9 (1979) 17–20.

10. Milan Zeleny, Managers without management science?, Interfaces 5(4) (1975) 41.

16

Where Have All the Leaders Gone?

WARREN G. BENNIS

Where have all the leaders gone? They are, as a paraphrase of that haunting song reminds us, "long time passing."

All the leaders whom the young respect are dead. F.D.R., who could challenge a nation to rise above fear, is gone. Churchill, who could demand and get blood, sweat, and tears, is gone. Eisenhower, the most beloved leader since Washington, is gone. Schweitzer, who from the jungles of Lambarene could inspire mankind with a reverence for life, is gone. Einstein, who could give us that sense of unity in infinity, is gone. Gandhi, the Kennedys, Martin Luther King, all lie slain, as if to prove the mortal risk in telling us that we can be greater, better than we are.

The landscape is littered with fallen leaders. A President re-elected with the greatest plurality in history resigns in disgrace. The Vice President he twice chose as qualified to succeed him is driven from office as a common crook. Since 1973 the governments of all nine Common Market countries have changed hands—at least once. In the last year over a dozen major governments have fallen. Shaky coalitions exist in Finland, Portugal, Argentina, Belgium, Holland, and Israel. Minority governments rule precariously in Britain, Denmark, and Sweden. In Ethiopia, the King of Kings died captive in his palace.

The leaders who remain, the successors and the survivors—the struggling corporate chieftains, the university presidents, the city managers and mayors, the state governors—all are now seen as an "endangered species," because of the whirl of events and circumstances beyond rational control.

Reprinted with permission from *Technology Review,* 75:9 (March–April 1977), pp. 3–12. Copyright © 1977.

There is a high turnover, an appalling mortality—whether occupational or actuarial—among leaders. In recent years the typical college president has lasted about four years; in the decade of the 1950s, the average tenure was over eleven years. Men capable of leading institutions often refuse to accept such pressures, such risks. We see what James Reston of the *New York Times* calls "burnt out cases," the debris of leaders. We see Peter Principle leaders rising to their final levels of incompetence. It has been said that if a Martian were to demand, "Take me to your leader," Earthlings would not know where to take him. Administrative sclerosis around the world, in political office, in all administrative offices breeds suspicion and distrust. A bumper sticker in Massachusetts summed it up: "Impeach Someone!"

In business the landscape is equally flat. The great leaders that come to mind—Ford, Edison, Rockefeller, Morgan, Schwab, Sloan, Kettering—are long gone. Nixon's business chums were either entrepreneurs "outside" the business Establishment, like Aplanalp the Aerosol King, or they had no widespread acceptance as business leaders or spokesmen. President Ford seemed to get on best with the Washington vice presidents of major corporations (a vice president syndrome as it were). *Fortune* magazine reveals the absence of business leaders in New York University's Hall of Fame. Of the ninety-nine individuals selected, only ten are business leaders.

The peril of the present situation is not exaggerated. Dr. John Platt, a scientist at the University of Michigan, recently stated what he considers to be the ten basic dangers to world survival. Of greatest significance was the possibility of some kind of nuclear war or accident which would destroy the entire human race. The second greatest danger is the possibility of a worldwide epidemic, famine or depression. He sees as the world's third greatest danger a general failure in *the quality of the management and leadership of our institutions.*

Where have all the leaders gone? Why have they become "endangered species?"

Falling Out of Control

Something's happened, that's clear; something that bewilders. As I write this, for example, it can be noted that our technology brings together, at 600 m.p.h. speeds, people who left Los Angeles, San Francisco, Denver, Chicago, Atlanta, at lunch, only to have them all blown to smithereens by a bomb left in a baggage locker at an airport.

It's as if mankind, to paraphrase Teilhard de Chardin, is *falling suddenly out of control of its own destiny.* Perhaps only a new Homer or Herodotus would be able, later on, to show us its patterns and designs, its coherences and contours. We still lack that historical view. What we hear and discern now is not one voice or signal but a confusing jim-jangle of cords. All we know for sure is that we cannot wait a generation for the historian to tell us what happened; we must try to make sense out of the jumble of voices now. Indeed, the first test for any leader today is to discover just *what* he or she does confront; only then will it be possible to devise the best ways of making that reality—the multiple realities—potentially manageable.

The most serious threat to our institutions and the cause of our diminishing sense of able leadership is the steady erosion of institutional autonomy. Time was when the leader could decide—period. A Henry Ford, an Andrew Carnegie, a Nicholas Murray Butler could issue a ukase—and all would automatically obey. Their successors' hands are now tied in innumerable ways—by governmental requirements, by various agencies, by union rules, by the moral and sometimes legal pressures of organized consumers and environmentalists. For example, before David Mathews became Secretary of Health, Education, and Welfare, and speaking as President of the University of Alabama, he characterized federal regulations as threatening to

> ... bind the body of higher education in a Lilliputian nightmare of forms and formulas. The constraints emanate from various accrediting agencies, Federal bureaucracies, and state boards, but their effects are the same ... a loss of institutional autonomy, and a serious threat to diversity, creativity, and reform. Most seriously, that injection of more regulations may even work against the accountability it seeks to foster, because it so dangerously diffuses responsibility.

The external forces that impinge and impose upon the perimeter of our institutions—the incessant concatenation of often contrary require-ments—are the basic reasons for the loss of their self-determination. Fifty years ago this external environment was fairly placid, like an ocean on a calm day, forecastable, predictable, regular, not terribly eventful. Now that ocean is turbulent and highly inter-dependent—and makes tidal waves. In my own institution right now the key people for me to reckon with are not only the students, the faculty, and my own management group, but people external to the university—the city manager, city council members, the state legislature, accrediting and professional associations, the federal government, alumni, and parents. There is an incessant, dissonant clamor out there. And because the university is a brilliant example of an institution that has blunted and diffused its main purposes through a proliferation of dependence on "external patronage structures," its autonomy has declined to the point where our boundary system is like Swiss cheese. Because of these pressures, every leader must create a department of "external affairs," a secretary of state, as it were, to deal with external constituencies.

Accompanying all this is a new kind of populism, not the barn burners of the Grange days, not the "free silver" of Bryanism ("The crown of thorns"), but the fragmentation, the caucusization of constituencies. My own campus is typical; we have over 500 organized governance and pressure groups. We have a coalition of women's groups, a gay society, black organizations for both students and faculty, a veterans' group, a continuing education group for women, a handicapped group, a faculty council on Jewish affairs, a faculty union organized by the American Association of University Professors, an organization for those staff members who are neither faculty nor administrators, an organization of middle-management staff members, an association of women administrators, a small, elite group of graduate fellows.

This fragmentation, which exists more or less in all organizations, marks the end not only of community, a sense of shared values and symbols, but of consensus, an agreement reached despite differences. It was Lyndon Johnson's tragedy to plead, "Come let us reason together," at a time when all these groups scarcely wanted to *be* together, much less reason together.

These pressure groups are fragmented. They go their separate and often conflicting ways. They say: "No, we don't want to be part of the mainstream of America—we just want to be us," whether they're blacks, Chicanos, women, the third sex, or Menominee Indians seizing an empty Catholic monastery. They tell us that the old dream of "the melting pot," of assimilation does not work—or never was. They have never been "*beyond* the melting pot" (as Glazer and Moynihan wrote about it); they have been *behind* it.

So what we have now is a new form of politics—King Caucus, who has more heads than Cerberus, and contending Queens who cry, "Off with their heads!" as they play croquet with flamingos. It is *the politics of multiple advocacies*—vocal, demanding, often "out of sync" with each other. They represent people who are fed up with being ignored, neglected, excluded, denied, subordinated. No longer do they march on cities, on bureaus, or on organizations they view as sexist, racist, anti-Semitic, or whatever. Now, they file suit. The law has suddenly emerged as the court of first resort.

A Litigious Society: "Is the Wool Worth the Cry?"

And so, we have become a litigious society where individuals and groups—in spectacularly increasing numbers—bring suits to resolve issues which previously might have been settled privately. A hockey player, injured in his sport, bypasses the institutional procedures to bring formal suit. The club owners are outraged that one of "its own" would take the case "outside." College students, unhappy with what they are learning on campus, are turning to the courts as well. A lawsuit against the University of Bridgeport may produce the first clear legal precedent. It was filed last spring by a woman seeking $150 in tuition, the cost of her books, and legal fees because a course required of secondary education majors was "worthless" and she "didn't learn anything." A law review has been sued for rejecting an article. In New Jersey, a federal judge has ordered twenty-eight state Senators to stand trial for violating the constitutional rights of the twenty-ninth member, a woman, by excluding her from their party caucus. They did so because, they claimed, she was "leaking" their deliberations to the press. In a Columbus, Ohio, test case, the U.S. Supreme Court recently ruled that secondary-school students may not be suspended, disciplinarily, without formal charges and a hearing, that the loss of a single day's education is a deprivation of property. A federal court in Washington has just awarded $10,000 to each of the thousands of May, 1970, anti-war demonstrators whom it found had been illegally arrested and confined at the behest of Attorney General Mitchell.

Aside from the merits of any particular case, the overriding fact is clear that the hands of all administrators are increasingly tied by real or potential legal issues. I find I must consult our lawyers over even small, trivial decisions. The university has so many suits against it (40 at last count) that my mother calls me, "My son, the defendant."

The courts and the law are, of course, necessary to protect individual rights and to provide recourse for negligence, breach of contract, and fraud. But a "litigious society" presents consequences that nobody bargained for, not the least the rising, visible expense of legal preparation plus the invisible costs of wasted time.

Far more serious than expense, however, is the confusion, ambiguity, and lack of subtlety of the law and what that does to institutional autonomy and leadership. To take the example of consumer protection, we see that lawsuits are forcing universities to insert a railroad-timetable disclaimer in their catalogues—e.g., "Courses in this catalogue are subject to change without notice"—in order to head off possible lawsuits. At the same time, the Federal Trade Commission is putting pressure on doctors, architects, lawyers, and other professionals to revise their codes of ethics forbidding advertising. The Buckley amendment, which permits any student to examine his own file, tends to exclude from the file any qualitative judgments which would provide even the flimsiest basis for a suit.

The confusion, ambiguity, and complexity of the law—augmented by conflicting court interpretations—tend toward institutional paralysis. Equally forbidding is the fact that the courts are substituting their judgments for the expertise of the institution. Justice may prevail but at a price to institutional leadership so expensive, as we shall see, that one has to ask if the "wool is worth the cry."

One for the Seesaw

The incessant external forces and the teeming internal constituencies, each with their own diverse and often contrary expectations, demands, and pressure, are difficult enough for any leader to understand, let alone control: at their best, leaders serve as quiet and efficient custodians.

The problem is made infinitely more complex when the goals and values of the internal and external forces seem not merely divergent, but irreconcilable. Their collision, or "boundary clash," tends to isolate or crush the "man at the top."

The College of Medicine of a large urban, but state affiliated, university accepts 187 applicants out of 8,000. Immediately some 23,000 people are angered, the rejected applicants and their parents. Although admissions decisions are the prerogative of the faculty, the president of the university finds himself deluged by phone calls and letters from parents, alumni, friends of the regents, and legislators. He feels, however, that "The president shouldn't butt in. . . ." Meanwhile, the issue grows more political. Disgruntled persons write their legislators. The legislators demand an informal commitment that the College of Medicine accept only state residents. Next they propose a bill that only state residents receive support. The president is forced to become involved. He talks to the governor, the legislators, and the media, and he amasses political support to oppose the state-only bill. Eventually, the bill is dropped.

The legislators provide a large share of the revenues of the university (which happens to be the University of Cincinnati—but it could be legion), and their support has a direct relation to how their constituents react to our internal decisions. Patronage structures blanket the social geography of our environment, as they do that of other institutions. Whether these structures consist of taxpayers or consumers, they are demanding, often fickle, and always want their way. In any case, their generosity or miserliness reflects the degree of respect which they feel for the institution, and whether they like what we're doing for them or their relatives. It's as simple as that.

Let me cite a classic confrontation between these internal and external constituencies, mirroring a divergence in their goals and values. It concerns the policy of "open admission" which has created bewilderment and confusion on many campuses. Open admission makes it difficult to understand what we're about, what our "basic" mission is. It makes it almost impossible to define with any precision the educational stands that we must take from time to time. It's hard to determine just what students need or want and what our responsibility to them should be. As one Appalachian student told his humanities professor: "Sure, I'll be glad to read Dante with you, as soon as everybody in my family has a pair of shoes."

The public's uneasiness is often verbalized through code words or phrases (at least according to my mail and the letters-to-the-editor columns) like "lowering of academic standards" or "cheapening the degree." These concerns often (but not always) reflect the public's foreboding about mass education and its concomitant, "equal opportunity" for minorities and women in higher education. While "Affirmative Action" is the mandated vehicle for implementing equal education and work opportunities, in practice it has proved to be more a case study of how difficult it is to force profound changes in an institution as complex, prestigious, slow-moving—and sensitive to economic forces—as a university.

Whatever the reality of Affirmative Action, some citizens are uneasy about this development and use the rhetoric of "lowering standards" or "quotas" to question sharply its validity. And to make matters more complicated, another, increasingly vocal, group feels dissatisfied at the seeming lack of progress. Each of these viewpoints is held by our various publics, and this in turn leads to a situation where "both sides" are dissatisfied with our progress—some because we are doing too little, others because we are trying too much. In either case, we are in the middle and neither side is happy with the university. Or its president.

The university is, in a sense, an anvil on which a fragmented society hammers.

Yes, provide a broad, liberal arts, humanistic education.

No, teach people practical things, so as to guarantee them jobs.

Yes, focus on research and education for the elite.

No, train dental technicians, hotel managers, accountants, but also provide professional education for lawyers, doctors, and engineers.

Yes, stop lowering academic standards, but be sure and enroll more minorities and the poor as a way of creating a more egalitarian society.

And also, while you're at it, provide compensatory education for those victimized by inadequate public schooling, provide opportunities for part-time students, especially for women caught in the homemaker's trap, provide continuing education as job enrichment for workers and executives, and, by the way, become the vehicle through which income redistribution can be achieved.

Obviously, we do not possess the resources to achieve all of these aims. We couldn't, even if we wanted to. By providing a complete menu for every taste we would inevitably and quickly alienate one or another public who would feel disaffected or threatened by one or another of our academic programs and would, actively or passively, turn off its support.

All of our institutions, both public *and* private, confront similar conflict between internal and external environments. In Cincinnati, Procter and Gamble and Federated Department Stores, two of our nation's most successful and well-managed enterprises, must now consider (indeed, are on occasion forced by law to consider) *both* external and internal conflicts, whether nitrates or price-labeling.

The root problem contains profound and grave consequences. It isn't only a matter of a loss of *consensus* over basic values; it is a *polarization* of these values. The university problem is basically a reflection of society's problems, a fact so obvious that we tend to forget it. Education and society are indivisible and cannot be detached from each other. Similarly, Business, with a large "B," is the concentrated epitome of our culture—and is inseparable from it. Coolidge was right that America's business *is* business, and Engine Charlie Wilson was not far wrong with his memorable "what's good for General Motors" remark: business thrives or sickens along with our nation's destiny. All of our institutional fates are correlated with our nation's.

What seems to have happened is this: the environmental encroachments and turbulence, the steady beat of litigation, the fragmentation of constituencies along with their new found eloquence and power, multiple advocacy, win-lose adversarial conflicts between internal and external forces—all of this—has led to a situation where our leaders are "keeping their heads below the grass," as L.B.J. once put it, or paralyzed, or resembling nothing so much as acrobatic clowns. Whatever metaphor one prefers, to grow and stay healthy an institution must strike a proper balance between openness to the environment and protection from too much permeability. Achieving the proper trading relationship without being colonialized is the delicate balance leaders must achieve.

Having to look both ways—in and out, back and forth—was the special gift of Janus, and is required for all leaders today. The "Janus Phenomenon" is a relatively new example of organizational turbulence and leadership optics. Today's leader is surrounded by constituent groups, from inside and outside, as well as by numerous individuals who at any moment, discovering some supposed mutual interest, may suddenly coalesce into some new constituency. In either case, people need slight stimulus to become vocal, organized advocates and activists.

The Cat's Cradle

We know what overstimulation by external forces does to an individual; a total reliance on external cues, stimuli, rewards, and punishments leads to an inability to control one's own destiny. People in this state tend to avoid any behavior for which there is no external cue. Without signals, they vegetate. With contrary signals, they either become catatonic—literally too paralyzed to choose, let alone *act* on a choice, for fear of risk—or, conversely, they lunge at anything and everything, finally contorting themselves into enervated pretzels.

When we apply this analysis to organizations and their leadership, we can observe the same effects. While these coercive political and legal regulations are more pronounced in the public sector than in the private sector, in the latter area the market mechanism has heretofore been the linking pin between the firm and environment, the source of feedback regarding rewards and punishments, and the reflection of the success or failure of decisions. Whether the organization is private or public, whether the controls are legitimate or not, there is only one natural conclusion: an excess of (even well-intended) controls will lead inexorably to lobotomized institutions.

What neither lawmakers nor politicians seem to realize is that law and regulation deal primarily with sins of commission. Sins of omission are more difficult to deal with, partly, as Kenneth Boulding points out, because it is just damned hard in practice to distinguish between honest mistakes and deliberate evil. Which is another way of saying that legitimate risk-taking can land you in jail. On the other hand, by "playing it safe," by living up to the inverted proverb, "Don't just do something, sit there," an institution, a leader, a person can avoid error, and if continued long enough, they can *almost* avoid living.

As the legal and political systems become increasingly concerned with sins of commission—a fact exemplified in the dramatic switch from *caveat emptor* to *caveat vendor,* in the deluge of consumer protection legislation, in malpractice suits, in the environmental protection movement, in the court decisions awarding damages to purchasers of faulty products—we can get to a point where no producer, no organization will do anything at all, like the California surgeons who quit operating on any but emergency patients. Why should they? The costs of uncertainty and honest mistakes are now unbearable and far too costly.

At my own and many other universities, for example, we are now in the process of rewriting our catalogues so carefully that it will be virtually impossible for any student (read: consumer) to claim that we haven't fulfilled our end of the bargain. At the same time, because we have to be so careful, we can never express our hopes, our dreams, and our bold ideas of what a university experience could provide for the prospective student. I suspect that in ten years or so, college catalogues, rarely a publication which faculty, students, or administrators are wild about in any case, will devolve into statements that resemble nothing more than the finely printed cautions and disclaimers on the back of airline tickets—just the opposite of what education is all about: an adventurous and exciting odyssey of the mind.

All this—all of the litigation, legislation, and *caveat vendor*—not only diminish the potency of our institutions, but lead to something more pernicious and possibly irrecoverable. We seek comfort in the delusion that all of our troubles, our failures, our losses, our insecurities, our "hangups," our missed opportunities, our incompetence can be located "somewhere else," can be blamed on "someone else," can be settled in the seamless, suffocating, and invisible "system." How convenient, dear Brutus.

Just think: at a certain point, following our current practices and national mood, any sense of individual responsibility will rapidly erode. And along with that, the volume of low-level "belly-aching" and vacuous preaching about "the system" will grow more strident. The result: those leaders who are around either will be too weak or will shy away from the inevitable risks involved in doing anything good, bad, or indifferent.

I am *not* arguing the case against regulations and controls. I am painfully conscious that some of them are necessary if we are to realize our nation's values (e.g., equality of opportunity for all); without them, I fear, our basic heritage would have long ago been indelibly corrupted. (And it is not hard to understand why campaign finances have come under control recently. How do we deal with Gulf's $12 million bribes, including one to L.B.J. in 1962 when he was Vice President?) I am also aware that many of our institutions have, through inactive, corrupt, and inhumane actions, brought on themselves regulations which today they claim are unnecessary.

All the same, when it comes to protecting people from their exploiters we have an extra responsibility to be so vigilant, so careful that we don't end up in a situation where *everyone* is enmeshed by a cat's cradle of regulations erratically tangled together with the filaments of "good intentions."

As Justice Brandeis put it many years ago:

> Experience should teach us to be most on guard to protect liberty when the governments' purposes are beneficient. Men born to freedom are naturally alert to repel invasion of their liberty by evil-minded rulers. The greatest dangers to liberty lurk in insidious encroachments by men of zeal, well-meaning, but without understanding.

Variations on a Theme

Memorandum to the People of Ohio's 13th Congressional District:
Summary: Being the Congressman is rigorous servitude, ceaseless
enslavement to a peculiar mix of everyone else's needs, demands and
whims, plus one's own sense of duty, ambition or vanity. It is that from
which Mrs. Mosher and I now declare our personal independence, to
seek our freedom, as of January 3, 1977.

It is a Congressman's inescapable lot, his or her enslavement, to be
never alone, never free from incessant buffeting by people, events,
problems, decisions. . . . It is a grueling experience, often frustrating,
discouraging, sometimes very disillusioning. . . . House debates, caucuses,
briefings, working breakfasts, working lunches, receptions, dinners, home-
work study, and even midnight collect calls from drunks. . . . you name
it!

I am for opting out. I shall not be a candidate for reelection in 1976.

Charles A. Mosher,
Representative
13th Congressional District
State of Ohio
December 19, 1975

The basic problem is that leaders are facing a set of conditions that seemed to take shape suddenly, like an unscheduled express train looming out of the night. Whoever would have forecast the post-Depression development in the public sector of those areas of welfare, social service, health, and education? Who, save for a Lord Keynes, could have predicted the scale and range of the multi-national corporations? Prophetically he wrote: "Progress lies in the growth and the recognition of semi-auton-omous bodies within the states. Large business corporations when they have reached a certain age and size, approximate the status of public corporations rather than that of the individualistic private enterprise."

The Keynesian prophecy is upon us. When David Rockefeller goes to London, he is greeted as if he were a chief of state (and some of his empires *are* bigger than many states). But in addition to the growth of semi-autonomous, often global, corporations which rival governments, we also have public-sector institutions which Keynes could scarcely have imagined. The largest employment sector of our society, and the one growing at the fastest rate, is local and state government. Higher education, which less than twenty years ago was 50 percent private–50 percent public, is now about 85 percent public and is expected to be 90 percent public by 1980. And, where a century ago 90 percent of all Americans were self-employed, today 90 percent work in what can be called bureaucracies, members of some kind of corporate family. They might be called "juristic" persons who work within the sovereignty of a legal entity called a corporation or agency. Juristic persons, not masters of their own actions, cannot place the same faith in themselves that self-employed persons did.

These are the problems of leadership today. We have the important emergence of a Roosevelt-Keynes revolution, the new politics of multiple advocacy, new dependencies, new constituencies, new regulatory controls, new values. And how do our endangered species, the leaders, cope with these new complications and entanglements? For the most part, they do not; that is, they are neither coping nor leading. One reason, I fear, is that many of us misconceive what leadership is about. Leading does not mean managing; the difference between the two is crucial. I know many institutions that are very well *managed* and very poorly *led*. They may excel in the ability to handle the daily routine, and yet they may never ask whether the routine should be done at all. To lead, the dictionary informs us, is to go in advance of, to show the way, to influence or induce, to guide in direction, course, action, opinion. To manage means to bring about, to accomplish, to have charge of or responsibility for, to conduct. The difference may be summarized as activities of vision and judgment versus activities of efficiency.

In his decisionmaking, the leader today is a multidirectional broker who must deal with four estates—his own management team, constituencies within his organization, forces outside his organization, and the media. While his decisions and actions affect the people of these four estates, their decisions and actions, too, affect him. The fact is that the concept of "movers and shakers"—a leadership elite that determines the major decisions—is an outdated notion. Leaders are as much the "shook" as the shakers. Whether the four estates force too great a quantity of problems on the leader or whether the leader takes on too much in an attempt to prove himself, the result is what I call "Bennis' First Law of Pseudodynamics," which is that routine work will always drive out the innovational.

When the well-known author, John Hersey, was permitted to sit for a week in the Oval Office and its antechambers, recording all he saw and heard, he counted (in five working days) more than 4,000 visitors— Indian tribal chiefs, bishops and rabbis, woolgrowers and cattlemen, labor leaders and businessmen, students, blacks—flowing through the President's office in an unending stream. Just to handle the millions of pieces of mail pouring in and out of the White House took some 250 employees. The daily "news summary" occupied six full-time staffers. To collect and screen the names of possible candidates for the 4,000 positions the President controls, there was a staff of 30. The speech-writing team, which turned out 746,000 words during Ford's first 10 months in office, numbered 13, and Ron Nessen's news staff included eight deputies plus 38 other assistants apparently needed to handle the 1,500 news correspondents covering the White House.

During Lincoln's presidency there was a total of 50 on the White House staff—and that included telegraph operators and secretaries. Roosevelt inherited three secretaries from Hoover; now there are over 3,000. During the Eisenhower and Kennedy years, the staff of the Office of the President increased 13 percent under each. L.B.J. increased his another 13 percent, and Nixon increased his by 25 percent in his first term. Unhappily, the White House overload can be duplicated over the entire corporate and public bureaucratic landscapes. Little wonder there are burnt-out cases or that Congressman Mosher should declare his independence from "rigorous servitude, ceaseless enslavement."

Leading Through Limits

We are now experiencing a transition period that may aptly be called an "era of limits." After the Club of Rome warned us of *The Limits of Growth,* the Arab petroleum boycott, soaring fuel costs, and the continuing energy crisis have confirmed the brutal fact that our national goals have outrun our present means. Some political and institutional leaders exploit this mood by turning the public's disenchantment with growth into a political asset. They want to follow the popular mood, rather than lead it.

The National Observer calls California's young Governor Edmund G. Brown "the hottest politician in America," and quotes him thus: "Growth in California has slowed down . . . the feeling is strongly antigrowth. Once people seemed to think there were no limits to the growth of California. Now Californians are moving to Oregon and Colorado. . . . There are limits to everything—limits to this planet, limits to government mechanisms, limits to any philosophy or idea. And that's a concept we have to get used to. Someone called it the Europeanization of America. That's part right. You take an empty piece of land and you fill it up with houses and soon the land is more scarce and the air is more polluted and things are more complicated. That's where we are today. . . ." *The National Observer* says his rhetoric works: "Over 90 percent of the people in California applaud his performance." (November 29, 1975, pp. 1, 16)

Compared with the grandiose rhetoric of a quarter-century about the apostolic conviction that size and scale plus technological "know-how" could solve all society's basic problems, the management of decline, as presented by Governor Brown, sounds at least respectably sane, and especially so when compared with a pronunciamento by one of the leaders of the European Economic Community, Dr. Sicco Mansholt: "More, further, quicker, richer are the watchwords of present day society. We must adapt to this for there is no alternative." *That* kind of rhetoric, especially when at brutal odds with present reality, denies the very nature of the human condition.

Thus, growing in popularity, and becoming more sophisticated in its approach, is a new movement. I call it "cameo leadership," which aspires to carve things well, but smaller. It preaches a "homecoming," a less complicated time, a communal life, a radical decentralization of organizational life, a return to Walden before the Pond was polluted, before the Coke stand made its appearance, before *Walden* itself was required reading . . . when things were compassable.

A chief spokesman for this counter-technology movement is E. F. Schumacher, a former top economist and planner for England's National Coal Board. In his book, *Small is Beautiful,* he writes: "We are poor, not demi-gods. . . . We have plenty to be sorrowful about, and are not emerging into a golden age. . . . We need a gentle approach, a non-violent spirit, and small is beautiful. . . ."

Governor Brown of California is an avid disciple of Dr. Schumacher's "Buddhist economics." Small *is* beautiful. Sometimes. Perhaps it is beautiful more often than big is beautiful. When big gets ugly, we see human waste, depersonalization, alienation, possibly disruption. When small gets ugly, which never crosses Schumacher's mind, it leads to a decentralization bordering on anarchy; also to poverty, famine, and disease.

Small is beautiful. The era of limits is upon us. Who can argue? Nevertheless, these are slogans as empty as they are both appealing and timely. Because they are appealing we fail to see that they represent no specific programs for change. In fact, rather than opening up the possibilities for solutions, they close them with brevity and an exclamation mark. Basically, they reflect the symptoms now afflicting us by setting rhetorical opposites against each other. Small is beautiful, so big must be ugly. A grain of sand may be more beautiful than a pane of glass. But must we trade the glass for sand (as well as the life expectancy of those protected by glass for that of a Bedouin out admiring that ultimate decentralization, the desert)?

The real point is not one of beauty. The real point is whether leaders can face up to and cope with our present crises, worries, and imperatives. The real problem is how we can lead institutions in a world of over three billion people, millions of whom will starve while other millions can't find work; and for many who do find work it's either boring or underpaid. Many whose work is exciting and provides meaning live with quiet desperation in armed fortresses in fear of "the others." The real question is: How do we provide the needed jobs, and, after that, how do we learn to lead so that people can work more cooperatively, more sensibly, more humanely with one another? How can we lead in such a way that the requisite interdependence—so crucial for human survival and economic resilience—can be realized in a humane and gentle spirit?

Coda

Where have all the leaders gone? They're consulting, pleading, trotting, temporizing, putting out fires, either avoiding—or, more often—taking too much heat, and spending too much energy in doing both. They are peering at a landscape of "bottom lines," ostentatiously taking the bus to work (with four bodyguards, rather than the one chauffeur they might need if they drove) to demonstrate their commitment to energy conservation. They are money changers lost in a narrow orbit. They resign. They burn out. They decide not to run or serve. They read Buddhist economics, listen to prophets of decentralization and then proceed to create new bureaucracies to stamp out old ones. (Nixon's "Anti-Big Government" one was bigger than Johnson's.) They are organizational Houdinis, surrounded by sharks or shackled in a water cage and manage to escape, miraculously, while the public marvels at the feat and then longs for something more than "disappearing acts." They are motivating people through fear, or by cautiously following the "trends," or by posing as Reality through adopting a "Let's Face It" cynicism. They are all characters in a dreamless society. Groping in the darkness, learning how to "retrench," as if that were an art like playing the violin. And they are all scared.

And who can blame them? Sweaty palms are understandable, even natural. That is the final irony. Precisely at the time when the trust and credibility of our leaders is at an all-time low and when survivors in leadership feel most inhibited in exercising the potentiality of power, we most need individuals who can lead. We need people who can shape the future, not just barely manage to get through the day.

There is no simple solution. But there are some things we must recognize:

• Leaders must develop the vision and strength to call the shots. There are risks in taking the initiative. The greater risk is to wait for orders. We need leaders at every level who can lead, not just manage.

• This means that institutions (and followers) have to recognize that they *need* leadership, that their need is for vision, energy, and drive, rather than for blandness and safety.

• This means that the leader must be a "conceptualist" (not just someone to tinker with the "nuts and bolts"). A conceptualist is more than an "idea man." He must have an entrepreneurial vision, a sense of perspective, the time and the inclination to think about the forces and raise the fundamental questions that will affect the destiny of both the institution and the society within which it is embedded.

• This means that he must have a sense of continuity and significance in order, to paraphrase the words of Shelley, to see the present in the past and the future in the present. He must, in the compelling moments of the present, be able to clarify problems—elevate them into understandable choices for the constituents—rather than exploit them; to define issues, not aggravate them.

In this respect leaders are essentially educators. Our great political leaders, such as Jefferson, Lincoln, and Wilson tried to educate the people about problems by studying the messy existential groaning of the people and transforming murky problems into understandable issues. A leader who responds to a drought by attacking the lack of rainfall is not likely to inspire a great deal of confidence. What we see today is sometimes worse: leaving the problem as a problem (e.g., "the economy" or "the energy crisis") or allowing the problem to get out of control until it sours and becomes a "crisis." What is essential, instead, are leaders who will get at the underlying issues and present a clear alternative. Dr. Martin Luther King, Jr. provided this perspective for black people. We sorely need the same leadership for the whole nation.

• A leader must get at the truth and learn how to filter the unwieldy flow of information into coherent patterns. He must prevent the distortion of that information by over-eager aides who will tailor it to what they consider to be his prejudices or vanities. The biggest problem of a leader—any leader—is getting the truth. Pierre du Pont said well in a long-ago note to his brother Irenée, "One cannot expect to know what will happen, one can only consider himself fortunate if he can know what *has* happened." The politics of bureaucracy tend to interfere with rather than facilitate truth gathering.

That's mainly true because the huge size of our organizations and the enormous overload burdening every leader make it impossible for him to verify all his own information, analyze all of his own problems, or always decide who should or should not have his ear or time. Since he must rely for much of this upon his key assistants and officers, he would not feel comfortable in so close and vital a relationship with men (women, unfortunately, would not even be considered!) who were not at least of kindred minds and of compatible personalities.

Of course, this is perfectly human, and up to a point understandable. But the consequences can be devastating for it means that the leader is likely to see only that highly selective information, or those carefully screened people that his key assistants decide he should see. And he may discover too late that he acted on information that was inadequate or inaccurate, or that he has been shielded from "troublesome" visitors who wanted to tell him what he should have known, or that he had been protected from some problem that should have been his primary concern.

Given the character of today's institutions with their multiple dependencies and advocacies, picking a team of congenial and compatible associates may be deadly, a replay of Watergate. The most striking thing and most obvious impression I remember from the early Watergate hearings is how much all the Nixon aides looked alike. I had trouble telling Dean from Magruder, Porter from Sloan, Strachan from Haldeman. In appearance, they are almost mirror images of the younger Nixon of the 1940s, as if they were that spiritual or ghostly double called doppelganger. It is easy enough to cry shame on Watergate without perceiving its interconnections with our own lives and organizations and, in lesser degree, our conduct.

For in too many institutions a very few people are filtering the facts, implicitly skewing reality, and selecting information that provides an inaccurate picture on which decisions may be based. Such skewing can affect history: Barbara Tuchman in her recent book on China tells how, in the 1940s, Mao Tse Tung wanted very much to visit Roosevelt, but Roosevelt cancelled the proposed meeting on the basis of incredibly biased information from Ambassador Pat Hurley. It was nearly thirty years later that another President sought out the meeting with Mao, which earlier conceivably could have averted many subsequent disasters.

So the leader cannot rely exclusively on his palace guards for information. Hard as it is to do, he must have multiple information sources and must remain accessible, despite the fact that accessibility in modern times seems one of the most under-rated political virtues. The Romans, who were the greatest politicians of antiquity, and probably also the busiest men, valued that quality highly in their leaders. Cicero, in praising Pompey, commented on his ready availability, not only to his subordinates, but to the ordinary soldiers in his command.

A later Roman historian recounted this even more telling anecdote about the Emperor Hadrian. The emperor, who at that time ruled almost the entire civilized world, was riding into Rome in his chariot when an old woman blocked his path. The woman asked him to hear a grievance. Hadrian brushed her aside, saying that he was too busy. "Then you're too busy to be emperor," she called after him. Whereupon he halted his chariot and heard her out.

A pebble dropped in Watergate has its ripple throughout the complex organizational society, and by the same token it is the excesses, the concealments, the arrogance and half-truths of a thousand faceless doppelgangers, in innumerable large organizations, that make a Watergate, an Attica, a Selma possible.

• The leader must be a social architect who studies and shapes what is called the "culture of work"—those intangibles that are so hard to discern but are so terribly important in governing the way people act, the values and norms that are subtlely transmitted to individuals and groups and that tend to create binding and bonding. In whatever goals and values the leader pursues he must proceed toward their implementation by designing a social architecture which encourages understanding, participation, and ownership of the goals. He must, of course, learn about and be influenced by those who will be affected by the decisions which contain the day-to-day realization of the goals. At the very least, he must be forever conscious that the culture can facilitate or subvert "the best laid plans. . . ."

The culture of an organization dictates the mechanisms by which conflict can be resolved, and how costly, humane, fair, and reasonable the outcomes will be. It can influence whether or not there is a "zero-sum" mentality that insists upon an absolute winner or an absolute loser or whether there is a climate of hope. There can be no progress without hope, and there can be no hope if our organizations view conflict as a football game, a win-lose (or possibly tie) situation. While zero-sum situations are extremely rare, most leaders (and followers) tend to respond to most conflicts as if there has to be only one winner and only one loser. In reality, organizations and nations are involved in a much different kind of contest, resembling not so much football as it does the remarkable Swedish game, Vasa Run, in which many take part, some reach the finish line earlier than others and are rewarded for it, but all get there in the end.

Lots of things go into producing a culture: the particular technology of the institution, its peculiar history and geography, the characteristics of the people, and its social architecture. The leader must understand these things; he must have the capacities of an amateur social anthropologist so that he can understand the culture within which he works and which he himself can have some part in creating and maintaining.

• The task of the leader is to lead. And to lead others he must first of all know himself. His ultimate test is the wise use of power. As

Sophocles says in *Antigone:* "It is hard to learn the mind of any mortal, or the heart, till he be tried in chief authority. Power shows the man." So he must learn, most of all, to listen to himself. He must integrate his ideal with his actions and, even when a crackling discrepancy exists, learn how to tolerate this ambiguity between the desirable and the necessary, but not so much tolerance that the margins between them become undiscernible. When that happens, the leader is unwittingly substituting an authentic ideal for an evasion of convenience. Soon he'll forget about the goal—and even feel "comfortable" with an illusion of progress. He must learn how to listen to understand, not to evaluate. He must learn to play, to live with ambiguity and inconsistency. And, most of all, the test of any leader is whether he can ride and direct the process of change and, by so doing, build new strengths in the process.

17

The Antileadership Vaccine

JOHN W. GARDNER

It is generally believed that we need enlightened and responsible leaders—
at every level and in every phase of our national life. Everyone says
so. But the nature of leadership in our society is very imperfectly
understood, and many of the public statements about it are utter nonsense.

This is unfortunate because there are serious issues of leadership
facing this society, and we had better understand them.

The Dispersion of Power

The most fundamental thing to be said about leadership in the United
States is also the most obvious. We have gone as far as any known
society in creating a leadership system that is *not* based on caste or
class, nor even on wealth. There is not yet equal access to leadership
(witness the remaining barriers facing women and Negroes), but we
have come a long, long way from the family- or class-based leadership
group. Even with its present defects, ours is a relatively open system.

The next important thing to be said is that leadership is dispersed
among a great many groups in our society. The President, of course,
has a unique, and uniquely important, leadership role, but beneath him,
fragmentation is the rule. This idea is directly at odds with the notion
that the society is run by a coherent power group—the Power Elite, as
C. Wright Mills called it, or the Establishment, as later writers have
named it. It is hard not to believe that such a group exists. Foreigners
find it particularly difficult to believe in the reality of the fluid, scattered,

Reprinted from "The Antileadership Vaccine" by John W. Gardner, Carnegie Corporation
of New York annual report essay, 1965.

shifting leadership that is visible to the naked eye. The real leadership, they imagine, must be behind the scenes. But at a national level this simply isn't so.

In many local communities and even in some states there *is* a coherent power group, sometimes behind the scenes, sometimes out in the open. In communities where such an "establishment," that is, a coherent ruling group, exists, the leading citizen can be thought of as having power in a generalized sense: he can bring about a change in zoning ordinances, influence the location of a new factory, and determine whether the local museum will buy contemporary paintings. But in the dispersed and fragmented power system that prevails in the nation as a whole one cannot say "So-and-so is powerful," without further elaboration. Those who know how our system works always want to know, "Powerful in what way? Powerful to accomplish what?" We have leaders in business and leaders in government, military leaders and educational leaders, leaders in labor and in agriculture, leaders in science, in the world of art, and in many other special fields. As a rule, leaders in any one of these fields do not recognize the authority of leaders from a neighboring field. Often they don't even know one another, nor do they particularly want to. Mutual suspicion is just about as common as mutual respect—and a lot more common than mutual cooperation in manipulating society's levers.

Most of the significant issues in our society are settled by a balancing of forces. A lot of people and groups are involved and the most powerful do not always win. Sometimes a coalition of the less powerful wins. Sometimes an individual of very limited power gets himself into the position of casting the deciding ballot.

Not only are there apt to be many groups involved in any critical issue, but their relative strength varies with each issue that comes up. A group that is powerful today may not be powerful next year. A group that can cast a decisive vote on question A may not even be listened to when question B comes up.

The Nature of Leadership

People who have never exercised power have all kinds of curious ideas about it. The popular notion of top leadership is a fantasy of capricious power: the top man presses a button and something remarkable happens; he gives an order as the whim strikes him, and it is obeyed.

Actually, the capricious use of power is relatively rare except in some large dictatorships and some small family firms. Most leaders are hedged around by constraints—tradition, constitutional limitations, the realities of the external situation, rights and privileges of followers, the requirements of teamwork, and most of all the inexorable demands of large-scale organization, which does not operate on capriciousness. In short, most power is wielded circumspectly.

There are many different ways of leading, many kinds of leaders. Consider, for example, the marked contrasts between the politician and the intellectual leader, the large-scale manager and the spiritual leader. One sees solemn descriptions of the qualities needed for leadership without any reference at all to the fact that the necessary attributes depend on the kind of leadership under discussion. Even in a single field there may be different kinds of leadership with different required attributes. Think of the difference between the military hero and the military manager.

If social action is to occur, certain functions must be performed. The problems facing the group or organization must be clarified, and ideas necessary to their solution formulated. Objectives must be defined. There must be widespread awareness of those objectives, and the will to achieve them. Often those on whom action depends must develop new attitudes and habits. Social machinery must be set in motion. The consequences of social effort must be evaluated and criticized, and new goals set.

A particular leader may contribute at only one point to this process. He may be gifted in analysis of the problem, but limited in his capacity to communicate. He may be superb in communicating, but incapable of managing. He may, in short, be an outstanding leader without being good at every aspect of leadership.

If anything significant is to be accomplished, leaders must understand the social institutions and processes through which action is carried out. And in a society as complex as ours, that is no mean achievement. A leader, whether corporation president, university dean, or labor official, knows his organization, understands what makes it move, comprehends its limitations. Every social system or institution has a logic and dynamic of its own that cannot be ignored.

We have all seen men with lots of bright ideas but no patience with the machinery by which ideas are translated into action. As a rule, the machinery defeats them. It is a pity, because the professional and academic man can play a useful role in practical affairs. But too often he is a dilettante. He dips in here or there; he gives bits of advice on a dozen fronts; he never gets his hands dirty working with one piece of the social machinery until he knows it well. He will not take the time to understand the social institutions and processes by which change is accomplished.

Although our decentralized system of leadership has served us well, we must not be so complacent as to imagine that it has no weaknesses, that it faces no new challenges, or that we have nothing to learn. There are grave questions to be answered concerning the leadership of our society. Are we living up to standards of leadership that we have achieved in our own past? Do the conditions of modern life introduce new complications into the task of leadership? Are we failing to prepare leaders for tomorrow?

Here are some of our salient difficulties.

Failure to Cope with the Big Questions

Nothing should be allowed to impair the effectiveness and independence of our specialized leadership groups. But such fragmented leadership does create certain problems. One of them is that it isn't anybody's business to think about the big questions that cut across specialties—the largest questions facing our society. Where are we headed? Where do we *want* to head? What are the major trends determining our future? Should we do anything about them? Our fragmented leadership fails to deal effectively with these transcendent questions.

Very few of our most prominent people take a really large view of the leadership assignment. Most of them are simply tending the machinery of that part of society to which they belong. The machinery may be a great corporation or a great government agency or a great law practice or a great university. These people may tend it very well indeed, but they are not pursuing a vision of what the total society needs. They have not developed a strategy as to how it can be achieved, and they are not moving to accomplish it.

One does not blame them, of course. They do not see themselves as leaders of the society at large, and they have plenty to do handling their own specialized role.

Yet it is doubtful that we can any longer afford such widespread inattention to the largest questions facing us. We achieved greatness in an era when changes came more slowly than now. The problems facing the society took shape at a stately pace. We could afford to be slow in recognizing them, slow in coping with them. Today, problems of enormous import hit us swiftly. Great social changes emerge with frightening speed. We can no longer afford to respond in a leisurely fashion.

Our inability to cope with the largest questions tends to weaken the private sector. Any question that cannot be dealt with by one of the special leadership groups—that is, any question that cuts across special fields—tends to end up being dealt with by government. Most Americans value the role played by nongovernmental leadership in this country and would wish it to continue. In my judgment it will not continue under the present conditions.

The cure is not to work against the fragmentation of leadership, which is a vital element in our pluralism, but to create better channels of communication among significant leadership groups, especially in connection with the great issues that transcend any particular group.

Failure of Confidence

Another of the maladies of leadership today is a failure of confidence. Anyone who accomplishes anything of significance has more confidence than the facts would justify. It is something that outstanding executives have in common with gifted military commanders, brilliant political leaders, and great artists. It is true of societies as well as of individuals. Every great civilization has been characterized by confidence in itself.

Lacking such confidence, too many leaders add ingenious new twists to the modern art which I call "How to reach a decision without really deciding." They require that the question be put through a series of clearances within the organization and let the clearance process settle it. Or take a public opinion poll and let the poll settle it. Or devise elaborate statistical systems, cost-accounting systems, information-processing systems, hoping that out of them will come unassailable support for one course of action rather than another.

This is not to say that leadership cannot profit enormously from good information. If the modern leader doesn't know the facts he is in grave trouble, but rarely do the facts provide unqualified guidance. After the facts are in, the leader must in some measure emulate the little girl who told the teacher she was going to draw a picture of God. The teacher said, "But, Mary, no one knows what God looks like"; and Mary said, "They will when I get through."

The confidence required of leaders poses a delicate problem for a free society. We don't want to be led by Men of Destiny who think they know all the answers. Neither do we wish to be led by Nervous Nellies. It is a matter of balance. We are no longer in much danger, in this society, from Men of Destiny. But we *are* in danger of falling under the leadership of men who lack the confidence to lead. And we are in danger of destroying the effectiveness of those who have a natural gift for leadership.

Of all our deficiencies with respect to leadership, one of the gravest is that we are not doing what we should to encourage potential leaders. In the late eighteenth century we produced out of a small population a truly extraordinary group of leaders—Washington, Adams, Jefferson, Franklin, Madison, Monroe, and others. Why is it so difficult today, out of a vastly greater population, to produce men of that caliber? It is a question that most reflective people ask themselves sooner or later.

There is no reason to doubt that the human material is still there, but there is excellent reason to believe that we are failing to develop it—or that we are diverting it into nonleadership activities.

The Antileadership Vaccine

Indeed, it is my belief that we are immunizing a high proportion of our most gifted young people against any tendencies to leadership. It will be worth our time to examine how the antileadership vaccine is administered.

The process is initiated by the society itself. The conditions of life in a modern, complex society are not conducive to the emergence of leaders. The young person today is acutely aware of the fact that he is an anonymous member of a mass society, an individual lost among millions of others. The processes by which leadership is exercised are not visible to him, and he is bound to believe that they are exceedingly intricate. Very little in his experience encourages him to think that he might some day exercise a role of leadership.

This unfocused discouragement is of little consequence compared with the expert dissuasion the young person will encounter if he is sufficiently bright to attend a college or university. In those institutions today, the best students are carefully schooled to avoid leadership responsibilities.

Most of our intellectually gifted young people go from college directly into graduate school or into one of the older and more prestigious professional schools. There they are introduced to—or, more correctly, powerfully indoctrinated in—a set of attitudes appropriate to scholars, scientists, and professional men. This is all to the good. The students learn to identify themselves strongly with their calling and its ideals. They acquire a conception of what a good scholar, scientist, or professional man is like.

As things stand now, however, that conception leaves little room for leadership in the normal sense; the only kind of leadership encouraged is that which follows from the performing of purely professional tasks in a superior manner. Entry into what most of us would regard as the leadership roles in the society at large is discouraged.

In the early stages of a career, there is a good reason for this: becoming a first-class scholar, scientist, or professional requires single-minded dedication. Unfortunately, by the time the individual is sufficiently far along in his career to afford a broadening of interests, he often finds himself irrevocably set in a narrow mold.

The antileadership vaccine has other more subtle and powerful ingredients. The image of the corporation president, politician, or college president that is current among most intellectuals and professionals today has some decidedly unattractive features. It is said that such men compromise their convictions almost daily, if not hourly. It is said that they have tasted the corrupting experience of power. They must be status seekers, the argument goes, or they would not be where they are.

Needless to say, the student picks up such attitudes. It is not that professors propound these views and students learn them. Rather, they are in the air and students absorb them. The resulting unfavorable image contrasts dramatically with the image these young people are given of the professional who is almost by definition dedicated to his field, pure in his motives, and unencumbered by worldly ambition.

My own extensive acquaintance with scholars and professionals on the one hand and administrators and managers on the other does not confirm this contrast in character. In my experience, each category has its share of opportunists. Nevertheless, the negative attitudes persist.

As a result the academic world appears to be approaching a point at which everyone will want to educate the technical expert who advises the leader, or the intellectual who stands off and criticizes the leader, but no one will want to educate the leader himself.

Are Leaders Necessary?

For a good many academic and other professional people, negative attitudes toward leadership go deeper than skepticism concerning the leader's integrity. Many have real doubts, not always explicitly formulated, about the necessity for leadership.

The doubts are of two kinds. First, many scientific and professional people are accustomed to the kinds of problems that can be solved by expert technical advice or action. It is easy for them to imagine that any social enterprise could be managed in the same way. They envisage a world that does not need leaders, only experts. The notion is based, of course, upon a false conception of the leader's function. The supplying of technically correct solutions is the least of his responsibilities.

There is another kind of question that some academic or professional people raise concerning leadership: Is the very notion of leadership somehow at odds with the ideals of a free society? Is it a throwback to earlier notions of social organization?

These are not foolish questions. We have in fact outgrown or rejected several varieties of leadership that have loomed large in the history of mankind. We do not want autocratic leaders who treat us like inferior beings. We do not want leaders, no matter how wise or kind, who treat us like children.

But at the same time that we were rejecting those forms of leadership, we were evolving forms more suitable to our values. As a result our best leaders today are *not* out of place in a free society—on the contrary, they strengthen our free society.

We can have the kinds of leaders we want, but we cannot choose to do without them. It is in the nature of social organization that we must have them at all levels of our national life, in and out of government— in business, labor, politics, education, science, the arts, and every other field. Since we must have them, it helps considerably if they are gifted in the performance of their appointed task. The sad truth is that a great many of our organizations are badly managed or badly led. And because of that, people within those organizations are frustrated when they need not be frustrated. They are not helped when they could be helped. They are not given the opportunities to fulfill themselves that are clearly possible.

In the minds of some, leadership is associated with goals that are distasteful—power, profit, efficiency, and the like. But leadership, properly conceived, also serves the individual human goals that our society values so highly, and we shall not achieve those goals without it.

Leaders worthy of the name, whether they are university presidents or senators, corporation executives or newspaper editors, school superintendents or governors, contribute to the continuing definition and articulation of the most cherished values of our society. They offer, in short, moral leadership.

So much of our energy has been devoted to tending the machinery of our complex society that we have neglected this element in leadership. I am using the word "moral" to refer to the shared values that must undergird any functioning society. The thing that makes a number of individuals a society rather than a population or a crowd is the presence of shared attitudes, habits and values, a shared conception of the enterprise of which they are all a part, shared views of why it is worthwhile for the enterprise to continue and to flourish. Leaders can help in bringing that about. In fact, it is required that they do so. When leaders lose their credibility or their moral authority, then the society begins to disintegrate.

Leaders have a significant role in creating the state of mind that is the society. They can serve as symbols of the moral unity of the society. They can express the values that hold the society together. Most important, they can conceive and articulate goals that lift people out of their petty preoccupations, carry them above the conflicts that tear a society apart, and unite them in the pursuit of objectives worthy of their best efforts.

18

Thinking About Leadership

THOMAS E. CRONIN

Leadership is one of the most widely talked-about subjects and at the same time one of the most elusive and puzzling. Americans often yearn for great, transcending leadership for their communities, their companies, the military, unions, universities, sports teams, and for the nation. However, we have an almost love-hate ambivalence about power wielders. And we especially dislike anyone who tries to boss us around. Yes, we admire the Washingtons and Churchills, but Hitler and Al Capone were leaders too—and that points up a fundamental problem. Leadership can be exercised in the service of noble, liberating, enriching ends, but it can also serve to manipulate, mislead, and repress.

"One of the most universal cravings of our time," writes James MacGregor Burns, "is a hunger for compelling and creative leadership." But exactly what is creative leadership? A *Wall Street Journal* cartoon had two men talking about leadership. Finally, one turned to the other in exasperation and said: "Yes, we need leadership, but we also need someone to tell us what to do." That is to say, leadership for most people most of the time is a rather hazy, distant, and even confusing abstraction. Hence, thinking about or defining leadership is a kind of intellectual leadership challenge in itself.

What follows are some thoughts about leadership and education for leadership. These thoughts and ideas are highly personal and hardly scientific. As I shall suggest below, almost anything that can be said about leadership can be contradicted with counter examples. Moreover, the whole subject is riddled with paradoxes. My ideas here are the product of my studies of political leadership and my own participation in politics from the town meeting level to the White House staff. Some

An essay initially presented at the Western Academy of Management, Colorado Springs, CO, April 3, 1982. Copyright © 1983 by Thomas E. Cronin. Reprinted by permission.

of my ideas come from helping to advise universities and foundations and the Houston-based American Leadership Forum on how best to go about encouraging leadership development. Finally, my thoughts have also been influenced in a variety of ways by numerous conversations with five especially insightful writers on leadership—Warren Bennis, James MacGregor Burns, David Campbell, Harlan Cleveland, and John W. Gardner.

* * *

Can we teach people to become leaders? Can we teach leadership? People are divided on these questions. It was once widely held that "leaders are born and not made" but that view is less widely held today. We also used to hear about "natural leaders" but nowadays most leaders have learned their leadership ability rather than inherited it. Still there is much mystery to the whole matter. In any event, many people think colleges and universities should steer clear of the whole subject. What follows is a set of reasons why our institutions of higher learning generally are "bashful about teaching leadership." These reasons may overstate the case, but they are the objections that serious people often raise.

First, many people still believe that leaders are born and not made, or that leadership is somehow almost accidental or at least that most leaders emerge from circumstances and normally do not create them. In any event, it is usually added, most people, most of the time, are not now and never will be leaders.

Second, American cultural values hold that leadership is an elitist and thus anti-American phenomenon. Plato and Machiavelli and other grand theorists might urge upon their contemporaries the need for winnowing out and training a select few for top leadership roles, but this runs against the American grain. We like to think that anyone can become a top leader here. Hence, no special training should be given to some special select few.

Third is the complaint that leadership training would more than likely be preoccupied with skills, techniques, and the *means* of getting things done. But leadership for what? Leadership in service of what ends? A focus on *means* divorced from *ends* makes people—especially intellectuals—ill at ease. They hardly want to be in the business of training future Joe McCarthys or Hitlers or Idi Amins.

Fourth, leadership study strikes many as an explicitly vocational topic. It's a practical and applied matter—better learned in summer jobs, in internships, or on the playing fields. You learn it on the job. You learn it from gaining experience, from making mistakes and learning from them. And you should learn it from mentors.

Fifth, leadership often involves an element of manipulation or deviousness, if not outright ruthlessness. Some consider it virtually the same as learning about jungle-fighting or acquiring "the killer instinct." It's just not a "clean" enough subject matter for many people to embrace. Plus, "leaders" like Stalin and Hitler or even our own Johnson and Nixon gave "leadership" a bad name. If they were leaders, then spare us from their clones or imitators.

Sixth, leadership in the most robust sense of the term is such an ecumenical and intellectually all-encompassing subject that it frightens not only the timid but even the most well-educated persons. To teach leadership is an act of arrogance. That is, it is to suggest one understands far more than even a well-educated person can understand—history, ethics, philosophy, classics, politics, biography, psychology, management, sociology, law, etc., and to be steeped deeply as well in the "real world."

Seventh, colleges and universities are increasingly organized in highly specialized divisons and departments all geared to train specialists. While the mission of the college may be to educate "the educated person" and society's future leaders, in fact the incentive system is geared to training specialists. Society today rewards the expert or the super specialist—the data processors, the pilots, the financial whiz, the heart surgeon, the special team punt returners, and so on. Leaders, however, have to learn to become generalists and usually have to do so well after they have left our colleges, graduate schools, and professional schools.

Eighth, leadership strikes many people (and with some justification) as an elusive, hazy, and almost mysterious commodity. Now you see it, now you don't. So much of leadership is intangible, you can't possibly define all the parts. A person may be an outstanding leader here, but fail there. Trait theory has been thoroughly debunked. In fact, leadership is highly situational and contextual. A special chemistry develops between leaders and followers and it is usually context specific. Followers often do more to determine the leadership they will get than can any teacher. Hence, why not teach people to be substantively bright and well-read and let things just take their natural course.

Ninth, virtually anything that can be said about leadership can be denied or disproven. Leadership studies, to the extent they exist, are unscientific. Countless paradoxes and contradictions litter every manuscript on leadership. Thus, we yearn for leadership, but yearn equally to be free and left alone. We admire risk-taking, entrepreneurial leadership but we roundly criticize excessive risk-taking as bullheadedness or plain stupidity. We want leaders who are highly self-confident and who are perhaps incurably optimistic—yet we also dislike hubris and often yearn for at least a little self-doubt (e.g., Creon in *Antigone*). Leaders have to be almost singleminded in their drive and commitment but too much of that makes a person rigid, driven, and unacceptable. We want leaders to be good listeners and to represent their constituents, yet as Walter Lippmann has put it, effective leadership often consists of giving the people not what they want but what they will learn to want. How in the world, then, can you be rigorous and precise in teaching leadership?

Tenth, leadership at its best comes close to creativity. And how do you teach creativity? We are increasingly made aware of the fact that creative thinking calls upon unconscious thinking, dreaming, and even fantasy. Some fascinating work is being done on intuition and the nonrational, but it is hardly a topic with which traditional disciplines in traditional colleges are comfortable.

*   *   *

A few other initial observations need to be made about leadership. Chief among these is that the study of leadership needs inevitably to be linked or merged with the study of followership. We cannot really study leaders in isolation from followers, constituents or group members. The leader is very much a product of the group, and very much shaped by its aspirations, values and human resources. The more we learn about leadership, the more the leader-follower linkage is understood and reaffirmed. A leader has to resonate with followers. Part of being an effective leader is having excellent ideas or a clear sense of direction, a sense of mission. But such ideas or vision are useless unless the would-be leader can communicate them and get them accepted by followers. A two-way engagement or two-way interaction is constantly going on. When it ceases, leaders become lost, out of touch, imperial or worse.

The question of leaders being linked with followers raises the question of the transferability of leadership. Can an effective leader in one situation transfer this capacity, this skill, this style to another setting? The record is mixed indeed. Certain persons have been effective in diverse settings. George Washington and Dwight Eisenhower come to mind. Jack Kemp and Bill Bradley, two well-known and respected members of Congress, were previously successful professional athletes. Scores of business leaders have been effective in the public sector and vice versa. Scores of military leaders have become effective in business or politics and some in both. However, there are countless examples of those who have not met with success when they have tried to transfer their leadership abilities from one setting to a distinctively different setting. Sometimes this failure arises because the new group's goals or needs are so different from those of the previous organization. Sometimes it is because the leadership needs are different. The leadership needs of a military officer leading a platoon up a hill in battle may well be very different from the leadership requirements of someone asked to change sexist attitudes and practices in a large corporation or to ease racist and ethnic hatred in an inner city. The leadership required of a candidate for office is often markedly different from that required of a campaign manager. Leadership required in founding a company may be exceedingly different from that required in the company's second generation.

Another confusing aspect of leadership is that leadership and management are often talked about as if they were the same. While it is true that an effective manager is often an effective leader and leadership requires, among other things, many of the skills of an effective manager, there are differences. Leaders are the people who infuse vision into an organization or a society. At their best, they are preoccupied with values and the longer range needs and aspirations of their followers. Managers are concerned with doing things *the right way*. Leaders are more concerned with identifying and then getting themselves and their organizations focused on *doing the right thing*. John Quincy Adams, Herbert Hoover, and Jimmy Carter were often good, sometimes excellent managers. Before coming to the White House, they were all recognized for being effective achievers. As businessmen, diplomats, governors, or cabinet members, they excelled. As presidential leaders, they were found wanting. None was invited back for a second term. While none was considered an outright failure, each seemed to fail in providing the vision needed for the times. They were unable to lift the public's spirit and get the nation moving in new, more desirable directions.

As this brief digression suggests, being a leader is not the same thing as being a holder of high office. An effective leader is someone concerned with far more than the mechanics of office. While a good manager is concerned, and justifiably so, with efficiency, with keeping things going, with the routines and standard operating procedures, and with reaffirming ongoing systems, the creative leader acts as an inventor, risk taker, and generalist entrepreneur, ever asking or searching for what is right, where we should be headed, keenly sensing new directions, new possibilities, and welcoming change. We need all the talented managers we can get, but we also need creative leaders. Ironically, too, an effective leader is not very effective for long unless he or she can recruit effective managers to help them make things work over the long run.

One of the most important things to be said about leadership is that it is commonly very dispersed throughout a society. Our leadership needs vary enormously. Many of the great breakthroughs occur because of people well in advance of their time who are willing to agitate for change and suggest fresh new approaches that are, as yet, unacceptable to majority opinion. Many of the leadership needs of our nations are met by persons who do not hold high office and who often don't look or even act as leaders. Which brings us to the question of defining leadership. Agreement on a definition is difficult to achieve. But for the purposes at hand, leaders are people who perceive what is needed and what is right and know how to mobilize people and resources to accomplish mutual goals.

Leaders are individuals who can help create options and opportunities, who can help clarify problems and choices, who can build morale and coalitions, who can inspire others and provide a vision of the possibilities and promise of a better organization or a better community. Leaders have those indispensable qualities of contagious self-confidence, unwarranted optimism, and incurable idealism that allows them to attract and mobilize others to undertake demanding tasks they never dreamed they could undertake. In short, leaders empower and help liberate others. They enhance the possibilities for freedom, both for people and for organizations. They engage with followers in such a way that many of the followers became leaders in their own right.

As implied above, many of the significant breakthroughs in both the public and the private sectors of this nation have been made by people who saw all the complexities ahead of them, but so believed in themselves and their purposes that they refused to be overwhelmed and paralyzed by doubts. They were willing to invent new rules and gamble on the future.

Good leaders, almost always, have been get-it-all-together, broken-field runners. They have been generalists. Tomorrow's leaders will very likely have begun life as trained specialists. Our society particularly rewards the specialist. On the long road up, most young would-be leaders become servants of what is rather than shapers of what might be. In the process of learning how various systems work, most young specialists are rewarded for playing within the intricate structure of existing rules. But only as creative generalists can these would-be leaders cope with the multitude of highly organized groups—subsystems within the larger system—fighting for special treatment, each armed with their own narrow definition of the public interest, often to the point of paralyzing *any* significant action.

Overcoming fears, especially fears of stepping beyond the boundaries of one's tribe, is a special need for the leader. A leader's task as a renewer of organizational goals and aspirations is to illuminate goals, to help reperceive their own and their organization's resources and strengths, to speak to people of what is only dimly recognized in their minds. The effective creative leader is one who can give voice and form so that people say, "Ah, yes—that's what I too have been feeling."

Note, however, that leaders are always aware of and at least partly shaped by the higher wants and aspirations and common purposes of their followers and constituents. Leaders consult and listen just as they educate and attempt to renew the goals of an organization. They know how "to squint with their ears." Civic leaders often emerge as we are able to agree upon goals. One analyst has suggested that it is no good for us to just go looking for leaders; we must first rediscover our own goals and values. If we are to have the leaders we need, we will first have to agree upon priorities. In one sense, if we wish to have leaders to follow, we will often have to show them the way.

In looking for leadership and in organizational affiliations people are looking for *significance, competence, affirmation, and fairness.* To join an organization, individuals have to give up some aspect of their uniqueness, some part of their souls. Thus, there is a price in affiliating and in following. The leader gives strength and serves as an attraction in the organization, but psychologically there is also a *repulsion* to the leader—in part because of dependence on the leader. John Steinbeck said of American presidents that the people believe that, "they were ours and we exercise the right to destroy them." Effective leaders must know how to absorb these hostilities, however latent they may be.

The leader also must be ever sensitive to the distinction between *power* and *authority.* Power is the strength or raw force to exercise control or coerce someone to do something, while authority is power that is *accepted* as legitimate by subordinates. The whole question of leadership raises countless issues about participation and the acceptance of power in superior-subordinate relationships. How much participation or involvement is needed, is desirable? What is the impact of participation on effectiveness? How best for the leader to earn moral and social acceptance for his or her authority? America generally prizes participation in all kinds of organizations, especially in civic and political life. Yet, we must realize too that a part of us yearns for charismatic leadership. Ironically, savior figures and charismatic leaders often—indeed almost always—create distance and not participation.

One of the most difficult tasks for those who would measure and evaluate leadership is the task of trying to look at the elements that make up leadership. One way to look at these elements is to suggest that a leader has various *skills,* also has or exercises a distinctive *style* and, still more elusive, has various *qualities* that may be pronounced. By skill, I mean the capacity to do something well. Something that is learnable and can be improved, such as speaking or negotiating or planning. Most leaders need to have *technical skills,* such as writing well; *human relations skills,* including the capacity to supervise, inspire, and build coalitions; and also what might be called *conceptual skills,* the capacity to play with ideas, shrewdly seek advice, and forge grand strategies. Skills can be examined. Skills can be taught. And skills plainly make up an important part of leadership capability. Skills alone, however, cannot guarantee leadership success.

A person's leadership style may also be critical to effectiveness. Style refers to how a person relates to people, to tasks, and to challenges. A person's style is usually a very individual and distinctive feature of their personality and character. A style may be democratic or autocratic, centralized or decentralized, empathetic or detached, extroverted or introverted, assertive or passive, engaged or remote. (This hardly exhausts the diverse possibilities, but is meant to be suggestive.) Different styles may work equally well in different situations. However, there is often a proper fit between the needs of an organization and the needed leadership style. A fair amount of research has been done in this area, but much more remains to be learned.

A person's *behavioral style* refers to one's way of relating to other people—to peers, subordinates, rivals, bosses, advisers, the press. A person's *psychological style* refers to one's way of handling stress, tensions, challenges to the ego, internal conflicts. Considerable work needs to be done in these areas, particularly if we are to learn how best to prepare people for shaping their leadership styles to diverse leadership situations and needs. But it is a challenge worth accepting.

James MacGregor Burns, in his book *Leadership,* offers us yet one additional distinction worth thinking about. Ultimately, Burns says, there are two overriding kinds of social and political leadership: *transactional* and *transformational leadership.* The transactional leader engages in an exchange, usually for self-interest and with short-term interests in mind. It is, in essence, a bargaining situation: "I'll vote for your bill if you vote for mine." Or "You do me a favor and I will shortly return it." Most pragmatic officeholders practice transactional leadership most of the time. It is commonly a practical necessity. It is the general way people do business and get their jobs done—and stay in office. The transforming or transcending leader is the person who, as briefly noted earlier, so engages with followers as to bring them to a heightened political and social consciousness and activity, and in the process converts many of those followers into leaders in their own right. The transforming leader, with a focus on the higher aspirations and longer range, is also a teacher, mentor, and educator, pointing out the possibilities and the hopes and the often only dimly understood dreams of people and getting them to undertake the preparation and the job needed to attain these goals.

Of course, not everyone can be a leader. And rarely can any one leader provide an organization's entire range of leadership needs. Upon closer inspection, most firms and most societies have all kinds of leaders and these diverse leaders, in turn, are usually highly dependent for their success on the leadership performed by other leaders. Some leaders are excellent at creating or inventing new structures. Others are great task leaders, helping to energize groups at problem solving. Others are excellent social (or affective) leaders, helping to build morale and renew the spirit of an organization or a people. These leaders are often indispensable in providing what might be called the human glue that holds groups together. Further, the most lasting and pervasive leadership of all is often intangible and noninstitutional. It is the leadership fostered by ideas embodied in social, political, or artistic movements, in books, in documents, in speeches, and in the memory of great lives greatly lived. Intellectual or idea leadership at its best is provided by those—often not in high political or corporate office—who can clarify values and the implications of such values for policy. The point here is that leadership is not only dispersed and diverse, but interdependent. Leaders need leaders as much as followers need leaders. This may sound confusing but it is part of the truth about the leadership puzzle.

*   *   *

In the second half of this essay, I will raise in a more general way some of the qualities I believe are central to leadership. Everyone has their own lists of leadership qualities. I will not be able to discuss all of mine, but permit me to offer my list and then describe a few of the more important ones in a bit more detail.

Leadership Qualities—A Tentative List

- Self-knowledge/self-confidence
- Vision; ability to infuse important, transcending values into an enterprise
- Intelligence, wisdom, judgment
- Learning/renewal
- World-mindedness/a sense of history and breadth
- Coalition-building/social architecture
- Morale-building/motivation
- Stamina, energy, tenacity, courage, enthusiasm
- Character, integrity/intellectual honesty
- Risk-taking/entrepreneurship
- An ability to communicate, persuade/listen
- Understanding the nature of power and authority
- An ability to concentrate on achieving goals and results
- A sense of humor, perspective, flexibility

Leadership consists of an upwards spiral, a spiral of self-improvement, self-knowledge, and seizing and creating opportunities so that a person can make things happen that would not otherwise have occurred. Just as there can be a spiral upwards, there can be a spiral downwards, characterized by failure, depression, self-defeat, self-doubt, and paralyzing fatalism.

If asked to point to key qualities of successful leadership, I would suggest these:

1. *Leaders are people who know who they are and know where they are going.* "What a man thinks about himself," Thoreau wrote, "that is what determines, or rather indicates his fate." One of the most paralyzing of mental illnesses is wrong perception of self. This leads to poor choosing, and poor choosing leads to a fouled-up life. In one sense, the trouble with many people is not what they don't know, it is what they do know, but it is misinformed or misinformation.

Leaders must be self-reliant individuals with great tenacity and stamina. The world is moved by people who are enthusiastic. Optimism and high motivation count for a lot. They can lift organizations. Most people are forever waiting around for somebody to light a fire under them. They are people who have not learned the valuable lesson that ultimately you are the one who is responsible for you. You don't blame others. You don't blame circumstances. You simply take charge and help move the enterprise forward.

I am sure many of you have been puzzled, as I have been, about why so many talented friends of ours have leveled off earlier than needs to be the case. What is it that prevents people from becoming the best they could be? Often it is a lack of education, a physical handicap, or a disease such as alcoholism. Very often, however, it is because people have not been able to gain control over their lives. Various things nibble away at their capacity for self-realization or what Abraham Maslow called self-actualization. Family problems, inadequate financial planning, and poor health or mental health problems are key factors that damage self-esteem. Plainly, it is difficult to handle life, not to mention leadership responsibilities, if a person feels they do not control their own lives. This emotional feeling of helplessness inevitably leads people to believe they aren't capable, they can't do the job. It also inhibits risk-taking and just about all the qualities associated with creativity and leadership.

Picture a scale from, at one end, an attitude of "I don't control anything and I feel like the bird in a badminton game" to the other end of the scale where there is an attitude of "I'm in charge." Either extreme may be pathological, but plainly the higher up, relatively, toward the "I'm in charge" end of the scale, the more one is able to handle the challenges of transforming or creative leadership.

Thus, the single biggest factor is motivating or liberating would-be leaders in their attitude toward themselves and toward their responsibilities to others.

Leaders also have to understand the situations they find themselves in. As observed in *Alice in Wonderland,* before we decide where we are going, we first have to decide where we are right now. After this comes commitment to something larger and longer term than just our own egos. People can achieve meaning in their lives only when they can give as well as take from their society. Failure to set priorities and develop significant personal purposes undermines nearly any capacity for leadership. "When a man does not know what harbor he is making for, no wind is the right wind."

2. *Setting priorities and mobilizing energies.* Too many people become overwhelmed with trivia, with constant close encounters of a third rate. Leaders have always to focus on the major problems of the day and on the higher aspirations and needs of their followers. Leadership divorced from an important transcending purpose becomes manipulation, deception and, in the extreme, is not leadership at all, but repression and tyranny.

The effective modern leader has to be able to live in an age of uncertainty. Priorities have to be set and decisions have to be made even though all the information is not in—this will surely be even more true in the future than it has been in the past. The information revolution has tremendously enlarged both the opportunities and the frustrations for leaders. Knowing what you don't know becomes as important as knowing what you do know. A willingness to experiment and explore possible strategies even in the face of uncertainty may become a more pronounced characteristic of the creative leader.

The creative priority setter learns both to encourage and to question his or her intuitive tendencies. Oliver Wendell Holmes, Jr., said that "to have doubted one's own first principles is the mark of a civilized man" and so it continues to be. The ability to look at things differently and to reach out for more and better advice is crucial. The ability to admit error and to learn from mistakes is also vitally important.

Leaders need to have considerable self-confidence, but they also must have a dose of self-doubt. Leaders must learn how to communicate the need for advice and help, how to become a creative listener, how to empathize and understand. In Sophocles' compelling play, *Antigone,* the tragic hero, King Creon, hears his son's advice but imprudently rejects it or perhaps does not even hear it. But Haemon's advice is advice any leader should take into account:

Let not your first thought be your only thought. Think if there cannot be some other way. Surely, to think your own the only wisdom, and yours the only word, the only will, betrays a shallow spirit, an empty heart. It is no weakness for the wisest man to learn when he is wrong, know when to yield. . . .
So, father, pause and put aside your anger. I think, for what my young opinion's worth, that good as it is to have infallible wisdom, since this is rarely found, the next best thing is to be willing to listen to wise advice.[1]

Leaders need to be able to discover their own strengths and the strengths of those with whom they work. They have to learn how to share and to delegate. They have to be able to make people believe they are important, that they are or can be winners. People yearn to think that what they are doing is something useful, something important. The transforming or creative leader knows how to nourish conviction and morale within an organization.

Good leaders know how to serve as morale-builders and renewers of purpose, able to get people to rededicate themselves to long-cherished but sometimes dimly understood values. Motivation is sometimes as much as 40 to 50 percent of the leadership enterprise. You can do very little alone with just faith and determination, yet you can do next to nothing without them. Organizations of all kinds need constantly to rediscover or renew their faith, direction, and sense of purpose.

3. *Leaders have to provide the risk-taking, entrepreneurial imagination for their organizations and communities.* Leaders are able to see things in a different and fresh context. Warren Bennis suggests that creative leadership requires the capacity to recontextualize a situation. Willis Harmon suggests that a leader is one who reperceives situations and challenges and comes up with new approaches, insights, and solutions.

A third grade class begins and the teacher says: "Class, take out your pencils and paper and draw a picture of anything you can think of." Students begin to draw—balls, trees, automobiles, and so forth. Teacher asks Sally, in the second row: "What are you drawing?" Sally says, "I'm drawing a picture of God." Teacher says: "But no one has ever seen God, we don't know what he looks like." An undaunted Sally responds: "Well, they sure will when I get through!"

This little story illustrates the sometimes irrational self-confidence and "failure is impossible" factor that motivates the galvanizing leader. The founding revolutionaries in America, Susan B. Anthony, Martin

Luther King, Jr., Saul Alinsky, and countless others had the vision of a better and newer society and they, in effect, said, "They'll know a better or more just society when we get through."

Mark Twain once said, "A man is viewed as a crackpot until his idea succeeds." We need a hospitable environment for the dissenter and the creative individual. We need to avoid killing the spark of individuality that allows creativity to flourish. We kill it with rules, red tape, procedures, standard operating restrictions, and countless admonitions "not to rock the boat."

Creativity is the ability to recombine things. To see a radio here and a clock there and put them together. Hence, the clockradio. Open-mindedness is crucial. Too many organizations are organized with structures to solve problems that no longer exist. Vested interest grows up in every human institution. People all too often become prisoners of their procedures.

Psychologist David Campbell points out that history records a long list of innovations that come from outside the "expert" organization. The automobile was not invented by the transportation experts of that era, the railroaders. The airplane was not invented by automobile experts. Polaroid film was not invented by Kodak. Handheld pocket calculators were not invented by IBM, digital watches were not invented by watchmakers. Apple computers and herbal tea are yet two more examples. The list is endless and the moral is vivid.

Leaders get organizations interested in what they are going to become, not what they have been. Creative leadership requires also not being afraid to fail. An essential aspect of creative leadership is curiosity. The best way to have inventive ideas is to have lots of ideas, and to have an organization that welcomes fresh ideas, whatever their merit. As any scientist knows, the art of research requires countless experiments and failures before you get the results you want or sometimes the unexpected result that constitutes the true breakthrough.

Leaders recognize the utility of dreaming, fantasy, and unconscious thinking. Unconscious thinking, thinking which you are unaware of, is often a major source of fresh ideas and approaches.

4. *Leaders need to have a sense of humor and a sense of proportion.* Leaders take their work seriously, but do not take themselves too seriously. Humor relieves strain and enables people to relax and see things in a slightly different or fresh light. Effective leaders usually can tell a joke, take a joke, and tell a good story. They also usually know the art of telling parables. Lincoln, F.D.R., and J.F.K. come quickly to mind, while Hoover, Nixon, and Carter were humorless men. Adlai Stevenson

put it this way, "If I couldn't laugh, I couldn't live—especially in politics."

In this same light, leaders need to be able to share the credit. Leadership sometimes consists of emphasizing the dignity of others and of keeping one's own sense of importance from becoming inflated. Dwight Eisenhower had a slogan he tried to live by, which went as follows: "There's no telling how much one can accomplish so long as one doesn't need to get all the credit for it."

Thus, leaders need to have a sense of proportion and a sense of detachment. They must avoid being workaholics and recognize that they will have to be followers in most of the enterprises of life and leaders only a small fraction of the time.

Humor, proportion, and also *compassion.* Being able to understand emotions and passion and at least on occasion to express themselves with passion and conviction. Enthusiasm, hope, vitality, and energy are crucial to radiating confidence.

5. *Leaders have to be skilled mediators and negotiators, but they also have to be able to stir things up and encourage healthy and desired conflict.* An old *Peanuts'* cartoon has a dejected Charlie Brown coming off a softball field as the game concludes. In exasperation he whines, "How can we lose when we are so sincere?" Sincerity or purity of heart are not enough to succeed in challenging leadership jobs.

The strength of leaders often lies in their tenacity, in knowing how to deal with competing factions, knowing when to compromise, when to amplify conflict, and when to move an organization or a community away from paralyzing divisiveness and toward a vision of the common good.

Most citizens avoid conflict and find conflicts of any kind painful. The truly effective leader welcomes several kinds of conflict and views conflict as an opportunity for change or revitalization.

Stirring things up is often a prerequisite for social and economic breakthrough. Women's rights, black rights, consumer protection, tax reform movements, and even our election campaigns are occasions for division and conflict. They are a reality the leader has to learn to accept, understand, and turn to his advantage. Harry Truman said, "A president who's any damm good at all makes enemies, makes a lot of enemies. I even made a few myself when I was in the White House, and I wouldn't be without them."

George Bernard Shaw and others have put it only slightly differently. Reasonable people, they observe, adjust themselves to reality and cope with what they find. Unreasonable people dream dreams of a different and better world and try to adapt the world to themselves. This discontent or unreasonableness is often the first step in the progress of a person as well as for a community or nation.

But be aware that "stirrer uppers" and conflict-amplifiers are often threatening in any organization or society. In the kingdom of the blind, the one-eyed man is king. This may well be as the proverb has it, but in the kingdom of the one-eyed person, the two-eyed person is looked upon with considerable suspicion and may even be considered downright dangerous.

Thus, it takes courage and guts as well as imagination and stamina to be the two-eyed person in a one-eyed world. Harlan Cleveland points out that just about every leader has had the experience of being in an office surrounded by experts. The sum of the meeting will be, "Let's do nothing, cautiously." The leader is the one who has to say, "Let's take the first step." He or she is the functional equivalent of the first bird off the telephone wire, or what Texans call the "Bell cow." The experts always have an excuse. They are like the losing tennis player whose motto is: "It's not whether you win or lose, it's how you place the blame."

6. *An effective leader must have integrity.* This has been suggested earlier in several implicit ways, but it is perhaps the most central of leadership qualities. A leader must be able to see people in all of their relationships, in the wholeness of their lives and not just as a means of getting a job done, as a means for enhanced productivity.

Some may call it character, others would call it authenticity, compassion or empathy. Whatever we call it, character and integrity are much easier kept than recovered. People can see through a phony. People can readily tell whether a person has respect for others. Respect and responsibility generally migrate to those who are fair, compassionate, and who care about the values, beliefs, and feelings of others. Those who cannot rise above their own prejudices usually fail. A person who permits a shell to be built up around his or her heart will not long be able to exercise creative leadership. Michael Maccoby captures this concern.

> The exercise of the heart is that of experiencing, thinking critically, willing, and acting, so as to overcome egocentrism and to share passion with other people . . . and to respond to their needs with the help one can give. . . . It requires discipline, learning to concentrate, to think critically, and to communicate. The goal, a developed heart, implies integrity, a spiritual center, a sense of "I" not motivated by greed or fear, but by love of life, adventure and fellow feelings.[2]

A leader's integrity requires also that he or she not be captured by peer pressures, protocol, mindless traditions, or conventional rules. The truly effective leader is able to see above and beyond normal constraints to discern proper and desirable ends. The leader also possesses a sense of history and a concern for posterity. This exceptional capacity for disregarding external pressures is the ability that separates leaders from followers.

7. *The leader has to have brains and breadth.* In the future, even more so than in the past, only the really bright individuals will be leaders. Harlan Cleveland highlights this quality well when he writes:

> It used to be that a leader was a two-fisted businessman who chopped up the jobs that needed to be done, then left everyone alone and roared at them if they didn't work right. . . .
> Loud commands worked if one person knew all things, but because of the way we [now] make decisions, through committees, a person charging around with a loud voice is just in the way.[3]

Today's leaders must widen their perspectives and lengthen the focal point of their thinking. Leaders today have to learn how to thread or weave together disparate parts and move beyond analytical to integrative thinking. This will require well-read, well-traveled persons who can rise above their specialties and their professions. It will require as well persons who are not afraid of politics, but who rather view the art of politics as the art of bringing about the difficult and the desirable.

The creative political leader must work in a tension-filled world between unity and dissent, majority rule and minority rights, and countless other contradictions. De Tocqueville said of us, "These Americans yearn for leadership, but they also want to be left alone and free." The political leader is always trying to reconcile this and other paradoxes, but the important point is to be able to live with the paradoxes and dilemmas. And beyond this, the political leader must also be able to create, and preserve, a sense of community and shared heritage, the civic bond that ties us disparate and fiesty rugged individualists together.

Effective leaders of today and tomorrow also know how to vary their styles of leadership depending on the maturity of their subordinates. They involve their peers and their subordinates in their responsibility networks. They must be good educators and good communicators. They also have to have that spark of emotion or passion that can excite others to join them in the enterprise.

Most effective leaders will also be effective communicators: good writers, good speakers, and good conversationalists. A few noted scientists may get by with mumbling, but they are the exception. For so much of leadership consists nowadays in persuading and informing that someone who cannot communicate well, cannot succeed. If people cannot communicate well, they cannot think well, and if they cannot think well, others will do their thinking for them.

America is especially good at training experts, specialists, and managers. We have plenty of these specialist leaders, but they are almost always one-segment leaders. We are in special need of educating multisegment leaders—persons who have a global perspective and understand that the once tidy lines between domestic and international, public and private are irretrievably blurred. Indispensable to a leader is a sense of breadth, the intellectual capacity to handle complex mental tasks, to see relationships between apparently unrelated objects, to see patterns in incomplete information, to draw accurate conclusions from inchoate data.

Vision is the ability to see all sides of an issue and to eliminate biases. Vision and breadth of knowledge put one in a strategic position— preventing the leader from falling into the traps that short-sightedness and mindless parochialism often set for people.

None of these qualities can guarantee creative leadership, but they can, when encouraged, provide a greater likelihood of it. We need all of the leadership we can get—in and out of government. The vitality of nongovernmental America lies in our ability to educate and nourish more citizen-leaders. Those of us who expect to reap the blessings of freedom and liberty must undergo the fatigues of supporting it and provide the leadership necessary to sustain it.

*   *   *

Permit me to return again to the question of whether leadership can be learned and possibly taught. My own belief is that students cannot usually be taught to be leaders. But students, and anyone else for that matter, can profitably be exposed to leadership, discussions of leadership skills and styles, and leadership strategies and theories. Individuals can learn in their own minds the strengths as well as limitations of leadership. People can learn about the paradoxes, contradictions, and ironies of leadership, which however puzzling, are central to appreciating the diversity and the dilemmas of problem-solving and getting organizations and nations to function.

Learning about leadership means recognizing bad leadership as well as good. Learning about leadership means understanding the critical linkage of ends and means. Learning about leadership also involves the study of the special chemistry that develops between leaders and followers, not only the chemistry that existed between Americans and Lincoln, but also between Mao and the Chinese peasants, Lenin and the Bolsheviks, between Martin Luther King, Jr., and civil rights activists, between Jean Monnet and those who dreamed of a European Economic Community.

Students can learn to discern and define situations and contexts within which leadership has flourished. Students can learn about the fallibility of the trait theory. Students can learn about the contextual problems of leadership, of why and when leadership is sometimes transferable, and sometimes not. Students can learn about the crucial role that advisors and supporters play in the leadership equation. Students can also learn about countless problem-solving strategies and theories, and participate in role-playing exercises that sharpen their own skills in such undertakings.

Students of leadership can learn widely from reading biographies about the best and the worst leaders. Plutarch's *Lives* and Shakespeare's plays would be good places to start. Much can be learned from mentors and from intern-participant observing. Much can also be learned about leadership by getting away from one's own culture and examining how leaders in other circumstances go about the task of motivating and mobilizing others. Countless learning opportunities exist that can sharpen a student's skills as a speaker, debater, negotiator, problem clarifier, and planner. Such skills should not be minimized. Nor should anyone underestimate the importance of history, economics, logic, and a series of related substantive fields that help provide the breadth and the perspective indispensable to societal leadership.

Above all, students of leadership can make an appointment with themselves and begin to appreciate their own strengths and deficiencies. Personal mastery is important. So too the ability to use one's intuition, and to enrich one's creative impulses. It's what you learn after you know it all that really counts. Would-be leaders learn to manage their time more wisely. Would-be leaders learn that self-pity and resentment are like toxic substances. Would-be leaders learn the old truth that most people are not for you or against you but are rather preoccupied with themselves. Would-be leaders learn to break out of their comfortable imprisonments; they learn to cast aside dull routines and habits that enslave most of us. Would-be leaders learn how to become truly sharing and caring people—in their families, their professions, and in their communities. And would-be leaders constantly learn that they have more to give than they have ever given, no matter how much they have given.

Let me conclude by paraphrasing from John Adams: "We must study politics [and leadership] and war [and peace] that our sons [and daughters] have the liberty to study mathematics and philosophy, geography, natural history and naval architecture, navigation, commerce, and agriculture, in order to give their children a right to study painting, poetry, music, architecture, statuary, tapestry, and porcelain."

Notes

1. Sophocles, *The Theban Plays* (New York: Penguin, 1947), p. 145.
2. Michael Maccoby, *The Gamesman* (New York: Simon and Shuster, 1976), p. 182.
3. Harlan Cleveland, *Houston Business Journal,* March 1, 1982, p. 13.

Part Four

MILITARY LEADERSHIP: CHALLENGE AND OPPORTUNITY

At this point, we would like to examine the contemporary issues that affect leader behavior in the military. This subject is particularly important in preparing young men and women for the challenges and opportunities of leadership in the future. We may or may not change your concept of leadership, but your ideas on how we should prepare people for the responsibilities of leadership will surely be affected. This is not a prescription for the military (or for any other single organization, for that matter); rather, we have tried to identify the contemporary concerns of society and discuss attempts that have been made to deal with these concerns.

We noted earlier that the gap between leaders and followers has narrowed. For better or worse, we must acknowledge that there will be greater sophistication among the followers in the military. There is strong evidence to suggest that the services must spend more time and effort training these people, for in doing so, leader candidates will enjoy a more realistic training ground—be more in touch with their subordinates, if you will. Followers will also be able to set more reasonable expectations for their leaders—to paraphrase Gertrude Stein, a leader is a follower is a leader. Better developed followers may result in greater successes from their leaders.

Encouraging more creativity may well yield two very positive results. First, by developing creativity in future leaders, we shed the constraints described in Part 2 that have fostered management at the expense of leadership. Creativity implies a broader view of the world, freedom to be intuitive, and the willingness to take risks. There are costs; not all creativity leads to success. The second outcome is better reactions to the ever-increasing rate of technological change—creativity fosters an entrepreneurial spirit, a vision of the future that ensures flexibility in problem solving. Our military leaders must be capable of such vision if we are to remain an effective fighting force.

A definite masculine image permeates the military literature. This is hardly a criticism; it merely reflects the reality that, until recently, there has been little chance of women achieving key leadership roles. As the number of women in the military increases, we must make sure that our concept of leadership does not hold stereotypical images. Our focus must be on leaders as people.

Finally, we must give leader candidates the chance to fail. If leadership is a process that nurtures slowly, we must allow people an opportunity to test their skills and gain the confidence of experience. Perfection at every step of the way is an unrealistic expectation—particularly in light of the complexities that characterize the military mission. This suggests different leader behaviors for people in the military as they mature and grow in their responsibilities.

In Chapter 19, "Leadership Through Followership," William Litzinger and Thomas Schaefer propose that effective leadership may be primarily an achievement of the followers; able leaders may emerge only from the ranks of able followers. They draw upon the philosophy of Aristotle, Plato, and particularly Hegel to support their argument that a good personal history of effective followership may be a significant factor in leadership, although it is not the final determinant of leadership success. Some mastery of followership is a necessary condition for successful leadership, but not by itself a sufficient condition. Still, they write, followership deserves stronger consideration by leadership theorists. We agree.

James MacGregor Burns is one of the most acknowledged contemporary writers on leadership. Chapter 20, an excerpt from his book *Leadership,* expands on the link between leadership and followership. He defines leadership as the leader inducing followers to opt for certain goals that represent shared (leader and followers) values and motivations. Two key notions are introduced: transactional leadership and transforming leadership. In a sense, the relationship between leader and follower ranges from one of power to one of interdependence. The differences are dramatic, having a strong impact on the effectiveness of the military leader.

Chapter 21 examines individual creativity, a personal quality that is often said to be a distinguishing characteristic of the successful leader. Morgan W. McCall, Jr., conjectures about and examines some hypothetical descriptions of creative leaders: crafty, grouchy, dangerous, feisty, contrary, evangelistic, prejudiced, and spineless. He goes on to suggest that despite their "horrible" characteristics, creative leaders have fun in their organizations because success is fun. Playfulness, according to McCall, does not necessarily lead to creativity, but successful, creative organizations have a great deal of fun because there is nothing more exciting than to succeed at what you are doing—surely an interesting view of leader behavior. Although work is not all "fun," hard work is the one quality that is most often rewarded, particularly in bureaucratic organizations.

Warren G. Bennis then examines another personal characteristic that is often ascribed to successful leaders. In "False Grit" (Chapter 22) he declares that the idea that one must be macho to get ahead in today's organization is just that—false grit. He argues that it is time to move beyond sex roles and sex differences to a more sophisticated understanding of women and men in organizations. We must recognize the organization as a culture that governs behavior because leadership success depends greatly upon being able to diagnose the organizational culture and to develop the flexibility to respond and initiate within that structure. There is nothing sex-related about it. It is a grave error, according to Bennis, to fall into the trap of attributing leadership success to toughness or softness, assertiveness or sensitivity, masculinity or femininity, or any other irrelevant set of criteria. As more women assume critical leadership roles, these stereotypes will disappear. We feel this is particularly true of military organizations.

In "How Do Leaders Get to Lead?" (Chapter 23), Michael M. Lombardo of the Center for Creative Leadership draws upon Tom Wolfe's *The Right Stuff* to make his point: If having skills and capabilities to become a leader is not as important as the opportunity to develop and demonstrate them, then many managers may never have a chance. By creating opportunities for more young managers and by avoiding premature decisions on managerial careers, organizations can increase their chances of developing the best possible leaders for the future. For a variety of reasons many managers who have the "right stuff" may never be presented with the background experiences and skills that would enable them to show it. Lombardo suggests that before deciding that some managers don't have it, superiors should first answer the question, "Have they ever been in a position where they could show it?"

Once again, we offer no prescriptions. Our thrust has been to highlight the ambiguities of leadership. We see the lack of a clear-cut definition as evincing the richness of leader development, particularly in the military. The ability to cope with uncertainties encompasses all of the attributes of leadership that have survived over time. That ability assumes flexibility in face of change in order to meet the opportunities and challenges of the future. Perhaps the basic tenets of leadership have not and will not be altered, but rather our ability to perpetuate leader success in the military will depend on how we encourage people to develop. Our image of leadership must be dynamic, reflecting the changing environments and the society in which we live.

19

Leadership
Through Followership

WILLIAM LITZINGER
THOMAS SCHAEFER

Not long ago, we posed a question to a group of officers, most of whom were on the West Point faculty, and many of whom were themselves graduates of the Academy. "Since developing leadership is what this place is all about," we asked, "how do you go about doing that task?" Their answer surprised us. "We begin by teaching them to be followers."

This insight prompted us to undertake a study, not of the nature of leadership (a subject which has been widely discussed), but of the notion that leadership may be chiefly an achievement of followers—that able leaders may emerge only from the ranks of able followers. Because of the genesis of our idea, we call it the West Point Thesis. Our concern is the developmental question of how leaders emerge and, particularly, how the mastery of followership may prepare and qualify one for leadership.

Contemporary authors seem to say little or nothing about what leaders must have done yesterday to become leaders today. Yet the ground of leadership can lie only in the leader's personal history.

Much earlier writers seem to have realized this. Plato's *Republic* analyzes what the king must do from his earliest years to become the sovereign. In the *Politics,* Aristotle laments the rarity of virtue among aspirants to statesmanship, and insists that only by training from youth may subjects grow to leadership. Much later, the philosopher Hegel required of the mature leader the most intimate understanding of his

Reprinted by permission from *Business Horizons,* 25:5 (September–October 1982), pp. 78–81. Copyright © 1982 by the Foundation for the School of Business at Indiana University.

followers, achievable only by passage through the experience of servitude. In his *Phenomenology of Mind,* Hegel so strongly affirms the mastery of followership as the sine qua non of leadership—our "West Point Thesis"—that an outline of his ideas is critical here.

Leadership/Followership

Hegel's "dialectic of master and slave" is a significant episode in the history of leadership theory. Leadership is possible, says Hegel, not only on the condition that followership has been learned, but on the more radical condition that the leader has known subjection and thralldom. The mature leader not only must have known the travail of the follower; he must here and now incorporate within himself all that the follower is. The school for leadership is indeed followership, a followership that is fully preserved within leadership, but transformed for having moved beyond itself. The leader, in short, must not merely have been a follower. He must, here and now, be a follower in the fullest sense; in a sense, paradoxically, that the follower cannot be. The leader is more a follower than the follower.

In the curious Hegelian dialectic, where opposites pass constantly into one another, the recognition that there is "followership in the leader" demands the recognition that there is "leadership in the follower." Believers in participative leadership would agree; "management by objectives," especially, through insisting that none manage "by objectives" who do not "control themselves," affirms a need for "leadership in the follower."[1] In MBO, leadership is a shared effort in which all, leader and follower alike, not only struggle for goals, but also set them. A central purpose of MBO is to substitute for the supervisor's role of judge that of "helper." This connects the "followership of the leader" with the "leadership of the follower." MBO receives "good grades" in the school of Hegel.

The paradoxes of Hegel's thought may be less unsettling when we recall how the Pope of the Catholic church designates his own leadership; he is "The Servant of the Servants of God." Where leader and follower alike are held to obedience to defined doctrine, neither may act on his own autonomous will alone. Leadership endures so long as it assumes a posture of humility, a spirit of followership.

Epitomizing the Group's Values

Argument from authority is notoriously weak. Plato and Aristotle, Hegel and others have propounded the "thesis," but does it prove out in practice?

In fact, many fine leaders *have* been excellent followers. The young Churchill distinguished himself as a faithful taker of orders, as did the young Bismarck, and the youthful Caesar. Even figures who are despised because they were not good followers of societal norms—such as Stalin, Hitler, Idi Amin—were good followers of some other code. Though he "marched to a different drummer," Hitler was an excellent "follower" of National Socialism in Germany. He was not above showing obsequiousness to those whom he judged to be arbiters of his rise to power. Mussolini, beloved of the Fascists, was a beast to the Allies, as was Ghengis Khan to the people of Europe.

The leader, then, appears to be a poor follower when judged by norms other than his own. When perceived in the context of his own organization, he is its obedient servant. Adversary organizations (gangs, revolutionary groups) demand more rigid conformity to group norms than do their legitimate counterparts. In prison societies, for example, an "inmate code" demands that leaders conform more perfectly to group norms than do their followers. Leaders who were notoriously "poor followers" of societal norms are typically heads of opposition groups that replaced, or threatened, another regime. They are, of course, poor followers of the enemy regime, but excellent followers of their own. "Mavericks," like Zapata, who became leaders, may appear to have been bad followers. They are, in fact, good followers of an orthodoxy other than the one by which the majority judges them. Zapata's organization exacted the strictest possible obedience from all, including Zapata himself.

Whether adversary or orthodox, an organization demands common acceptance of values. In this lies the link between obedience and command. The commander cannot break the link without destroying the legitimacy of his rule. Richard Nixon broke the link and had to relinquish command. In this sense, surely, followership is the school of leaders. To have internalized an organization's values, to have become, even, an embodiment of them, is to have the potential to be a leader. And, assuming an infallible awareness among the organization's members that one among them is an incarnation of its values, that member will be elected to leadership. No less certainly will abandonment of these values by the leader bring his decline and eventual fall.

There has been broad recognition of what we are calling the West Point Thesis throughout history. For centuries in China, leaders were chosen on the basis of their obedience to and knowledge of Confucian principles. The British Civil Service, like virtually all armies, has linked faithful service at the lower ranks to advancement to leadership. The idea, in fact, is inseparable from the conception of hierarchy. To stand at the pinnacle, one must have ascended some series of steps. Ascent demands not merely effort but upward progress. This occurs by gaining a foothold at each level, mastering each higher step. It requires the art of followership.

Applying the West Point Thesis

How might the West Point Thesis mesh with present-day concepts? Chester Barnard's well-known Acceptance Theory of Authority strongly asserts the followership-leadership link.

"The decision as to whether an order has authority or not lies with the persons to whom it is addressed, and does not reside in 'persons of authority' or those who issue these orders."[2]

With the ground of authority in the followers' granting or withholding obedience, leaders are constrained to lead in ways construed by followers to be consistent with the goals of the organization. "A person will accept a communication as authoritative only when . . . he believes that it is not inconsistent with the purposes of the organization," says Barnard. The leader, then, must also "follow," that is, follow goals as understood by those under him. Followers hold power over the leader since they judge whether the leader leads, that is, conducts them to their goal.

The leader turns out to *be* a follower, and "a truer follower than the followers" in that he is held to a greater fidelity in followership than are the followers. So great is the requirement of faithful followership for the leader that he ceases to exercise command the moment this "faith" is judged wanting by his followers. Such a situation arises when a command lies outside the "zone of indifference," that group of commands which are unquestionably acceptable. Presumably, if the follower perceives an order as conducive to the goal and *still* disobeys, the threat to organization is not nearly so great as it is when the leader commands action that does not conform to the goal. Again: mastery of followership is even more important in the leader than in the follower.

Barnard's ideas, then, support the West Point Thesis. Our thesis would illuminate the Acceptance Theory by focusing on the followership exercised by the leader. How is the leader's followership like, and how is it unlike, that of the followers? Pursuit of these questions could be fruitful in clarifying the Acceptance Theory, and in drawing out the meaning of the West Point Thesis. In any case, if followership as a subordinate is a propaedeutic for followership as a leader, then surely, as Aristotle claimed, "who would learn to command must first of all learn to obey." Theorists are well aware of the "reciprocality" between leader and follower, realizing that "poor" subordinates affect leadership style profoundly.

Yet the kind of follower the leader was may affect how he leads as significantly as the kinds of followers the leader now commands. We argue here that this dimension should be brought into any dialogue about leadership.

How might a more explicit awareness of "The West Point Thesis" enrich modern theories of leadership? We now grope for some idea of how "the thesis" might open some dimensions within existing theory.

"X- and Y-Style" Followership?

McGregor's distinction invites concern over which leadership style is best in particular circumstances. Whatever style may be appropriate, however, distinct styles of leadership must elicit distinct styles of followership. Appropriate types of followership will be expected as responses to, and support for, particular styles of leadership. Should we designate a follower's response to autocratic leaders as "X-style followership," or would the nuances of the concept require a separate designation? Whatever the answer, identifying followership styles seems a condition for understanding the kind of follower the leader was, which is crucial for knowing the kind of leader he is now. The most appropriate followership training needed for a specific style of leadership will probably depend on the style of leadership in question.

The ways in which the arts of followership and leadership are related will probably vary as a function of the degree of centralization, extent of specialization, type of technology, location on the product-life cycle trajectory, and other factors in the organization. A past mastery of followership probably would be increasingly important for leadership as one moves along a continuum from loosely controlled, decentralized organization to tightly controlled, centralized types. While the followership and leadership arts would prove always linked in some way, logic suggests that in the tightly structured organization the link would be very strong, while in the loosely structured organization, with decision-making at the lowest possible levels, the link would be found weaker.

Choice of a Followership Pattern

Does the "right" choice of a leadership pattern presuppose that subordinates must have learned to choose a "right" followership pattern? Is flexibility in the choice of "followership style" possible in anything like the way in which flexibility is possible in choosing one's leadership style? Although followership may be a necessary prelude to leadership in some organizations, is it necessary in all?

This last question prompts the reflection that, while a personal history of good followership may be one significant factor in leadership, it is not the final determinant of leadership success. Some mastery of followership is a *necessary* condition for leadership, but not a *sufficient* condition. A good record of followership is far from a guarantee that one will make a fine leader. Something more than being an "obedient servant" is needed to create the leader. There were others among the tribes of Israel as obedient as Moses, but none with his "fire."

Still, followership deserves a larger place among those items now attracting the attention of leadership theorists. The perennial affirmation of the idea through history should be enough to prompt more serious consideration of it. Its greater integration into contemporary theory will provide new insights into the phenomena of leadership.

Notes

1. In the chapter, "Management by Objectives and Self-Control" in *The Practice of Management* (New York: Harper and Row, 1954), Peter Drucker affirms this point strongly: "It [MBO] motivates the manager to action not because somebody tells him to do something . . . but because the objective needs of his task demand it. *He acts not because somebody wants him to but because he himself decides that he has to—he acts, in other words, as a free man.*" p. 136. (Italics are ours.)

2. Chester I. Barnard, *The Functions of the Executive* (Cambridge, Mass.: Harvard Press, 1938): 82.

20

Leadership
and Followership

JAMES MACGREGOR BURNS

Leadership is an aspect of power, but it is also a separate and vital process in itself.

Power over other persons, we have noted, is exercised when potential power wielders, motivated to achieve certain goals of their own, marshal in their power base resources (economic, military, institutional, or skill) that enable them to influence the behavior of respondents by activating motives of respondents relevant to those resources and goals. This is done in order to realize the purposes of the *power wielders, whether or not these are also the goals of the respondents.* Power wielders also exercise influence by mobilizing their own power base in such a way as to establish direct physical control over others' behavior, as in a war of conquest or through measures of harsh deprivation, but these are highly restricted exercises of power, dependent on certain times, cultures, and personalities, and they are often self-destructive and transitory.

Leadership over human beings is exercised when persons with certain motives and purposes mobilize, in competition or conflict with others, institutional, political, psychological, and other resources so as to arouse, engage, and satisfy the motives of followers. This is done in order to realize goals mutually held by *both* leaders and followers, as in Lenin's calls for peace, bread, and land. In brief, leaders with motive and power bases tap followers' motives in order to realize the purposes of both leaders and followers. Not only must motivation be relevant, as in power generally, but its purposes must be realized and satisfied. Leadership is exercised in a condition of *conflict* or *competition* in which leaders

Reprinted by permission from *Leadership* (New York: Harper and Row Publishers, Inc., 1978), pp. 18–23. Copyright © 1978 by James MacGregor Burns.

contend in appealing to the motive bases of potential followers. Naked power, on the other hand, admits of no competition or conflict—there is no engagement.

Leaders are a particular kind of power holder. Like power, leadership is relational, collective, and purposeful. Leadership shares with power the central function of achieving purpose. But the reach and domain of leadership are, in the short range at least, more limited than those of power. Leaders do not obliterate followers' motives though they may arouse certain motives and ignore others. They lead other creatures, not things (and lead animals only to the degree that they recognize animal motives—i.e., leading cattle to shelter rather than to slaughter). To control *things*—tools, mineral resources, money, energy—is an act of power, not leadership, for things have not motives. Power wielders may treat people as things. Leaders may not.

All leaders are actual or potential power holders, but not all power holders are leaders.

These definitions of power and of leadership differ from those that others have offered. Lasswell and Kaplan hold that power must be relevant to people's valued things; I hold that it must be relevant to the *power wielder's* valued things and may be relevant to the *recipient's* needs or values only as necessary to exploit them. Kenneth Janda defines power as "the ability to cause other persons to adjust their behavior in conformance with communicated behavior patterns." I agree, assuming that those behavior patterns aid the purpose of the power wielder. According to Andrew McFarland, "If the leader causes changes that he intended, he has exercised power; if the leader causes changes that he did not intend or want, he has exercised influence, but not power. . . ." I dispense with the concept of influence as unnecessary and unparsimonious. For me the leader is a very special, very circumscribed, but potentially the most effective of power holders, judged by the degree of intended "real change" finally achieved. Roderick Bell et al. contend that power is a relationship rather than an entity—an entity being something that "could be smelled and touched, or stored in a keg"; while I agree that power is a relationship, I contend that the relationship is one in which some entity—part of the "power base"—plays an indispensable part, whether that keg is a keg of beer, of dynamite, or of ink.

The crucial variable, again, is *purpose*. Some define leadership as leaders making followers do what *followers* would not otherwise do, or as leaders making followers do what the *leaders* want them to do; I define leadership as leaders inducing followers to act for certain goals that represent the values and the motivations—the wants and needs, the aspirations and expectations—*of both leaders and followers*. And the genius of leadership lies in the manner in which leaders see and act on their own and their followers' values and motivations. Leadership, unlike naked power-wielding, is thus inseparable from followers' needs and goals. The essence of the leader-follower relation is the interaction of persons with different levels of motivations and of power potential, including skill, in pursuit of a common or at least joint purpose. That interaction, however, takes two fundamentally different forms. The first I will call *transactional* leadership. . . . Such leadership occurs when one person takes the initiative in making contact with others for the purpose of an exchange of valued things. The exchange could be economic or political or psychological in nature: a swap of goods or of one good for money; a trading of votes between candidate and citizen or between legislators; hospitality to another person in exchange for willingness to listen to one's troubles. Each party to the bargain is conscious of the power resources and attitudes of the other. Each person recognizes the other as a *person*. Their purposes are related, at least to the extent that the purposes stand within the bargaining process and can be advanced by maintaining that process. But beyond this the relationship does not go. The bargainers have no enduring purpose that holds them together; hence they may go their separate ways. A leadership act took place, but it was not one that binds leader and follower together in a mutual and continuing pursuit of a higher purpose.

Contrast this with *transforming* leadership. Such leadership occurs when one or more persons *engage* with others in such a way that leaders and followers raise one another to higher levels of motivation and morality. . . . Their purposes, which might have started out as separate but related, as in the case of transactional leadership, become fused. Power bases are linked not as counterweights but as mutual support for common purpose. Various names are used for such leadership, some of them derisory: elevating, mobilizing, inspiring, exalting, uplifting, preaching, exhorting, evangelizing. The relationship can be moralistic, of course. But transforming leadership ultimately becomes *moral* in that it raises the level of human conduct and ethical aspiration of both leader and led, and thus it has a transforming effect on both. Perhaps the best modern example is Gandhi, who aroused and elevated the hopes and demands of millions of Indians and whose life and personality were enhanced in the process. Transcending leadership is a dynamic leadership in the sense that the leaders throw themselves into a relationship with followers who will feel "elevated" by it and often become more active themselves, thereby creating new cadres of leaders. Transcending leadership is leadership *engagé*. Naked power-wielding can be neither transactional nor transforming; only leadership can be.

Leaders and followers may be inseparable in function, but they are not the same. The leader takes the initiative in making the leader-led connection; it is the leader who creates the links that allow communication and exchange to take place. An office seeker does this in accosting a voter on the street, but if the voter espies and accosts the politician, the voter is assuming a leadership function, at least for that brief moment. The leader is more skillful in evaluating followers' motives, anticipating their responses to an initiative, and estimating their power bases, than the reverse. Leaders continue to take the major part in maintaining and effectuating the relationship with followers and will have the major role in ultimately carrying out the combined purpose of leaders and followers. Finally, and most important by far, leaders address themselves to followers' wants, needs, and other motivations, as well as to their own, and thus they serve as an *independent force in changing the makeup of the followers' motive base through gratifying their motives.*

Certain forms of power and certain forms of leadership are near-extremes on the power continuum. One is the kind of absolute power that, Lord Acton felt, "corrupts absolutely." It also coerces absolutely. The essence of this kind of power is the capacity of power wielders, given the necessary motivation, to override the motive and power bases of their targets. Such power objectifies its victims; it literally turns them into objects, like the inadvertent weapon tester in Mtésa's court. Such power wielders, as well, are objectified and dehumanized. Hitler, according to Richard Hughes, saw the universe as containing no persons other than himself, only "things." The ordinary citizen in Russia, says a Soviet linguist and dissident, does not identify with his government. "With us, it is there, like the wind, like a wall, like the sky. It is something permanent, unchangeable. So the individual acquiesces, does not dream of changing it—except a few, few people...."

At the other extreme is leadership so sensitive to the motives of potential followers that the roles of leader and follower become virtually interdependent. Whether the leadership relationship is transactional or transforming, in it motives, values, and goals of leader and led have merged. It may appear that at the other extreme from the raw power relationship, dramatized in works like Arthur Koestler's *Darkness at Noon* and George Orwell's *1984,* is the extreme of leadership-led merger dramatized in novels about persons utterly dependent on parents, wives, or lovers. Analytically these extreme types of relationships are not very perplexing. To watch one person absolutely dominate another is horrifying; to watch one person disappear, his motives and values submerged into those of another to the point of loss of individuality, is saddening. But puzzling out the nature of these extreme relationships is not intellectually challenging because each in its own way lacks the qualities of complexity and conflict. Submersion of one personality in another is not genuine merger based on mutual respect. Such submersion is an example of brute power subtly applied, perhaps with the acquiescence of the victim.

More complex are relationships that lie between these poles of brute power and wholly reciprocal leadership-followership. Here empirical and theoretical questions still perplex both the analysts and the practitioners of power. One of these concerns the sheer measurement of power (or leadership). Traditionally we measure power resources by calculating each one and adding them up: constituency support plus access to leadership plus financial resources plus skill plus "popularity" plus access to information, etc., all in relation to the strength of opposing forces, similarly computed. But these calculations omit the vital factor of motivation and purpose and hence fall of their own weight. Another controversial measurement device is *reputation*. Researchers seek to learn from informed observers their estimates of the power or leadership role and resources of visible *community* leaders (projecting this into national arenas of power is a formidable task). Major questions arise as to the reliability of the estimates, the degree of agreement between interviewer and interviewee over their definition of power and leadership, the transferability of power from one area of decisionmaking to another. Another device for studying power and leadership is *linkage theory,* which requires elaborate mapping of communication and other interrelations among power holders in different spheres, such as the economic and the military. The difficulty here is that communication, which may expedite the processes of power and leadership, is not a substitute for them.

My own measurement of power and leadership is simpler in concept but no less demanding of analysis: *power and leadership are measured by the degree of production of intended effects.* This need not be a theoretical exercise. Indeed, in ordinary political life, the power resources and the motivations of presidents and prime ministers and political parties are measured by the extent to which presidential promises and party programs are carried out. Note that the variables are the double ones of *intent* (a function of motivation) and of *capacity* (a function of power base), but the test of the extent and quality of power and leadership is the degree of *actual accomplishment* of the promised change.

Other complexities in the study of power and leadership are equally serious. One is the extent to which power and leadership are exercised not by positive action but by *inaction* or *nondecision*. Another is that power and leadership are often exercised not directly on targets but indirectly, and perhaps through multiple channels, on multiple targets.

We must ask not only whether P has the power to do X to R, but whether P can induce or force R to do Y to Z. The existence of power and leadership in the form of a stream of multiple direct and indirect forces operating over time must be seen as part of the broader sequences of historical causation. Finally, we must acknowledge the knotty problem of events of history that are beyond the control of identifiable persons capable of foreseeing developments and powerful enough to influence them and hence to be held accountable for them. We can only agree with C. Wright Mills that these are matters of fate rather than power or leadership.

We do well to approach these and other complexities of power and leadership with some humility as well as a measure of boldness. We can reject the "gee whiz" approach to power that often takes the form of the automatic presumption of "elite control" of communities, groups, institutions, entire nations. Certain concepts and techniques of the "elitist" school of power are indispensable in social and political analysis, but "elitism" is often used as a concept that *presupposes* the existence of the very degree and kind of power that is to be estimated and analyzed. Such "elite theorists" commit the gross error of equating power and leadership with the assumed power bases of preconceived leaders and power holders, without considering the crucial role of *motivations* of leaders and followers. Every good detective knows that one must look for the motive as well as the weapon.

21

Conjecturing About Creative Leaders

MORGAN W. McCALL, JR.

I will frankly admit to you that both the terms creative and leadership confuse me. I have learned to be relatively comfortable with some of the ambiguities and outrages of leadership research, but I have always been afraid to confront the nebulousness of creativity, much less to try to put creativity and leadership together. So it is my hope to share a few thoughts with you, not based in science. Abraham Maslow once said that "science is a means whereby noncreative people can create." So I will avoid data. My intention here is to stir up some controversy, and I think that is almost assured. I am certainly not giving prescriptions; in fact, maybe you should do the opposite of what I suggest if you want to be a creative leader.

In preparing for this talk, I drew heavily on Karl Weick (1974, 1976, 1978) and Michael Cohen and Jim March (1974), who to me are among the most creative of the social scientists writing today. I'll try to give them credit where it is due. I also drew on John Steinbeck (1962) who is one of the most creative persons whom I have ever encountered in print. And finally, I drew on David Ogilvy (1965) who is the head of a major advertising firm and has written some very interesting things.

What I am going to be talking about is leaders in organizations. I am going to be talking about managers, administrators, presidents, foremen, supervisors; I am not going to be talking about the research and development types, or isolated staff specialists, or independent creative people. What I am going to do is to try to reflect on what creative leadership might be in a nonreflective, fast-paced, constrained, goal-oriented system. In a real live organization what can creative leadership possibly mean?

Reprinted by permission from *The Journal of Creative Behavior*, 14:4 (1979), pp. 225–234.

I think one way to start is with the Second Law of Thermodynamics. Entropy is a natural law that things tend to run down, fly apart, return to their natural disorganized state. One way to look at managers is as manifestations of negative entropy, because managers are the glue that keeps systems from flying apart, running down, and disorganizing.

Cohen and March studied the presidents of 42 universities. What they had to say about the lives of those people is relevant to other managers as well. They described them as reactive, parochial, conventional, and living an illusion (Cohen & March, 1974). By reactive, Cohen and March could be talking about Warren Bennis (he was then President of the University of Cincinnati) who described some 500 interest groups with which he had to deal. Most of his job was reacting to the demands and concerns of other people. By parochial, they mean that if you look at where college presidents come from, you discover that they have similar backgrounds, similar experiences, and relatively narrow views of the world. If you look at upwardly mobile corporate managers, some of those same characteristics apply. They mean conventional in the sense that many people have expectations about what a president, or manager, or chief executive officer will do; people have certain expectations of what leaders will do and they tend to be conventional expectations. Leaders will handle the budget, will administer, will be fair, and so forth. Finally, the illusion Cohen and March write about is that presidents think they have a lot of control, when the reality is that presidents have only modest control over events. The main things affecting universities are far beyond the power of any individual to do much about. They may be things as esoteric as the birthrate 20 years ago. And the same thing is true for leaders of corporations, and particularly for the President of the United States.

Leaders work in an environment that sees creativity as a threat, especially creativity defined as a deviant response. The deviant response is something that could ruin an organization as easily as it could move it forward. So organizations tend to be designed for survival, not for creativity. And managers are imbedded in an organization that runs contrary to most of the things that we know about creativity. In fact, most organizations might have a sign that says "stamp out creativity." Many organizations deal with creativity by isolating it, controlling it, judging it, and, at times, even eliminating it.

What is a creative leader in this kind of environment, and what is that creative leader trying to do? It is probably useful to describe a simple series of steps that creative leaders are involved with. One thing that they are trying to do is generate, or stimulate others to generate original, creative ideas, and so come up with new processes, new ways of doing things. The second thing that they have to do as managers is to find out somehow what all these ideas are, collect them in some way, and then evaluate them, because in an on-going organization you can't just let ideas float around indefinitely. Then, having evaluated and picked a few of them, creative leaders have to convince the organization that an idea is worth the investment and worth the trouble to implement. Now that is a very simple model, not profound; but I would suggest to you, for the sake of heresy, that there are already so many ideas, and so much information, and so many different opinions running around in organizations that the real challenge of creative leadership is in the last two steps. Nonetheless, there is some value in trying to produce more ideas; so how might we describe one of these creative leaders in an ongoing organization? I am going to describe creative leaders as being crafty, grouchy, dangerous, feisty, contrary, inconsistent, evangelistic, prejudiced, and spineless. (I'm indebted to Karl Weick [1976] who used a similar series of adjectives to describe organizations.) Let me try to justify these descriptions one at a time.

Crafty

My feeling is that creativity itself, and certainly the evaluation of whether something is good or bad, involves a value judgment. If I were to put up six pieces of modern art and ask you which were creative and which were good, I would get a lot of differences of opinion. So the first thing about creativity is that, because value judgments are involved, people will disagree about whether an idea is good or bad, or whether it is even creative. The second aspect is that organizations are political systems. The evidence is overwhelming; all of you live in organizations, and you see the political activities all around you. So you put those two together, and you have a value judgment being made in a political system. That is why I suggest to you that creative leaders are crafty. There is a good deal of cunning involved, first in helping others to create something, and, second, in being able to create something oneself in a political environment. This means that leaders out there who are creative are, in fact, able to negotiate very well; they are able to circumvent constraints; they are very sensitive to the tactical issues involved in the use of power. Although power is a different topic, I don't think you can talk about creative leadership in organizations without talking about power, because power is unevenly distributed; and whether or not the people who are trying to push through a creative idea have power is going to make a lot of difference in their effectiveness. The literature on power includes a variety of tactics, some subtle, some blatant—and I suspect that creative leaders are well versed in how to use the power that they have.

Another interesting aspect of craftiness is that, in organizations, managers have to survive failures. We have interviewed a lot of managers, and we have discovered that a manager is usually permitted one or two boners. After that he or she is in trouble. The nature of creativity requires taking a series of half-baked ideas, pushing for them, and getting them implemented. Because of power structures, if creative leaders are to survive, they have to be able to disassociate with failures and associate with successes. Thus, creative leaders are probably manipulative, even Machiavellian. They probably use structure, create structure, disband structure, and change structure. They probably also use people; in short, they are probably extremely political.

Grouchy

I suspect that complacency is the enemy of creativity. There has been a lot of research done on the issue of satisfaction, and some people have claimed that if your employees are satisfied, your employees will be more productive. The accumulated research evidence is heavily against that. There are few consistent relationships between the satisfaction of individual employees and their productivity. Sometimes the relationship is negative, sometimes it is positive, but most of the time there is no relationship at all. In fact, when there is a causal relationship between employee satisfaction and performance, it usually goes the other way: high performing employees are more satisfied; more satisfied employees are not necessarily more productive. So I would suspect that our grouchy, creative leader can be quite demanding and controlling, and may, in fact, have exorbitant standards.

This brings us to the issue of complaints. One of Maslow's interesting suggestions is that the number of complaints in an organization is relatively constant; that no matter how good you are to people, the number of complaints will remain the same. What happens is that complaints will change in level. Karl Weick elaborated on this idea when he suggested that we consider the level of complaint in an organization. If people are complaining about conditions of work and job security, you have a relatively low level of complaint going on in your organization. However, if people are complaining about not getting praised, or about threats to their self-esteem, then you have a higher level of complaint. It means you have evolved as an organization. Weick goes on to say that in the effective organization, a large number of complaints focus on perfection, truth, beauty, and other higher ideals. To give you an example of what I mean, I'll quote from Maslow (cited by Weick, 1976):

To complain about the garden programs in the city where I live, to have committees heatedly coming in and saying that the rose gardens in the parks are not sufficiently cared for, is in itself a wonderful thing; because it indicates the height of life at which the complainers are living. To complain about rose gardens means that your belly is full, that you have a good roof over your head, that your furnace is working, that you are not afraid of bubonic plague, that you are not afraid of assassination, that the police and fire departments work well and many other pre-conditions are already satisfied. This is the point, the high level complaint is not to be taken simply like any other complaint. It must be used to indicate all the pre-conditions which have been satisfied in order to make the height of his complaint theoretically possible.

So we may have some grouches out there who are trying to keep people from being complacent by moving them to a different level of noncomplacency, if such a thing is possible.

We have done some research using Mintzberg's ten managerial roles. One, leadership, concerns what is called "consideration and initiating structure" in our jargon, and means creating a warm, supportive climate for subordinates, structuring their work, and setting goals. This is the only one of the ten roles negatively related to both level in the organization and promotion rate within the organization in a sample of 2,700 managers. I suspect that creative leaders are, in fact, a bit grouchy, that they do prod people, and that they probably won't worry as much about the satisfaction of their people as might be suspected.

Dangerous

From an organizational perspective, creative leaders are indeed dangerous. As I said before, creative ideas are something new, something untried, something different that a leader is going to get implemented. In most organizations implementing a major new idea means millions of dollars, new plants, commitments for years ahead. So new ideas represent a threat to organization survival. Take, for example, a new technology. An organization taking advantage of new technology may have to build a plant before they even know if the new product will sell. Failure might sink the organization; success could make it great. Maybe that is why research and development tends to be isolated on a hill somewhere. In most companies they do that; they build a little cage and put all their creative people in it, and then when an idea comes out they take it back to the management committee and evaluate it in the cold light of day-to-day realities. But creative leaders can be dangerous because they tend to take risks first and ask questions later.

From an organizational point of view, the unpredictability of this can be disturbing.

Feisty

I suspect that creative leaders deliberately create conflict—not to increase competition necessarily but to create sparks that contain ideas. If you have ever read Oliver Wendell Holmes, you may remember the notion of the dice and marbles (Weick, 1974). You can take two positions and visualize them as dice. They have sharp corners and they are very distinct. The noncreative leader takes a rasp and files all the sharp corners off so that they roll around, and anybody who wants to can roll them. In fact, some people have argued that compromise is the worst possible strategy because the result is the most inane parts of two ideas—the parts that everybody can agree on; you lose what was really dramatically different about them. I suspect that creative leaders, rather than trying to suppress conflict, sometimes generate it and often try to control and direct it. The real challenge is to make that conflict useful.

Another reason that creative leaders may be feisty is that in an organization, it is tough to get resources, so they are fighting for resources and the power to implement ideas. To protect people out there having weird ideas takes a lot of work—it takes some fighting. Some of the managers that we talked to, the ones that struck us as creative, markedly loved to straighten out messes, to get involved in conflicts, and make conflicts productive.

Contrary

By contrary I simply mean that some of the creative leaders out there must be contrary to our laws of human nature. Let me give you five of these contradictions out of Cohen and March (1974). Creative leaders might treat:

1. goals as hypotheses;
2. intuition as reality;
3. hypocrisy as transition;
4. memory as an enemy; and
5. experience as theory.

Most of us like to have a concrete goal, something that we are working for; but apparently some people, who are a little bit more creative than most of us, treat goals as hypotheses. They are not wedded to a particular point of view, a particular thing that they are after.

As for treating intuition as reality—intuition can be viewed as an excuse for doing something you can't justify. However, creative leaders see it as a real factor and will go on a hunch. As I said before, they will take a risk and see what happens: they'll learn by experience.

Creative leaders treat hypocrisy as transition. Now there is a thought-provoking idea. Most of us in our lives try to balance our attitudes and values with what we do. We are uncomfortable when we believe one thing and do a different thing. We try to balance. It is called "cognitive balance" in the jargon. If I like Mary, and Mary likes John, then I want to like John—because if I don't I have an imbalance. Cohen and March argue that when people behave differently than they believe they are ripe for change. And there is good research evidence to say that behavior creates attitudes, not the reverse. What you think is a poor predictor of what you do, but what you do is an excellent predictor of what you will eventually think. So creative leaders may be out there trying to get people to behave differently and, in so doing, may be creating new values.

Memory is treated as an enemy. Habit, folklore, and myth are as prevalent in organizations as anywhere else, so creative leaders try not to be susceptible to them. And finally, creative leaders treat experience as a theory. They act before thinking rather than think before acting. So there are five ways in which creative leaders may be contrary.

Inconsistent

We envision managers having things highly integrated, with lots of rules, processes, and control. The survival of the organization depends on its different pieces being interdependent and being controlled and being watched. However, creative leaders may try to keep the system flexible so the different pieces can do different things. John Steinbeck (1962) has talked about that, and he puts it in terms of integration. As we integrate organizations—make them more interdependent, more controlled—we drive out the possibility that different parts of the organization can do things differently. Steinbeck says:

> We thought that perhaps our species thrives best and most creatively in a state of semi-anarchy, governed by loose rules and half-practiced mores. To this we added the premise that overintegration in human groups might parallel the law in paleontology that over-armor or over-ornamentation are symptoms of decay and disappearance. Indeed, we thought, over-integration *might be* the symptom of human decay. We thought: there is

no creative unit in the human save the individual working alone. In pure creativeness, in art, in music, in mathematics, there are no true collaborations. The creative principle is a lonely and an individual matter. Groups can correlate, investigate, and build, but we could not think of any group that has ever created or invented anything. Indeed, the first impulse of the group seems to be to destroy the creation and the creator. But integration, or the designed group, seems to be highly vulnerable.

He then goes on to give some examples which suggest that we don't want integrated systems, and then says:

Consider the blundering anarchic system of the United States; the stupidity of some of its lawmakers, the violent reaction, the slowness of its ability to change. Twenty-five key men destroyed could make the Soviet Union stagger, but we could lose our Congress, our President, and our general staff and nothing much would have happened. We could go right on. In fact we might be better for it.

In any case I suspect that creative leaders might have to fight the urge to integrate, to solidify, to make everything interdependent. They want to keep the pieces loose enough so that they could lose a few and the organization would still survive.

Evangelistic

Karl Weick once said, "Leaders are evangelists, not accountants." By that he meant that creative leaders manipulate symbols for the rest of the organization. If you walk into an organization that is bottom-line oriented, what you are walking into is a symbol; this is the way we punctuate reality in this organization, this is the reality we strive for. Creative leaders create the myths and symbols by which other people operate. In that sense, they are evangelists, preaching a cause, saying it is alright to be creative, saying that the organization prefers this to that, using a reward system to make people who do something bizarre-but-effective a symbol for the whole organization. It is the suggestion box raised to a level at which it becomes a symbolic part of the people in the organization.

Prejudiced

When I suggest that creative leaders are prejudiced, I don't mean sex bias or race bias; they may or may not be prejudiced in those ways. I do suspect, though, that creative leaders are prejudiced about competence. They use it and discriminate with it. If they have different kinds of people, they match them to jobs so that the creative ones are not mixed in with the Philistines. There is some evidence in the leadership research that leaders rarely treat all of their subordinates the same way. They have in-groups and out-groups, and when you look at their relationships with individual subordinates, they are, in fact, discriminating. There is a quote from Ogilvy that I want to share with you. At one time he worked in a French kitchen and apparently the head chef was a real tyrant. Ogilvy (1965) said this about him:

> M. Pitard did not tolerate incompetence. He knew that it is demoralizing for professionals to work alongside incompetent amateurs. I saw him fire three pastry cooks in a month for the same crime: They could not make the caps on their brioches rise evenly. Mr. Gladstone would have applauded such ruthlessness; he held that the first essential for a prime minister is to be a good butcher. M. Pitard taught me exorbitant standards of service.

While creative leaders are prejudiced, they are not at all egalitarian. This idea has been expanded on by Craig Lundberg (1978) who has talked about Lieutenants, about how effective leaders in organizations find an ally with whom they work closely. They may exclude others; they may fight the selection system. So I suggest that any creative leaders out there would be far from egalitarian or participative in the way they make decisions.

Spineless

One of the crucial things about living in a complex organizational environment and being able to deal with it is to be a listener, an absorber, a monitor. The data we have indicates a positive correlation between monitoring information and promotion rate in the organization. In a recent essay, Karl Weick (1978) makes a point about managers being a media. To demonstrate this point, he uses a contour gauge. You can set it down on a corner, press on it, and you'll come away with a precise image of the corner. Weick elaborates on this analogy by pointing out that each one of the little spines in the contour gauge operates independently of the others. In much the same way, he says, creative leaders are out there absorbing all kinds of different things, but not necessarily connecting them. The interesting irony of all this is that creative leaders are also able to act. They can turn their absorbing, monitoring functions around and use all that differentiation to make something happen. It is almost like being on the other side of the contour gauge when you push it down.

So, these are some hypothetical characteristics of creative leaders: they may be crafty, grouchy, dangerous, feisty, contrary, evangelistic, prejudiced, and spineless.

I suspect that some of the creative leaders in organizations would appear two-faced to an outsider, because on the one hand, they are playing the traditional organizational game so that they can stay in the system and continue to do something with it, while on the other hand they are moving ahead, gaining credits, and being generally outrageous.

Finally, I believe that people have fun in organizations in spite of these "horrible" characteristics of creative leaders. My proposition would be that success is the fun. Playfulness does not necessarily lead to creativity, but successfully creative organizations have a great deal of fun because there is nothing more exciting than to succeed at what you are doing.

Let me close by reminding you that I started out with Cohen and March describing managers as reactive, parochial, conventional, and living an illusion. Because I think there are many oxymorons in creative leadership, and because the nature of creativity is making opposites fit and frames of reference clash, what we really may be talking about is reactive reflection, broad parochialism, unorthodox conventionalism, and solid illusions.

References

Cohen, D. & March, J. G. *Leadership and ambiguity.* NYC: McGraw-Hill, 1974.

Lundberg, C. The unreported leadership research of Dr. G. Hypothetical. In McCall, M. & Lombardo, M. (eds.), *Leadership: where else can we go?* Durham, NC: Duke University Press, 1978.

Ogilvy, D. M. The creative chef. In Steiner, G. A. (ed.), *The creative organization.* Chicago: University of Chicago Press, 1965.

Steinbeck, J. *The log from the sea of Cortez.* NYC: Viking, 1962.

Thomas, L. *The lives of a cell.* NYC: Bantam, 1974.

Weick, K. E. Reward concepts: dice or marbles. Presented at the School of Industrial and Labor Relations, Cornell University, Ithaca, NY, 1974.

Weick, K. E. On re-punctuating the problem of organizational effectiveness. Paper presented at a conference on organizational effectiveness at Carnegie-Mellon University, Pittsburgh, 1976.

Weick, K. E. The spines of leaders. In McCall, M. & Lombardo, M. (eds.), *Leadership: where else can we go?* Durham, NC: Duke University Press, 1978.

22

False Grit

WARREN G. BENNIS

There's a mythology of competence going around that says the way for a woman to succeed is to act like a man. One proponent of this new "man-scam" is Marcille Gray Williams, author of *The New Executive Woman: A Guide to Business Success,* who advises women to "learn to control your tears. Mary Tyler Moore may be able to get away with it, but you can't. Whatever you do, don't cry." Women in increasing numbers are enrolling in a variety of training and retraining programs which tell them that if they dress properly (dark gray and dark blue) and talk tough enough (to paraphrase John Wayne, "A woman's got to do what a woman's got to do"), they'll take another step up the ladder of success. Which explains why training programs for women (and men too) have become a booming growth industry.

What we see today are all kinds of workshops and seminars where women undergo a metaphorical sex change, where they acquire a tough-talking, no-nonsense, sink-or-swim macho philosophy. They're told to take on traits just the opposite of those Harvard psychoanalyst Dr. Helen H. Tartakoff assigns to women: "endowments which include the capacity for mutuality as well as for maternity . . . for creativity as well as receptivity. In short," she sums up, "women's feminine heritage, as caretaker and peacemaker, contains the potential for improving the human condition."

Ironically, men are simultaneously encouraged to shed the same masculine character traits that women are trying to imitate through their own form of nonassertiveness and in sensitivity training programs. So it's O.K., even better than O.K., for old Charlie to cry in his office. How marvelous. How liberating. Women impersonate the macho male stereotype and men impersonate the countermacho stereotype of the women.

Reprinted with permission from *Savvy,* 1:6 (June 1980), pp. 43–47.

It's time to move beyond "sex differences" and "sex roles," beyond the myths of female and male impersonations, to a more sophisticated understanding of women in organizations. Instead of retraining women *as individuals* to acquire appropriate dress or assertiveness, we have to face up to the organization as a culture—as a system which governs behavior. For, according to research findings, the impact of the organization on success or failure is much greater than that of personality characteristics—or, for that matter, sex differences.

This realization avoids the "blame the victim" approach which explains executive success in terms of individual dispositions (whether created by temperament or socialization). The villains of the piece turn out to be complex organizations, whose power structures and avenues for opportunity routinely disadvantage those people not particularly sophisticated about how such organizations work. More often than not, those people are women, since they tend to have had less experience in learning the ropes of organizational life. This perspective suggests a different kind of strategy for the elimination of sex discrimination than the "sex roles" school of thought. Instead of retraining women (or men, for that matter) and trapping all concerned in a false dream, it's necessary to take a look at the very nature of complex organizations. It is these systems and the roles within them that women must understand. And it is, at bottom, these complex organizations which should bear the burden of change, not the women subjected to weekend bashes where male-chauvinist Pygmalion games are played to the tune of "Why Can't a Woman Be More Like a Man?"

Alfred North Whitehead cautioned us wisely: "Seek simplicity and then distrust it." To put it kindly, the trouble with too many sex-difference, sex-role training programs is that they seek simplicity but forget to distrust it. And no wonder. Simplicity is easier. It's easier to transform individuals than to transform creaky, complex systems with their bureaucratic sludge and impenetrable webs of self-interest. It's a lot easier to change an Eliza Doolittle than Victorian England's class structure. The trouble is: When Eliza returns to her old habitat in Covent Garden, the old familiar behaviors return almost immediately, and everything she learned from Professor Higgins is extinguished in days. This "fade out" effect has occurred wherever individuals are trained or re-educated outside the organizational context. What's easier can be dangerously off target.

When I discussed this with Boris Yavitz, Dean of Columbia University's Graduate School of Business, he told me, "What I fear is that women will try to take on the attributes of men in a wrong-headed attempt to disprove the old stereotypes." The women he sees in his program have all the intellectual equipment necessary for success in business; they're motivated, directed, purposeful. "We never set out eight years ago to bring in women by making it easy," says Yavitz, "and yet in the last eight years our female enrollment has increased from 5 percent to 40 percent of the school. We are holding exactly the same standards we have always held, and the women are doing superbly." As they are, by the way, in all top graduate schools of management. M.I.T. accepts from 25 percent to 40 percent as do Harvard, Stanford, Chicago and Wharton, the bastions of management-education excellence in this country. Women's competence is well documented. From all reports, they are capable on the job—and, Yavitz adds, "They prove their competence without the need for sporting hair on their chests."

Organizations, thankfully, are too complicated for the popular delusion of simplicity and certainty, the false-grit tunnel vision of a John Wayne. The fact is that there is no one set of rules, of programmed behavior, dress or skills that can apply to women or men in their attempts to succeed. Perhaps the most convincing documentation of this point is a study of 1,800 successful managers recently completed by The American Management Associations (A.M.A.). From this study, a profile emerges: Effective managers are social initiators; they anticipate problems and possible solutions. They build alliances, bring people together, develop networks. Their competencies cluster in several areas: *social-emotional maturity* (composed of such traits as self-control, spontaneity, perceptual objectivity, accurate self-assessment, stamina, adaptability); *entrepreneurial abilities* (efficiency, productivity); *intellectual abilities* (logical thought, conceptual ability, the diagnostic use of ideas and memory); and *interpersonal abilities* (self-presentation, interest in the development of others, concern with impact, oral communication skills, the use of socialized power, and concern with relationships).

The A.M.A. study is, without question, some of the most complete, systematic research ever undertaken on the attributes of the good manager. I see nothing in its findings that would give men or women (with whatever "natural endowments" one attributes to sex roles) an edge. I would also wager that most astute observers of the managerial landscape would agree with the study. Yavitz, for one, describes the effective manager as possessing "the ability for true communication—I don't mean the glib view, that you're communicating when you make a great pitch." He insists that two-way communication is imperative:

A manager must be perceptive, must understand what she's hearing, and then be able to convey the ideas clearly to others . . . must be flexible enough to acknowledge that there are competing constituencies and must be sensitive enough to listen to the emotion and spirit behind the words as well as to the content . . . and she must be able to synthesize what she's heard, to put together something as close to the optimal solution as possible, something that makes sense.

The manager must be able to persuade, explain, convince others why this solution is more sensible and beneficial for the whole cluster of constituencies than another solution. I surmise that a high sense of responsibility and commitment, ability to cope with ambiguity, and a continuing sense of curiosity and willingness to learn are critical attributes for the successful manager.

Does either sex have a monopoly on the constellation of traits identified by the A.M.A. research or by Dean Yavitz?

A better explanation of success, it seems to me, is that those who are favorably placed in organizational structures are more likely to be successful, independent of gender, than those less favorably placed. By "favorably placed" I mean: 1) having the support of one's subordinates, 2) having clear goals and a similarly clear path to them and 3) being empowered by the organization with appropriate means to reward and punish one's subordinates. When these conditions are present, we have what scholars refer to as "situational favorableness."

Complex organizations vary enormously. Specifically, they vary with respect to their "cultures." Some organizations are formalistic in nature, rigid, hierarchical; others are collegial, relying on agreement and consensus; while still others tend to be personalistic, concerned with the self-actualization of their employees. Within organizations, too, there can be great cultural differences. Just compare Bell Telephone's Murray Hill Labs with its international headquarters at Basking Ridge, New Jersey. It's hard to find a man without a beard or with a tie at the Bell Labs at Murray Hill, and equally hard to find a man without a tie and with a beard at Basking Ridge. Table 1 contrasts the values and behavior of three types of organizational systems.

Success depends greatly on being able to diagnose the particular organizational culture within which one is embedded and to develop the flexibility to respond and initiate within that structure. There's nothing sex-related about it. All that's required are the knowledge and the personal skills that most famous of all salesmen, Professor Harold Hill of "The Music Man," expounded: "Gotta know the territory."

From Hobbes to Freud, the special character of Western (most especially American) development has been an awareness of the heterogeneity of human experience and an accentuated consciousness of the power of the individual to overcome or shape his circumstances.

TABLE 1. Three Types of Organizational Cultures

	Formalistic	*Collegial*	*Personalistic*
Basis for decision	Direction from authority	Discussion, agreement	Directions from within
Form of control	Rules, laws, rewards, punishments	Interpersonal, group commitments	Actions aligned with self-concept
Source of power	Superior	What "we" think and feel	What *I* think and feel
Desired end	Compliance	Consensus	Self-actualization
To be avoided	Deviation from authoritative direction; taking risks	Failure to reach consensus	Not being "true to oneself"
Time perspective	Future	Near future	Now
Position relative to others	Hierarchical	Peer	Individual
Human relationships	Structured	Group oriented	Individually oriented
Basis for growth	Following the established order	Peer group membership	Acting on awareness of self

As Isaiah Berlin shows in his *Russian Thinkers,* the Russian tendency has always been for the system—always the senior partner to self-affirmation—to move toward hegemony. In the United States, that partnership has been reversed, with self-affirmation in the ascendence. There is, as Mounier, the French political writer, has warned us, a "madness in both those who treat the world as a dream and . . . a madness in those who treat the inner life as a phantom." To apply this to systems, there are those who view organizations as mirages, with no reality except that which we give them. This is one kind of madness. The other madness is that of those, like the Russians and some *echt* Marxist thinkers, who will not deal with, or even recognize, aspects of their personality, dispositions, if you will, that stem from our inner souls, or private lives. For the sake of our collective sanity, we must recognize the validity and reality of each—by organization and personality—for without that total embrace, our perspective will be dangerously skewed.

In any case, it would be a grave error to fall into the trap of underestimating the power of organizations and conceiving of executive success as dependent on toughness or softness, assertiveness or sensitivity, masculinity or femininity. That popular delusion has already caused too much damage, both to individuals who are impersonating males and females, and to the institutions for which they work.

23

How Do Leaders Get to Lead?

MICHAEL M. LOMBARDO

The question of whether leaders are born or made has vexed organizations throughout history. Even though about 75 percent of management development directors say real development occurs on the job, there is evidence that most organizations allow this development to occur for only a chosen few.

If having the skills and capabilities to become a leader is not as important as the opportunity to develop and demonstrate them, then many managers never have a chance.

The Early Years

A young man might go into military flight training believing that he was entering some sort of technical school in which he was simply going to acquire a certain set of skills. Instead, he found himself all at once enclosed in a fraternity. And in this fraternity, even though it was military, men were not rated by their outward rank as ensigns, lieutenants, commanders, or whatever. "The world was divided into those who had it and those who did not." This quality, this "it," was never named, however, nor was it talked about in any way.

—Tom Wolfe,
The Right Stuff

Organizations usually separate those who have "it" from those who do not during the early years of a career, and in so doing organizations favor as their future leaders young managers who demonstrate skills

Reprinted by permission from *Issues and Observations*, 2:1 (February 1982), pp. 1–4.

244   Michael M. Lombardo

and abilities they bring with them to the job. Abilities to work with others, handle conflict, analyze problems, run a meeting, set priorities and so forth are looked for early, and, if seen, can lead to anointment as a high-potential or fast-track manager. If the manager has the right background as well (e.g., an MBA and past positions of leadership), the odds of being dubbed a rising star increase further.

Organizations put confidence in this rite of anointment to reduce risk. The question of future leadership is a matter of survival. With the vicissitudes of competition, regulation, and the economy, businesses can't afford added uncertainty in the promotion of leaders.

To insure a steady stream of competent leaders, organizations therefore select and hone managers who demonstrate certain skills early. Since learning a management job takes about two years and learning a business takes several decades, organizations take the least risk possible. Although young managers cannot quickly understand the business, they can quickly demonstrate the skills necessary to learn it.

In short, it's easier to teach the objective components of business than it is to teach the murky clusters of behavior called skills, or even more difficult to teach abstractions like judgement.

There is more than logic to support the selection of future leaders from among the managers who demonstrate leadership skills early. In Bray and Howard's 20-year study of AT&T managers, there was a shocking finding: The average manager does not improve in managerial abilities over time. There is no evidence that managerial experience is a good teacher of management.

Critics can say that this finding holds for average managers but that those who get to the top are anything but average. Or they might attack the assessment center data on which the Bray and Howard findings are based, contending that the skills and abilities measured are too global to pick up the subtle learning and the refinement of skills that take place over 20 years. A manager who excelled in defining problems 20 years ago may have since developed subtle questioning techniques and ways of turning a problem inside out that a straightforward rating of "clearly defined the problem" might miss.

Still, there is the nagging suspicion that managers who have the skills to begin with have an edge that time only increases. Although most managers in the study indeed changed, becoming both more occupationally and family-oriented, less dependent on others, and more interested in achievement and influencing others, their skills didn't change much. Even for successful managers, interest in personal development and interpersonal skills tended to sag, but (and this is the source of the suspicion) their skills started higher and stayed higher than did the skills of those who were less successful.

It may be that even eventual leaders don't learn many new skills from experience. Instead, they bring their skills to the job, and, as some executives have insisted, rise to the top because their capabilities blossom when they are confronted with new situations. With this view, a manager who jumps in and handles a nasty conflict does so because the requisite skills are waiting within until they are needed.

The Self-Fulfilling Prophecy

If success as a leader were as simple as having the right skills and seizing opportunities to demonstrate them, this view of leadership development could be compelling. But even more important than having the right skills is having the right jobs. Once noticed, fast-movers get into, or are placed in, challenging jobs where they spend more time on projects involving top management, and work for managers who are themselves moving up.

This combination of access to the counsel of top management, working for a highly-regarded manager, and having a core job gives fast-movers the four edges that matter most:

- They learn the business more quickly.
- They learn the perspective of top managers on the business.
- They learn which kinds of jobs and experiences compose the core of the business.
- They more often have a highly-placed mentor to nudge and guide them.

As a result of being seen and being good, the highly-regarded move fast. Leaving their first position in less than two years (according to Veiga), they broaden their perspective with cross-divisional experiences and become expert in one segment of corporate operations.

While not as obvious as being knighted, there is apparently a self-fulfilling prophecy generated whereby success breeds success. By the third year or almost always by the third level of management, potential leaders have been spotted and from then on are exposed to jobs that provide experience relevant for higher-level jobs.

These experiences create expanding opportunities for high-potential managers to learn things far beyond management skills. One group of successful executives, reflecting on the significant learnings in their careers, came up with the following list:

- *Learning to delegate.* Many managers do it all until they pass middle-management, rarely delegating or keeping subordinates adequately informed. Once they become executives, however, a change in outlook must be made: Rather than enjoying doing something, executives must enjoy seeing it done. There must be a letting go of hands-on control in favor of in-out advice.
- *Learning how to get advice.* Many managers excel at aggressively seeking information and taking charge. Executives must learn how to communicate the need for advice and information, and how to listen to others' concerns.
- *Setting life goals.* Although managers may conduct their lives by just letting things happen, executives must learn to make career and life decisions based on specific, incremental goals.
- *Discovering strengths.* To take advantage of the opportunities that come to them, executives must learn what it is they are good at doing.
- *Dealing with adversity.* Executives must learn not to over-analyze the past when they are confronted with a failure. They must quickly understand what went wrong, accept responsibility for their part in the failure, and then move on.
- *Struggling with change.* Executives must learn how to take on new and demanding roles, to deal with a changing organization, new technology, and changing societal norms.

Managers not seen by their organizations as fast-trackers face a different experience. They leave their first position later (3–4 years), and often work in peripheral units for so-so managers. Although they, too, change jobs often, the pattern of their moves is less coherent.

They often switch across functional lines, garnering assignments that hinder the development of long-term business contacts (their network) and make it difficult to master any one segment of the business. (The opportunity to learn marketing or manufacturing or legal affairs in detail is critical to later success. In one study, presidents and board chairmen spent as much as two-thirds of their careers in the *same* function.)

The experiences that non-fast-trackers are exposed to are more narrow and specific. They learn how to implement decisions, set procedures, and master the technical side of management systems, but rarely do they have the opportunity to learn or practice the kinds of skills mentioned by more successful managers.

Haves and Have Nots

A man either had it or he didn't! There was no such thing as having most of it.

—Tom Wolfe,
The Right Stuff

Whether by nature or by nurture or by both, by about the third level of management, groups of "haves" and "have nots" form in many organizations. For the "haves," their past opportunities have helped them to develop patterns of behavior that are seen as effective in their present jobs and they remain eligible for the top.

For the "have nots"—those who lacked some of the skills to begin with—their problems have been compounded by dead-end, low-visibility jobs which further hinder the catching up they need to do. Real differences now exist between the groups, differences that were there to begin with and that have been exacerbated by later experiences. (See Table 1.)

For the "have nots," a self-defeating pattern emerges: They only listen long enough to categorize a problem, then they shoot from the hip with a standardized solution. If the problem reappears, thornier than ever, they waffle and shunt it off to a committee or they go to the other extreme and attempt to overwhelm the problem with a barrage of solutions. At no time do they stop and ask the questions that might tell them what the problem really is.

For the "haves," the essential difference is an ability to break set, to go against the grain of habit. Many managers who become successful embody an oppositeness of nature that enables them to pause long enough to listen to the music of organizational problems, heads craned for that one funny note, then, once they understand what's going on, to act quickly to hammer out the lyrics.

The Right Stuff?

. . . the idea was to prove at every foot of the way up that pyramid that you were one of the elected and anointed ones who had "the right stuff" and could move higher and higher and even—ultimately, God willing, one day—that you might be able to join that special few at the very top, that elite who had the capacity to bring tears to men's eyes, the very Brotherhood of the Right Stuff itself.

—Tom Wolfe,
The Right Stuff

Such divergent patterns beg the question of "Are these groups really

TABLE 1

Have Nots	Haves
Creatures of habit; tend to wing it based on what worked previously; management by cliché ("never fire-fight"; "the key to management is delegation")	Analyze each situation; may appear inconsistent because seemingly similar situations in fact aren't
Consistently err at the extremes of behavior—they may never get into detail, or may become obsessed with all details	May get into fine detail on one problem and totally ignore detail on the next; act according to the nature of the problem, not the nature of their habits
Work on whatever comes up (12 problems at once in one study)	Spend a third to a half of their time working on one or two priorities
Lack boldness; hesitate to make decisions on complex problems	Involve lots of people, listen to different views of the problem, play with ideas; once mind is made up, act quickly
Don't seek enough advice or help (limited network of contacts)	Extensive network of contacts who might be located anywhere inside or outside the organization
Personal and work-related blind spots resulting from inadequate feedback (e.g., believe they are superb delegators while their subordinates believe the opposite)	Job interests are balanced with family, friends, and other interests that provide helpful feedback

different or did they grow to be this way?" Or more simply, "Is there such a thing as the right stuff?"

There may well be. The problem is no one knows what the right stuff is, since it is the result of both the nature and the nurture of managers.

Most administrative and interpersonal skills are learnable, so these cannot form any unique set of talents. Conceptual abilities, however, are developed fairly early in life and although they can be modified a little, no one has as yet figured out how to improve them dramatically.

Teaching good judgement, or the ability to break set, or the ability to pick key problems, or the courage to make unpopular decisions is not something that can be reduced to simple formulas. Such abilities are terribly complex, and require dealing with ambiguity as a matter of course.

If there is such a thing as the right stuff, it probably lies in a certain comfort with the unknown, and in the ability to make sense of the discordant notes that most of us never even hear. But even if we assume that such an ineffable quality exists, many managers never get much opportunity to show it. Perhaps more important, they may never have had the life experiences that create the credentials that make them visible.

So What?

The point is this: By creating opportunities for more young managers, and by avoiding premature decisions on managerial careers, organizations can increase their chances of developing the best possible leaders for the future.

For a host of reasons, many managers who may have the right stuff will not have the background experiences and skills that will enable them to show it. Blacks, women, and "late-bloomers" are frequently mentioned as three talent pools who may have had inadequate opportunities to develop.

Here are some suggestions for ways to create opportunities for more managers.

- Have a committee of executives address the question, "What should our leaders look like 20 years from now?" (Otherwise, organizations run the risk of promoting only those managers who fit the model of leadership in use 20 years ago.) Decide what developmental experiences the leaders of the year 2000 could benefit from.
- Besides the traditional emphasis on skills and business training for young managers, conduct symposia on the significant events and major learnings of successful executives. These symposia should be small, informal, and conducted by the executives themselves.
- Many organizations have coaching and counseling programs for managers. Organizations could benefit from an executive mentoring program as well. Assign each management recruit to a mentor who meets with the recruit at least once a month for lunch. Ask the mentor to advise the recruit on the recruit's most pressing problems, at the same time injecting top management's perspective into the discussions. Besides getting advice, recruits may be able

to learn the business more quickly and understand how successful managers attack problems.

- Give young managers who have lightly-regarded bosses a chance to work with an effective role model at least part of the time.
- Before deciding that some managers don't have it, answer the question, "Have they ever been in a position where they could show it?"

None of these suggestions will produce miracles. Nor will they create wheat from chaff. They may, however, produce some pleasant surprises.

About the Authors

CHIEF MASTER SERGEANT OF THE AIR FORCE ARTHUR L. "BUD" ANDREWS is from Boston, Massachusetts. He enlisted in the Air Force in 1953 serving initially as a security policeman. Over the years he rose to First Sergeant and Senior Enlisted Advisor, and served as the seventh Chief Master Sergeant of the Air Force, until he retired late in 1983.

WARREN G. BENNIS is professor of research at the Graduate School of Business Administration, University of Southern California. He has written extensively on power and leadership in organizations. One of his books, *The Unconscious Conspiracy: Why Leaders Can't Lead,* was particularly influential in the editors' concept of leadership.

JAMES MACGREGOR BURNS is a political scientist and historian and a distinguished faculty member at Williams College. A Pulitzer Prize winner, he has written extensively on government, the presidency, and leadership. He was a combat historian during World War II and brings an eclectic experience to the study of leadership.

THOMAS E. CRONIN is a political scientist and writer. A former White House Fellow and candidate for Congress, he is president of CRC, Inc., and Adjunct Professor of Political Science at Colorado College. He is the author or coauthor of several books, including *The State of the Presidency, Government by the People, U.S. v. Crime in the Streets.*

JOHN W. GARDNER is the author of several books and former Secretary of Health, Education and Welfare. His service includes president of the Carnegie Foundation for the Advancement of Teaching, Urban Coalition, and Common Cause. He served with the Marine Corps during World War II and is the recipient of the USAF Exceptional Service Award.

CHARLES R. HOLLOMAN is a retired Air Force Lt. Colonel. Presently, he is the Grover C. Maxwell Professor of Organization Behavior at Augusta College, Georgia. He is the author of many articles about management and management development.

WILLIAM LITZINGER is Director of the Division of Management and Marketing at the University of Texas, San Antonio.

MICHAEL M. LOMBARDO is Behavioral Scientist/Project Manager at the Center for Creative Leadership. He is part of a research team examining how leaders get to the top and what they learn along the way.

GENERAL S.L.A. MARSHALL is a distinguished military historian. Rising to the rank of brigadier general in the Army, he was a combat historian in World War II. He also served in Korea and Vietnam. A syndicated columnist, he has also written numerous articles and books on the military. *The Armed Forces Officer* has been a classic book for military leadership and command.

MORGAN W. MCCALL, JR., is Senior Behavioral Scientist and Director of Research at the Center for Creative Leadership. In addition to several articles, he co-edited *Leadership: Where Else Can We Go?* and helped develop the "Looking Glass" management simulation. He also heads a program studying the careers of successful executives.

GENERAL EDWARD C. MEYER recently retired as the Army Chief of Staff, a post he held for the past four years. A graduate of West Point, he served in Korea and Vietnam. He was also a Brookings Institution Fellow.

ROBERT K. MUELLER is Chairman of the Board of Arthur D. Little, Inc. He has been Vice President of Monsanto Company and serves on the board of directors for several organizations. Writing for many scientific and business journals, he was also a Visiting Professor at Manhattan College.

JEFFREY PFEFFER, Professor of Organizational Behavior in the Graduate School of Business at Stanford University, has written over sixty articles and three books on topics in organization theory, organization design and power in organizations. During 1981–1982, he was the Thomas Henry Carroll–Ford Foundation Visiting Professor at the Harvard Business School.

GENERAL MATTHEW B. RIDGWAY graduated from West Point in 1917. During his distinguished career, he served in many command positions, culminating in his appointment as Army Chief of Staff from 1953 to 1955. His outstanding leadership in World War II and Korea is acknowledged with numerous U.S. and foreign decorations.

THOMAS SCHAEFER is Professor of Management at the University of Texas of the Permian Basin.

ADMIRAL JAMES BOND STOCKDALE is a retired Vice Admiral and recipient of the Congressional Medal of Honor. He is now a senior research fellow at the Hoover Institution on War and a classroom teacher and writer.

JAMES L. STOKESBURY is a professor of history at Acadia University in Nova Scotia. He served as an enlisted man in the U.S. Navy from 1953 to 1957. A prolific writer, he is very interested in military and naval history and he co-authored a 1975 book, *Masters of the Art of Command*.

WILLIAM E. TURCOTTE is the chairman of the Defense Economics and Decision Making Department at the Naval War college in Newport, Rhode Island. A graduate of the U.S. Naval Academy, he holds a doctorate from the Harvard Business School.

DAVID D. VAN FLEET is associate professor of management at Texas A&M University. An active consultant, he specializes in management development and leadership. He is a prolific author of leadership research and he is a member of several editorial review boards.

COLONEL ROY DALE VOORHEES is an associate professor in The School of Business Administration, Iowa State University. In the Air Force he served as a combat pilot, planner at Headquarters USAF, and embassy air attaché. He has published numerous articles in professional academic journals.

COLONEL MALHAM M. WAKIN is Associate Dean of the Faculty and Professor and Head of the Department of Philosophy and Fine Arts at the USAF Academy. He has flown as a navigator and he is well known throughout the military as a scholar of professional military ethics and morality and war. His works are widely published in military and academic journals.

ABRAHAM ZALEZNIK is Cahners-Rabb Professor of Social Psychology of Management at the Harvard University Graduate School of Business and a member of the Ogden Corporation, New York City. His books include *Power and the Corporate Mind* (1975) and *Human Dilemmas of Leadership* (1966).